Francis Turner Palgrave

The Children's Treasury of English Song

Francis Turner Palgrave

The Children's Treasury of English Song

ISBN/EAN: 9783744775038

Printed in Europe, USA, Canada, Australia, Japan

Cover: Foto ©Thomas Meinert / pixelio.de

More available books at **www.hansebooks.com**

THE CHILDREN'S TREASURY

OF

ENGLISH SONG.

> —This is an art
> Which does mend nature,—change it rather: but
> The art itself is nature.—
>
> Shakespeare: *Winter's Tale*

OF

ENGLISH SONG

SELECTED AND ARRANGED WITH NOTES BY

FRANCIS TURNER PALGRAVE
LATE FELLOW OF EXETER COLLEGE, OXFORD;
EDITOR OF THE 'GOLDEN TREASURY'

New York:
MACMILLAN AND CO.
1875

The Publishers owe their thanks to Mr. William Cullen Bryant for the use of his two poems "To a Waterfowl," and "The Death of the Flowers"; also to Messrs. James R. Osgood & Co. for permission to print Professor Longfellow's "The Wreck of the Hesperus," from their copyright edition of his works.

PREFACE

THIS selection is planned for children between nine or ten, and fifteen or sixteen years of age; the pleasure and advantage of the older students in Elementary, and the younger in Grammar and Public Schools, being especially kept in view. As it is meant for their own possession and study, not less than for use as a class-book in the teacher's hand, sufficient notes (it is thought) have been added to render the volume by itself fairly comprehensible to children of average intelligence : and the editor hopes that this object may be his excuse with those who may consider the annotations too numerous.

The scheme of choice followed has produced a selection different from any known to the editor. Suitability to childhood is, of course, the common principle of all. But, this quality secured (so far as individual judgment can), nothing has been here admitted which does not reach a high rank in poetical merit ; and the available stores of English poetry have been carefully reviewed for the purpose. The editor's wish has been to collect all songs, narratives, descriptions, or reflective pieces of a lyrical quality, fit to give pleasure, —high, pure, manly, (and therefore lasting)— to children in the stage between early childhood and early youth ; and no pieces which are not of this character. Poetry, for poetry's sake, is what he offers. To illustrate the history of our literature, to furnish specimens of leading or of less-known poets, to give useful lessons for this or the other life, to encourage a patriotic temper—each an aim fit to form the guiding principle of a selection—have here only an indirect and subsidiary recognition. It is, however, believed that, so far as the scope of the book coincides with such other aims, they may be more effectually served through the powerful operation of really good poetry, than when made the main object of a collection.

The standard of 'merit as poetry' (so far as the editor, aided by some friends distinguished by good judgment and scholarship, may have been successful in preserving it), has excluded a certain number of popular favourites. But the standard of 'suitability to childhood,' as here understood, has excluded many more pieces: pictures of life as it seems to middle-age—poems coloured by sentimentalism or morbid melancholy, however attractive to readers no longer children—love as personal passion or regret (not love as the groundwork of action)—artificial or highly allusive language—have, as a rule, been held unfit. The aim has been to shun scenes and sentiments alien from the temper of average healthy childhood, and hence of greater intrinsical difficulty than poems containing unusual words. Hence, although the rules of choice have given this book, as compared with many of its predecessors, an unfamiliar air, yet it is believed that the contents will in fact prove ultimately at least as comprehensible to children between the ages specified.

Poems suitable for readers in the latter half of these years are marked with a star in the index. Some pieces will be found admitted as examples leading up to the poetry appropriate to later education and the experience of life; but, looking to the small size of the collection, it has not been thought desirable to attempt ranging the contents in order of composition or of relative difficulty.

A few omissions have been made in order to render a poem more suitable for childhood, or to escape encroachment on the field of distinctly devotional verse; others, more copiously, when the poem could be thus strengthened in a vivid effectiveness. The North-country Ballads have thus been greatly shortened; a child (in the editor's judgment, especially one unfamiliar with dialect, being more likely to appreciate afterwards their charming antique garrulity, and the repetitions of phrase proper to orally-published poetry, if presented first with a tale in our more condensed modern manner. When, as here, poetry for poetry's sake is concerned, extracts in general appear wholly unsatisfactory to the editor; they are like fragments barbarously broken from statues. Such only have, therefore, been included which form in themselves complete works of art.

For some pieces, the editor has to thank the liberality of the copyright owners: regretting the refusal by which the present publisher of Mr. Alfred Tennyson's poems has deprived this book of a few brilliant pages, and its readers of an introduction to the writings of our greatest living poet.

The rule that no piece should be admitted, unless reaching a high rank in poetical merit, if carried out successfully, will have rendered this book fit also for older readers. Such will know that the treasures here collected are but a few drops from an ocean, unequalled in wealth and variety by any existing literature; that many illustrious names are, necessarily, altogether absent; that many others receive but a meagre and imperfect representation. Among the five (surviving) Imperial poets of the Western world, England claims two; but how faintly does a selection, limited as this, present the splendour of Shakespeare and Milton! Descending one or two steps, if Wordsworth and Scott, within this century, are fairly shown in a single region of their power, Keats, Shelley, Byron, Crabbe, on different grounds, must be nearly or wholly undisplayed. But, in truth, no selection should be planned or accepted as able to do more than open a glimpse into the 'Elysian fields' of song. Pleasant as has been the task of forming this book, in the hope that it may, in itself, prove a pleasure and a gain to the dear English and English-speaking children, all the world over, yet the editor will hold his work but half fulfilled, unless they are tempted by it to go on and wander, in whatever direction their fancy may lead them, through the roads and winding ways of this great and glorious world of English poetry. He aims only at showing them the path, and giving them a little foretaste of our treasures:—

To-morrow to fresh woods, and pastures new.

F. T. P.

May: 1875

The Children's Treasury

FIRST PART

* 1 *
A LAUGHING SONG

WHEN the green woods laugh with the voice of joy,
And the dimpling stream runs laughing by;
When the air does laugh with our merry wit,
And the green hill laughs with the noise of it;

When the meadows laugh with lively green,
And the grasshopper laughs in the merry scene;
When Mary, and Susan, and Emily,
With their sweet round mouths sing, 'Ha, ha, he!'

When the painted birds laugh in the shade,
Where our table with cherries and nuts is spread:
Come live, and be merry, and join with me
To sing the sweet chorus of 'Ha, ha, he!'
                                                W. Blake

* 2 *
THE PET LAMB

THE dew was falling fast, the stars began to blink;
I heard a voice; it said, 'Drink, pretty creature,
    drink!'
And looking o'er the hedge, before me I espied
A snow-white mountain lamb, with a maiden at its
    side.

Nor sheep, nor kine were near; the lamb was all
 alone,
And by a slender cord was tether'd to a stone;
With one knee on the grass did the little maiden
 kneel,
While to that mountain lamb she gave its evening
 meal.

The lamb, while from her hand he thus his supper
 took,
Seem'd to feast with head and ears; and his tail
 with pleasure shook:
'Drink, pretty creature, drink!' she said in such a tone
That I almost received her heart into my own.

'Twas little Barbara Lewthwaite, a child of beauty
 rare!
I watch'd them with delight, they were a lovely pair;
Now with her empty can the maiden turn'd away;
But ere ten yards were gone, her footsteps did she
 stay.

Right towards the lamb she look'd; and from that
 shady place
I unobserved could see the workings of her face;
If nature to her tongue could measured numbers
 bring,
Thus, thought I, to her lamb that little maid might
 sing:

'What ails thee, Young one? what? Why pull so
 at thy cord?
'Is it not well with thee? well both for bed and
 board?
'Thy plot of grass is soft, and green as grass can be;
'Rest, little Young one, rest; what is 't that aileth
 thee?

19 If she could write verse

'What is it thou wouldst seek? What is wanting to
    thy heart?
'Thy limbs are they not strong? and beautiful thou
    art!
'This grass is tender grass; these flowers they have
    no peers;
'And that green corn all day is rustling in thy ears.

'If the sun be shining hot, do but stretch thy
    woollen chain;
'This beech is standing by, its covert thou canst
    gain;
'For rain and mountain-storms!—the like thou
    need'st not fear,
'The rain and storm are things that scarcely can
    come here.

'Rest, little Young one, rest; thou hast forgot the
    day
'When my father found thee first in places far
    away;
'Many flocks were on the hills, but thou wert own'd
    by none,
'And thy mother from thy side for evermore was
    gone.

'He took thee in his arms, and in pity brought thee
    home:
'A blessèd day for thee!—then whither wouldst thou
    roam?
'A faithful nurse thou hast; the dam that did thee
    yean
'Upon the mountain-tops no kinder could have
    been.

27 *peers*, equals

'Thou know'st that twice a day I have brought thee
    in this can
'Fresh water from the brook, as clear as ever ran ;
'And twice in the day, when the ground is wet with
    dew,
'I bring thee draughts of milk, warm milk it is and
    new.

'Thy limbs will shortly be twice as stout as they are
    now,
'Then I'll yoke thee to my cart like a pony in the
    plough !
'My playmate thou shalt be ; and when the wind is
    cold
'Our hearth shall be thy bed, our house shall be
    thy fold.

'It will not, will not rest !—Poor creature, can it be
'That 'tis thy mother's heart which is working so in
    thee?
'Things that I know not of belike to thee are dear,
'And dreams of things which thou canst neither see
    nor hear.

'Alas, the mountain-tops that look so green and fair!
'I've heard of fearful winds and darkness that come
    there ;
'The little brooks that seem all pastime and all
    play,
'When they are angry, roar like lions for their prey.

'Here thou need'st not dread the raven in the sky ;
'Night and day thou art safe,--our cottage is
    hard by.
'Why bleat so after me? Why pull so at thy
    chain ?
'Sleep—and at break of day I will come to thee
    again !'

51 *belike*, probably

—As homeward through the lane I went with lazy
    feet,
This song to myself did I oftentimes repeat ;
And it seem'd, as I retraced the ballad line by line,
That but half of it was hers, and one half of it was
    mine.

Again, and once again, did I repeat the song;
' Nay,' said I, ' more than half to the damsel must
    belong !—
' For she look'd with such a look, and she spake
    with such a tone,
' That I almost received her heart into my own.'
                    W. Wordsworth

* 3 *

THE LAMB

  LITTLE Lamb, who made thee?
  Dost thou know who made thee?
  Gave thee life, and bade thee feed
  By the stream and o'er the mead ;
  Gave thee clothing of delight,
  Softest clothing, woolly, bright ;
  Gave thee such a tender voice,
  Making all the vales rejoice :
      Little Lamb, who made thee?
      Dost thou know who made thee?

     Little Lamb, I'll tell thee!
     Little Lamb, I'll tell thee.
     He is callèd by thy name,
     For He calls Himself a Lamb :—

6 3 retraced, repeated

He is meek, and He is mild ;
He became a little child :
I, a child, and thou, a lamb,
We are calléd by His name.
   Little Lamb, God bless thee;
   Little Lamb, God bless thee.

W. Blake

* 4 *

EPITAPH ON A HARE

HERE lies, whom hound did ne'er pursue,
   Nor swifter greyhound follow,
Whose foot ne'er tainted morning dew,
   Nor ear heard huntsman's halloo !

Old Tiney, surliest of his kind,
   Who, nursed with tender care,
And to domestic bounds confined,
   Was still a wild Jack-hare.

Though duly from my hand he took
   His pittance every night,
He did it with a jealous look,
   And, when he could, would bite.

His diet was of wheaten bread,
   And milk, and oats, and straw ;
Thistles, or lettuces instead,
   With sand to scour his maw.

On twigs of hawthorn he regaled,
   On pippin's russet peel ;
And when his juicy salads fail'd
   Sliced carrot pleased him well.

---

3 *tainted*, scented   10 *pittance*, portion   16 to make his food digest   18 *russet*, brown-red

A Turkey carpet was his lawn,
  Whereon he loved to bound,
To skip and gambol like a fawn,
  And swing his rump around.

His frisking was at evening hours,
  For then he lost his fear;
But most before approaching showers,
  Or when a storm drew near.

Eight years and five round-rolling moons
  He thus saw steal away,
Dozing out all his idle noons,
  And every night at play.

I kept him for his humour's sake,
  For he would oft beguile
My heart of thoughts that made it ache,
  And force me to a smile.

But now, beneath this walnut shade,
  He finds his long last home,
And waits, in snug concealment laid,
  Till gentler Puss shall come.

He, still more aged, feels the shocks
  From which no care can save :—
And, partner once of Tiney's box,
  Must soon partake his grave.

W. Cowper

* 5 *

THE WOUNDED HARE

INHUMAN man! curse on thy barbarous art,
And blasted be thy murder-aiming eye;
May never pity soothe thee with a sigh,
Nor ever pleasure glad thy cruel heart!

---

29 *moons*, months   34 *beguile*, cheat
1 *inhuman*, cruel; *barbarous art*, shooting for sport's sake

—Go, live, poor wanderer of the wood and field,
   The bitter little that of life remains ;
   No more the thickening brakes and verdant plains
To thee shall home, or food, or pastime yield.

Seek, mangled wretch, some place of wonted rest,
   No more of rest, but now thy dying bed !
   The sheltering rushes whistling o'er thy head,
The cold earth with thy bloody bosom prest.

Oft as by winding Nith, I, musing, wait
   The sober eve, or hail the cheerful dawn,
   I'll miss thee sporting o'er the dewy lawn,
And curse the ruffian's aim, and mourn thy hapless
   fate.   *R. Burns*

* 6 *

TO A SPANIEL ON HIS KILLING A YOUNG BIRD

A SPANIEL, Beau, that fares like you,
   Well fed, and at his ease,
Should wiser be than to pursue
   Each trifle that he sees.

But you have kill'd a tiny bird,
   Which flew not till to-day,
Against my orders, whom you heard
   Forbidding you the prey.

Nor did you kill that you might eat,
   And ease a doggish pain,
For him, though chased with furious heat,
   You left where he was slain.

9 *wonted*, where he had been before   13 *Nith*, river in Ayrshire
                        7 *thickening*, growing leafier

Nor was he of the thievish sort,
    Or one whom blood allures,
But innocent was all his sport
    Whom you have torn for yours.

My dog! what remedy remains,
    Since, teach you all I can,
I see you after all my pains
    So much resemble man?

Beau's Reply

Sir, when I flew to seize the bird
    In spite of your command,
A louder voice than yours I heard,
    And harder to withstand.

You cried—forbear!—but in my breast
    A mightier cried—proceed!
'Twas Nature, Sir, whose strong behest
    Impell'd me to the deed.

Yet, much as Nature I respect,
    I ventured once to break
(As you, perhaps, may recollect)
    Her precept for your sake;

And when your linnet, on a day,
    Passing his prison door,
Had flutter'd all his strength away,
    And, panting, press'd the floor;

Well knowing him a sacred thing,
    Not destined to my tooth,
I only kiss'd his ruffled wing,
    And lick'd the feathers smooth.

---

14 *allures*, tempts   17 *remedy*, cure   27 *behest*, command
28 *impell'd*, drove   32 *precept*, order   38 *destined*, meant for

Let my obedience then excuse
My disobedience now,
Nor some reproof yourself refuse
From your aggrieved Bow-wow;

If killing birds be such a crime
(Which I can hardly see),
What think you, Sir, of *killing time*,
With verse address'd to me?

W. Cowper

* 7 *

THE BLIND BOY

O SAY what is that thing call'd Light,
Which I must ne'er enjoy;
What are the blessings of the Sight:
O tell your poor blind boy!

You talk of wondrous things you see;
You say the sun shines bright;
I feel him warm, but how can he
Or make it day or night?

My day or night myself I make
Whene'er I sleep or play;
And could I ever keep awake
With me 'twere always day.

With heavy sighs I often hear
You mourn my hapless woe;
But sure with patience I can bear
A loss I ne'er can know.

Then let not what I cannot have
My cheer of mind destroy:
Whilst thus I sing, I am a king,
Although a poor blind boy.

C. Cibber

44 *aggrieved*, vexed 47 *killing*, wasting 14 *hapless*, unhappy

* 8 *

ALICE FELL

THE post-boy drove with fierce career,
For threatening clouds the moon had drown'd;
When, as we hurried on, my ear
Was smitten with a startling sound.

As if the wind blew many ways,
I heard the sound,—and more and more;
It seem'd to follow with the chaise,
And still I heard it as before.

At length I to the boy call'd out;
He stopp'd his horses at the word,
But neither cry, nor voice, nor shout,
Nor aught else like it, could be heard.

The boy then smack'd his whip, and fast
The horses scamper'd through the rain;
But hearing soon upon the blast
The cry, I bade him halt again.

Forthwith alighting on the ground,
'Whence comes,' said I, 'this piteous moan?'
And there a little girl I found,
Sitting behind the chaise alone.

'My cloak!' no other word she spake,
But loud and bitterly she wept,
As if her innocent heart would break;
And down from off her seat she leapt.

'What ails you, child?'—she sobb'd, 'Look
    here!'
I saw it in the wheel entangled,
A weather-beaten rag as e'er
From any garden scarecrow dangled.

There, twisted between nave and spoke,
It hung, nor could at once be freed;
But our joint pains unloosed the cloak,
A miserable rag indeed!

'And whither are you going, child,
'To-night, along these lonesome ways?'
'To Durham,' answer'd she, half wild—
'Then come with me into the chaise.'

Insensible to all relief
Sat the poor girl, and forth did send
Sob after sob, as if her grief
Could never, never have an end.

'My child, in Durham do you dwell?'
She check'd herself in her distress,
And said, 'My name is Alice Fell;
'I'm fatherless and motherless.

'And I to Durham, Sir, belong.'
Again, as if the thought would choke
Her very heart, her grief grew strong;
And all was for her tatter'd cloak.

The chaise drove on; our journey's end
Was nigh; and, sitting by my side,
As if she had lost her only friend,
She wept, nor would be pacified.

Up to the tavern-door we post:
Of Alice and her grief I told,
And I gave money to the host,
To buy a new cloak for the old.

'And let it be of duffil gray,
'As warm a cloak as man can sell!'
—Proud creature was she the next day,
The little orphan, Alice Fell!

W. Wordsworth

52 *pacified*, quieted   57 *duffil*, strong shaggy cloth

* 9 *

THE LITTLE GIRL LOST

IN the southern clime,
Where the summer's prime
Never fades away,
Lovely Lyca lay.

Seven summers old
Lovely Lyca told ;
She had wander'd long,
Hearing wild-birds' song.

' Sweet sleep, come to me
' Underneath this tree !
' Do father, mother, weep ?
' Where can Lyca sleep ?

' Lost in desert wild
' Is your little child !
' How can Lyca sleep
' If her mother weep ?

' If her heart does ache
' Then let Lyca wake :—
' If my mother sleep,
' Lyca shall not weep.

' Frowning, frowning, night
' O'er this desert bright,
' Let thy moon arise
' While I close my eyes !'

Sleeping Lyca lay :
While the beasts of prey
Come from caverns deep,
View'd the maid asleep.

The kingly lion stood,
And the virgin view'd :
Then he gamboll'd round
O'er the hallow'd ground.

Leopards, tigers, play
Round her as she lay;
While the lion old
Bow'd his mane of gold,

And [did] her bosom lick;
And upon her neck
From his eyes of flame
Ruby tears there came:

While the lioness
Loosed her slender dress;
And naked they convey'd
To caves the sleeping maid.

THE LITTLE GIRL FOUND

ALL the night in woe
Lyca's parents go,
Over valleys deep,
While the deserts weep.

Tired and woe-begone,
Hoarse with making moan,
Arm-in-arm seven days
They traced the desert ways.

Seven nights they sleep
Among shadows deep,
And dream they see their child
Starved in desert wild.

Pale through pathless ways
The fancied image strays,
Famish'd, weeping, weak,
With hollow piteous shriek

Rising from unrest
The trembling woman press'd
With feet of weary woe :
She could no further go.

In his arms he bore
Her, arm'd with sorrow sore ;
Till before their way
A couching lion lay.

Turning back was vain :
Soon his heavy mane
Bore them to the ground ;
Then he stalk'd around

Smelling to his prey ;
But their fears allay,
When he licks their hands,
And silent by them stands.

They look upon his eyes,
Fill'd with deep surprise ;
And wondering behold
A spirit arm'd in gold.

On his head a crown :
On his shoulders down
Flow'd his golden hair !
Gone was all their care.

' Follow me,' he said ;
' Weep not for the maid ;
' In my palace deep
' Lyca lies asleep.'

Then they followed
Where the vision led.
And saw their sleeping child
Among tigers wild.

To this day they dwell
In a lonely dell ;
Nor fear the wolvish howl,
Nor the lions' growl.

W. Blake

* 10 *

JOHN GILPIN

JOHN Gilpin was a citizen
   Of credit and renown,
A train-band captain eke was he
   Of famous London Town.

John Gilpin's spouse said to her dear,
   'Though wedded we have been
'These twice ten tedious years, yet we
   'No holiday have seen.

'To-morrow is our wedding-day,
   'And we will then repair
'Unto the Bell at Edmonton,
   'All in a chaise and pair.

'My sister and my sister's child,
   'Myself, and children three,
'Will fill the chaise ; so you must ride
   'On horseback after we.'

He soon replied, 'I do admire
   'Of womankind but one,
'And you are she, my dearest dear,
   'Therefore it shall be done.

---

3 *train-band*, militia

'I am a linendraper bold,
  'As all the world doth know,
'And my good friend, the Calender,
  'Will lend his horse to go.'

Quoth Mistress Gilpin, 'That's well said;
  'And, for that wine is dear,
'We will be furnish'd with our own,
  'Which is both bright and clear.'

John Gilpin kiss'd his loving wife;
  O'erjoy'd was he to find
That, though on pleasure she was bent,
  She had a frugal mind.

The morning came, the chaise was brought,
  But yet was not allow'd
To drive up to the door, lest all
  Should say that she was proud.

So three doors off the chaise was stay'd,
  Where they did all get in,
Six precious souls, and all agog
  To dash through thick and thin.

Smack went the whip, round went the wheels;
  Were never folks so glad:
The stones did rattle underneath,
  As if Cheapside were mad.

John Gilpin, at his horse's side,
  Seized fast the flowing mane,
And up he got, in haste to ride,
  But soon came down again;

For saddle-tree scarce reach'd had he,
  His journey to begin,
When, turning round his head, he saw
  Three customers come in.

23 *Calender*, cloth-dresser   44 a street in London
49 *saddle-tree*, bow of the saddle

So down he came; for loss of time
 Although it grieved him sore,
Yet loss of pence, full well he knew,
 Would trouble him much more.

'Twas long before the customers
 Were suited to their mind,
When Betty, screaming, came downstairs,
 'The wine is left behind!'

'Good lack!' quoth he, 'yet bring it me,
 'My leathern belt likewise,
'In which I bear my trusty sword
 'When I do exercise.'

Now Mistress Gilpin (careful soul!)
 Had two stone-bottles found,
To hold the liquor that she loved,
 And keep it safe and sound.

Each bottle had a curling ear,
 Through which the belt he drew,
And hung a bottle on each side,
 To make his balance true.

Then over all, that he might be
 Equipp'd from top to toe,
His long red cloak, well-brush'd and neat,
 He manfully did throw.

Now see him mounted once again
 Upon his nimble steed,
Full slowly pacing o'er the stones,
 With caution and good heed.

But finding soon a smoother road
 Beneath his well-shod feet,
The snorting beast began to trot,
 Which gall'd him in his seat.

64 as a soldier   74 *equipp'd*, dressed out

So, 'Fair and softly!' John he cried,
    But John he cried in vain;
That trot became a gallop soon,
    In spite of curb and rein.

So stooping down, as needs he must
    Who cannot sit upright,
He grasp'd the mane with both his hands,
    And eke with all his might.

His horse, who never in that sort
    Had handled been before,
What thing upon his back had got
    Did wonder more and more.

Away went Gilpin, neck or nought;
    Away went hat and wig;
He little dreamt, when he set out,
    Of running such a rig.

The wind did blow, the cloak did fly,
    Like streamer long and gay,
Till loop and button failing both,
    At last it flew away.

Then might all people well discern
    The bottles he had slung;
A bottle swinging at each side,
    As hath been said or sung.

The dogs did bark, the children scream'd,
    Up flew the windows all;
And every soul cried out—'Well done!'
    As loud as he could bawl.

Away went Gilpin—who but he?
    His fame soon spread around.
'He carries weight; he rides a race!
    'Tis for a thousand pound!'

92 *eke*, also

And still as fast as he drew near,
  'Twas wonderful to view
How in a trice the turnpike men
  Their gates wide open threw.

And now, as he went bowing down
  His reeking head full low,
The bottles twain behind his back
  Were shatter'd at a blow.

Down ran the wine into the road,
  Most piteous to be seen,
Which made his horse's flanks to smoke
  As they had basted been.

But still he seem'd to carry weight,
  With leathern girdle braced;
For all might see the bottle-necks
  Still dangling at his waist.

Thus all through merry Islington
  These gambols he did play,
Until he came unto the Wash
  Of Edmonton so gay;

And there he threw the Wash about
  On both sides of the way,
Just like unto a trundling mop,
  Or a wild goose at play.

At Edmonton his loving wife
  From the balcóny spied
Her tender husband, wondering much
  To see how he did ride.

'Stop, stop, John Gilpin!—Here's the house'—
  They all at once did cry;
'The dinner waits, and we are tired;'
  Said Gilpin, 'So am I!'

119 *trice*, moment 122 *reeking*, steaming 128 with gravy

But yet his horse was not a whit
   Inclined to tarry there;
For why? his owner had a house
   Full ten miles off, at Ware.

So like an arrow swift he flew,
   Shot by an archer strong;
So did he fly—which brings me to
   The middle of my song.

Away went Gilpin, out of breath,
   And sore against his will,
Till at his friend the Calender's
   His horse at last stood still.

The Calender, amazed to see
   His neighbour in such trim,
Laid down his pipe, flew to the gate,
   And thus accosted him.

'What news? what news? your tidings tell!
   'Tell me you must and shall—
'Say, why bare-headed you are come,
   'Or why you come at all?'

Now Gilpin had a pleasant wit,
   And loved a timely joke;
And thus unto the Calender
   In merry guise he spoke:

'I came, because your horse would come;
   'And, if I well forbode,
'My hat and wig will soon be here,
   'They are upon the road.'

The Calender, right glad to find
   His friend in merry pin,
Return'd him not a single word,
   But to the house went in;

149 *whit*, bit   164 *accosted*, spoke to   174 *forbode*, prophecy
                          173 *pin*, humour

Whence straight he came, with hat and wig,
  A wig that flow'd behind ;
A hat not much the worse for wear ;
  Each comely in its kind.

He held them up, and in his turn
  Thus show'd his ready wit :
'My head is twice as big as yours,
  'They therefore needs must fit.

'But let me scrape the dirt away,
  'That hangs upon your face ;
'And stop and eat, for well you may
  'Be in a hungry case.'

Said John, 'It is my wedding-day,
  'And all the world would stare,
'If wife should dine at Edmonton,
  'And I should dine at Ware !'

So, turning to his horse, he said,
  'I am in haste to dine ;
''Twas for your pleasure you came here,
  'You shall go back for mine.'

Ah, luckless speech, and bootless boast !
  For which he paid full dear ;
For, while he spake, a braying ass
  Did sing most loud and clear ;

Whereat his horse did snort, as he
  Had heard a lion roar,
And gallop'd off with all his might,
  As he had done before.

Away went Gilpin, and away
  Went Gilpin's hat and wig :
He lost them sooner than at first,
  For why ?—they were too big.

201 *bootless*, vain

Now Mistress Gilpin, when she saw
   Her husband posting down
Into the country far away,
   She pull'd out half-a-crown;

And thus unto the youth she said,
   That drove them to the Bell,
'This shall be yours, when you bring back
   'My husband safe and well.'

The youth did ride, and soon did meet
   John coming back amain;
Whom in a trice he tried to stop,
   By catching at his rein;

But not performing what he meant,
   And gladly would have done,
The frighten'd steed he frighten'd more,
   And made him faster run.

Away went Gilpin, and away
   Went postboy at his heels,
The postboy's horse right glad to miss
   The lumbering of the wheels.

Six gentlemen upon the road
   Thus seeing Gilpin fly,
With postboy scampering in the rear,
   They raised the hue and cry:—

'Stop thief!—stop thief!—a highwayman!'
   Not one of them was mute;
And all and each that pass'd that way
   Did join in the pursuit.

And now the turnpike gates again
   Flew open in short space:
The toll-men thinking as before
   That Gilpin rode a race.

And so he did, and won it too!
  For he got first to town;
Nor stopp'd, till where he had got up
  He did again get down.

— Now let us sing, Long live the King,
  And Gilpin, long live he;
And, when he next doth ride abroad,
  May I be there to see!

W. Cowper

* II *

WILLIAM AND MARGARET

'Twas at the silent, solemn hour
  When night and morning meet;
In glided Margaret's grimly ghost,
  And stood at William's feet.

Her face was like an April morn,
  Clad in a wintry cloud;
And clay-cold was her lily hand,
  That held her sable shroud.

So shall the fairest face appear
  When youth and years are flown:
Such is the robe that kings must wear,
  When death has reft their crown.

Her bloom was like the springing flower,
  That sips the silver dew;
The rose was budded in her cheek,
  Just opening to the view.

But love had, like the cankerworm,
  Consumed her early prime:
The rose grew pale, and left her cheek;
  She died before her time.

12 *reft*, taken

'Awake!' she cried, 'thy true Love calls,
  'Come from her midnight grave;
'Now let thy pity hear the maid,
  'Thy love refused to save!

'This is the dumb and dreary hour,
  'When injured ghosts complain;
'When yawning graves give up their dead,
  'To haunt the faithless swain.

'Bethink thee, William, of thy fault,
  'Thy pledge and broken oath!
'And give me back my maiden-vow,
  'And give me back my troth.

'Why did you promise love to me,
  'And not that promise keep?
'Why did you swear my eyes were bright,
  'Yet leave those eyes to weep?

'How could you say my face was fair,
  'And yet that face forsake?
'How could you win my virgin heart,
  'Yet leave that heart to break?

'Why did you say my lip was sweet,
  'And made the scarlet pale?
'And why did I, young witless maid!
  'Believe the flattering tale?

'That face, alas! no more is fair,
  'Those lips no longer red:
'Dark are my eyes, now closed in death,
  'And every charm is fled.

'The hungry worm my sister is;
  'This winding-sheet I wear:
'And cold and weary lasts our night,
  'Till that last morn appear.

28 *swain*, lover   32 *troth*, promise   48 *charm*, beauty

'But, hark! the cock has warn'd me hence;
'A long and late adieu!
'Come see, false man, how low she lies
'Who died for love of you!'

The lark sung loud; the morning smiled
With beams of rosy red:
Pale William quaked in every limb,
And raving left his bed.

He hied him to the fatal place
Where Margaret's body lay;
And stretch'd him on the green-grass turf
That wrapp'd her breathless clay.

And thrice he call'd on Margaret's name,
And thrice he wept full sore;
Then laid his cheek to her cold grave,
And word spake never more!

D. Mallet

* 12 *

THE TRUE SWEETHEART

A FAIR maid sat at her bower-door,
Wringing her lily hands;
And by it came a sprightly youth
Fast tripping o'er the strands.

'Where gang ye, young John,' she says,
'Sae early in the day?
'It gars me think, by your fast trip,
'Your journey's far away.'

He turn'd about with surly look,
And said, 'What's that to thee?
'I'm gaen' to see a lovely maid
'Mair fairer far than ye.'

54 *adieu*, good-bye   5 *gang*, go   7 *gars*, makes   12 *mair*, more

—' False Love, and hast thou play'd me this
   ' In summer among the flowers?
' I will repay thee back again
   ' In winter among the showers.

' Unless again, again, my Love,
   ' Unless you turn again;
' As you with other maidens rove,
   ' I'll smile on other men.'

—' O make your choice of whom you please,
   ' For I my choice will have;
' I've chosen a maid mair fair than thee,
   ' I never will deceive.'

She kilted up her clothing fine,
   And after him gaed she:
But aye he said, ' Turn back, turn back,
   ' No further gang with me!'

'—But again, dear Love, and again, dear Love,
   ' Will ye ne'er love me again?
' Alas for loving you sae weel,
   ' And you nae me again!'

The firstan town that they came till,
   He bought her brooch and ring;
But aye he bade her turn again,
   And no farther gang with him.

' But again, dear Love, and again, dear Love,
   ' Will ye ne'er love me again?
' Alas! for loving you sae weel,
   ' And you nae me again!'

The second town that they came till,
   His heart it grew more fain;
And he was as deep in love with her
   As she with him again.

25 *kilted*, tucked   31 *sae weel*, so well   33 *firstan*, first; *till*, to

The neistan town that they came till,
  He bought her wedding-gown ;
And made her lady of halls and bowers,
  In bonny Berwick town.

Unknown

* 13 *

THE GAY GOSHAWK

'O WELL is me, my gay goshawk,
  'That you can speak and flee ;
'For you can carry a love-letter
  'To my true Love from me.'

—'O how can I carry a letter to her?
  'Or how should I her know?
'I bear a tongue ne'er with her spake,
  'And eyes that ne'er her saw.'

—'O well shall ye my true Love ken
  'So soon as ye her see :
'For of all the flowers of fair England,
  'The fairest flower is she.

'And when she goes into the house,
  'Sit ye upon the whin ;
'And sit you there and sing our loves
  'As she goes out and in.'

Lord William has written a love-letter,
  Put it under his pinion gray :
And he's awa' to Southern land
  As fast as wings can gae.

And first he sang a low, low, note,
  And then he sang a clear ;
And aye the o'erword of the sang
  Was 'Your Love can no win here.'

---

45 *neistan*, next   1 *goshawk*, large hawk   14 *whin*, furze-bush
    23 *o'erword*, burden   24 *no win*, not come

'Feast on, feast on, my maidens all,
  'The wine flows you amang:
'While I gang to my shot-window
  'And hear yon bonnie bird's sang.'

O, first he sang a merry sang,
  And then he sang a grave:
And then he peck'd his feathers gray;
  To her the letter gave.

'Have there a letter from Lord William:
  'He says, he sent ye three;
'He can not wait your love longer,
  'But for your sake he'll die.'

—'I send him the rings from my white fingers,
  'The garlands of my hair;
'I send him the heart that's in my breast;
  'What would my Love have mair?
'And at Mary's kirk in fair Scotland,
  'Ye'll bid him wait for me there.'

She hied her to her father dear
  As fast as go could she:
'An asking, an asking, my father dear,
  'An asking grant you me!
'That if I die in fair England,
  'In Scotland bury me.

'At the first kirk of fair Scotland,
  'You cause the bells be rung;
'At the second kirk of fair Scotland,
  'You cause the mass be sung;

'And when ye come to Saint Mary's kirk,
  'Ye'll tarry there till night.'
And so her father pledged his word,
  And so his promise plight.

27 *shot-window*, window with shutter   41 *kirk*, church
    52 *mass*, service   56 *plight*, gave

The lady's gone to her chamber
　　As fast as she could fare ;
And she has drunk a sleepy draught
　　That she had mix'd with care.

And pale, pale, grew her rosy cheek,
　　And pale and cold was she :—
She seem'd to be as surely dead
　　As any corpse could be.

Then spake her cruel stepminnie,
　　'Take ye the burning lead,
'And drop a drop on her bosom,
　　'To try if she be dead.'

They dropp'd the hot lead on her cheek,
　　They dropp'd it on her chin,
They dropp'd it on her bosom white ;
　　But she spake none again.

Then up arose her seven brethren,
　　And hew'd to her a bier ;
They hew'd it from the solid oak ;
　　Laid it o'er with silver clear.

The first Scots kirk that they came to
　　They gart the bells be rung ;
The next Scots kirk that they came to
　　They gart the mass be sung.

But when they came to Saint Mary's kirk,
　　There stood spearmen in a row ;
And up and started Lord William,
　　The chieftain among them a'.

He rent the sheet upon her face
　　A little above her chin :
With rosy cheek, and ruby lip,
　　She look'd and laugh'd to him.

58 *fare*, go　　65 *minnie*, mother　　78 *gart*, made　　84 *a'*, all

—'A morsel of your bread, my lord!
  'And one glass of your wine!
'For I have fasted these three long days
  'All for your sake and mine!'

Unknown

* 14 *

THE MARINERS OF ENGLAND

YE Mariners of England
That guard our native seas!
Whose flag has braved, a thousand years,
The battle and the breeze!
Your glorious standard launch again
To match another foe:
And sweep through the deep,
While the stormy winds do blow;
While the battle rages loud and long
And the stormy winds do blow.

The spirits of your fathers
Shall start from every wave—
For the deck it was their field of fame,
And Ocean was their grave:
Where Blake and mighty Nelson fell
Your manly hearts shall glow,
As ye sweep through the deep,
While the stormy winds do blow;
While the battle rages loud and long
And the stormy winds do blow.

Britannia needs no bulwarks,
No towers along the steep;
Her march is o'er the mountain waves,
Her home is on the deep.
With thunders from her native oak
She quells the floods below—

---

5 *standard*, flag of England   15 *Blake*, admiral under the Commonwealth   21 Our island needs no coast fortifications

As they roar on the shore,
When the stormy winds do blow;
When the battle rages loud and long,
And the stormy winds do blow.

The meteor-flag of England
Shall yet terrific burn;
Till danger's troubled night depart
And the star of peace return.
Then, then, ye ocean-warriors!
Our song and feast shall flow
To the fame of your name,
When the storm has ceased to blow;
When the fiery fight is heard no more,
And the storm has ceased to blow.

T. Campbell

* 15 *

BEFORE BATTLE

THE signal to engage shall be
   A whistle and a hollo;
Be one and all but firm, like me,
   And conquest soon will follow!
You, Gunnel, keep the helm in hand—
   Thus, thus, boys! steady, steady
Till right a-head you see the land,—
   Then soon as we are ready,
     —The signal to engage shall be
       A whistle and a hollo;
     Be one and all but firm, like me,
       And conquest soon will follow!

Keep, boys, a good look out, d'ye hear?
   'Tis for Old England's honour;
Just as you brought your lower tier
   Broad-side to bear upon her,

---

31 *meteor-flag*, streaming like a flying star   15 *tier*, a row of cannon
     16 *bear upon*, be pointed towards

—The signal to engage shall be
  A whistle and a hollo ;
Be one and all but firm, like me,
  And conquest soon will follow !

All hands then, lads, the ship to clear ;
  Load all your guns and mortars ;
Silent as death th' attack prepare ;
  And, when you're all at quarters,
—The signal to engage shall be
  A whistle and a hollo ;
Be one and all but firm, like me,
  And conquest soon will follow !

C. Dibdin

· 16 ·

CASABLANCA

A True Story

THE boy stood on the burning deck,
  Whence all but he had fled ;
The flame that lit the battle's wreck,
  Shone round him o'er the dead ;
Yet beautiful and bright he stood
  As born to rule the storm !
A creature of heroic blood,
  A proud, though child-like form !

The flames roll'd on he would not go
  Without his Father's word ;
That Father, faint in death below,
  His voice no longer heard.
He call'd aloud : ' Say, father, say
  ' If yet my task is done ! '
He knew not that the chieftain lay
  Unconscious of his son.

22 *mortars,* guns to shoot bombs   7 *heroic,* noble   15 *chieftain,* admiral in command

'Speak, father!' once again he cried,
  'If I may yet be gone!'
And but the booming shots replied,
  And fast the flames roll'd on.
Upon his brow he felt their breath,
  And in his waving hair;
And look'd from that lone post of death
  In still, yet brave despair;

And shouted but once more aloud,
  'My father! must I stay?'
While o'er him fast through sail and shroud,
  The wreathing fires made way.
They wrapt the ship in splendour wild,
  They caught the flag on high,
And stream'd above the gallant child
  Like banners in the sky.

There came a burst of thunder-sound—
  The boy—O! where was he?
—Ask of the winds that far around
  With fragments strew'd the sea,
With mast, and helm, and pennon fair,
  That well had borne their part;
But the noblest thing which perish'd there
  Was that young faithful heart!

                F. Hemans

* 17 *

THE LOSS OF THE BIRKENHEAD:

Supposed to be told by a Soldier who survived

RIGHT on our flank the crimson sun went down;
The deep sea roll'd around in dark repose;
When, like the wild shriek from some captured
    town,
  A cry of women rose.

  19 *but*, only: *booming*, deep sounding   37 *pennon*, small flag
    1 *flank*, side 3 *captured*, taken in war

The stout ship Birkenhead lay hard and fast,
Caught without hope upon a hidden rock;
Her timbers thrill'd as nerves, when through them
    pass'd
      The spirit of that shock.

And ever like base cowards, who leave their ranks
In danger's hour, before the rush of steel,
Drifted away disorderly the planks
      From underneath her keel.

So calm the air, so calm and still the flood,
That low down in its blue translucent glass
We saw the great fierce fish, that thirst for blood,
      Pass slowly, then repass.

They tarried, the waves tarried, for their prey!
The sea turn'd one clear smile! Like things asleep
Those dark shapes in the azure silence lay,
      As quiet as the deep.

Then amidst oath, and prayer, and rush, and wreck,
Faint screams, faint questions waiting no reply,
Our Colonel gave the word, and on the deck
      Form'd us in line to die.

To die!—'twas hard, whilst the sleek ocean glow'd 25
Beneath a sky as fair as summer flowers:—
All to the boats! cried one:—he was, thank God,
      No officer of ours!

Our English hearts beat true:—we would not stir:
That base appeal we heard, but heeded not:
On land, on sea, we had our Colours, Sir,
      To keep without a spot!

They shall not say in England, that we fought
With shameful strength, unhonour'd life to seek;
Into mean safety, mean deserters, brought
      By trampling down the weak.

10 *rush of steel*, battle   14 *translucent*, transparent   15 *fish*, sharks

So we made women with their children go,
The oars ply back again, and yet again ;
Whilst, inch by inch, the drowning ship sank low,
    Still under steadfast men.

—What follows, why recall?—The brave who died,
Died without flinching in the bloody surf,
They sleep as well, beneath that purple tide,
    As others under turf : —

They sleep as well ! and, roused from their wild grave,
Wearing their wounds like stars, shall rise again,
Joint-heirs with Christ, because they bled to save
    His weak ones, not in vain.
Sir F. H. Doyle

* 18 *

THE 'NORTHERN STAR'

A Tynemouth Ship

The 'Northern Star'
  Sail'd over the bar
Bound to the Baltic Sea ;
  In the morning gray
  She stretch'd away :—
'Twas a weary day to me !

  For many an hour
  In sleet and shower
By the lighthouse rock I stray ;
  And watch till dark
  For the wingéd bark
Of him that is far away.

  The castle's bound
  I wander round,
Amidst the grassy graves :

---

11 *wingéd*, with sails 15 Tynemouth Castle, used as a graveyard

But all I hear
Is the north-wind drear,
And all I see are the waves.

The 'Northern Star'
Is set afar!
Set in the Baltic Sea:
And the waves have spread
The sandy bed ·
That holds my Love from me.

Unknown

· 19 ·

THE ADMIRAL'S GRAVE

THERE is in the lone, lone sea
A spot unmark'd but holy;
For there the gallant and the free
In his ocean-bed lies lowly.

Down, down, beneath the deep
That oft in triumph bore him,
He sleeps a sound and peaceful sleep
With the wild waves dashing o'er him.

He sleeps!— he sleeps! serene and safe
From tempest and from billow,
Where storms that high above him chafe
Scarce rock his peaceful pillow.

The sea and him in death
They did not dare to sever:
It was his home when he had breath:
'Tis now his home for ever!

Sleep on, sleep on, thou mighty dead!
A glorious tomb they've found thee;
The broad blue sky above thee spread:
The boundless ocean round thee.

Unknown

* 20 *

LOSS OF THE ROYAL GEORGE

TOLL for the Brave!
The brave that are no more!
All sunk beneath the wave
Fast by their native shore!

Eight hundred of the brave
Whose courage well was tried,
Had made the vessel heel
And laid her on her side.

A land-breeze shook the shrouds
And she was overset;
Down went the Royal George,
With all her crew complete.

Toll for the brave!
Brave Kempenfelt is gone;
His last sea-fight is fought,
His work of glory done.

It was not in the battle;
No tempest gave the shock;
She sprang no fatal leak,
She ran upon no rock.

His sword was in its sheath,
His fingers held the pen,
When Kempenfelt went down.
With twice four hundred men.

Weigh the vessel up
Once dreaded by our foes!
And mingle with our cup
The tears that England owes.

7 *heel*, lean over 9 *shrouds*, mast ropes 10 *sprang*, opened
25 *weigh*, lift 27 *cup*, rejoicing

Her timbers yet are sound,
And she may float again
Full charged with England's thunder,
And plough the distant main:

But Kempenfelt is gone,
His victories are o'er;
And he and his eight hundred
Shall plough the wave no more.

W. Cowper

* 21 *

THE SAILOR'S WIFE

AND are ye sure the news is true?
　And are ye sure he's weel?
Is this a time to think o' wark?
　Ye jades, lay by your wheel;
Is this the time to spin a thread,
　When Colin's at the door?
Reach down my cloak. I'll to the quay,
　And see him come ashore.
　　For there's nae luck about the house,
　　　There's nae luck at a';
　　There's little pleasure in the house
　　　When our gudeman's awa'.

And gie to me my bigonet,
　My bishop's satin gown;
For I maun tell the bailie's wife
　That Colin's in the town.
My Turkey slippers maun gae on,
　My stockin's pearly blue;
It's a' to pleasure our gudeman,
　For he's baith leal and true.

---

31 *thunder*, cannon　2 *weel*, well　4 *jades*, girls　10 *at a'*, at all
12 *gudeman*, master of the house　13 *bigonet*, little cap　15 *maun*,
　　must: *bailie*, magistrate　20 *leal*, faithful

Rise, lass, and mak a clean fireside,
    Put on the muckle pot;
Gie little Kate her button gown
    And Jock his Sunday coat;
And mak their shoon as black as slaes,
    Their hose as white as snaw;
It's a' to please my ain gudeman,
    For he's been long awa'.

There's twa fat hens upo' the coop
    Been fed this month and mair;
Mak haste and thraw their necks about,
    That Colin weel may fare;
And spread the table neat and clean,
    Gar ilka thing look braw,
For wha can tell how Colin fared
    When he was far awa'?

Sae true his heart, sae smooth his speech,
    His breath like caller air;
His very foot has music in't
    As he comes up the stair:—
And will I see his face again?
    And will I hear him speak?
I'm downright dizzy wi' the thought,
    In troth I'm like to greet.

If Colin's weel, and weel content,
    I hae nae mair to crave,
And gin I live to keep him sae,
    I'm blest aboon the lave:
And will I see his face again,
    And will I hear him speak?
I'm downright dizzy wi' the thought,
    In troth I'm like to greet.

---

22 *muckle*, big 25 *slaes*, sloes 31 *thraw*, twist 34 *gar*, make: *ilka*, every; *braw*, smart 38 *caller*, fresh 44 *greet*, cry 47 *gin*, if 48 *aboon the lave*, beyond every one else

For there's nae luck about the house,
There's nae luck at a';
There's little pleasure in the house
When our gudeman's awa'.
      W. J. Mickle

* 22 *

A SEA DIRGE

FULL fathom five thy father lies:
Of his bones are coral made;
Those are pearls that were his eyes:
Nothing of him that doth fade,
But doth suffer a sea-change
Into something rich and strange;
Sea-nymphs hourly ring his knell:
Hark! now I hear them—
Ding, Dong, Bell.
      W. Shakespeare

* 23 *

A LAND DIRGE

CALL for the robin-redbreast and the wren,
Since o'er shady groves they hover,
And with leaves and flowers do cover
The friendless bodies of unburied men.
Call unto his funeral dole
The ant, the field mouse, and the mole
To rear him hillocks that shall keep him warm,
And (when gay tombs are robb'd) sustain no harm:
But keep the wolf far thence, that's foe to men:
For with his nails he'll dig them up again.
      J. Webster

1 Full five fathoms under water   7 *sea-nymphs*, fairies   8 *gay*, splendid   5 *dole*, feast

* 24 *

THE SOLITUDE OF ALEXANDER SELKIRK

I AM monarch of all I survey;
  My right there is none to dispute;
From the centre all round to the sea
  I am lord of the fowl and the brute.
O Solitude! where are the charms
  That sages have seen in thy face?
Better dwell in the midst of alarms
  Then reign in this horrible place.

I am out of humanity's reach,
  I must finish my journey alone,
Never hear the sweet music of speech;
  I start at the sound of my own.
The beasts that roam over the plain
  My form with indifference see;
They are so unacquainted with man,
  Their tameness is shocking to me.

Society, Friendship, and Love,
  Divinely bestow'd upon man,
O had I the wings of a dove
  How soon would I taste you again!
My sorrows I then might assuage
  In the ways of religion and truth,
Might learn from the wisdom of age,
  And be cheer'd by the sallies of youth.

Ye winds that have made me your sport,
  Convey to this desolate shore
Some cordial endearing report
  Of a land I shall visit no more:—
My friends, do they now and then send
  A wish or a thought after me?
O tell me I yet have a friend,
  Though a friend I am never to see!

6 *sages*, wise people   9 *humanity*, human creatures   21 *assuage*, heal.
24 *sallies*, lively talk   27 *report*, news

How fleet is a glance of the mind !
    Compared with the speed of its flight,
The tempest itself lags behind,
    And the swift-wingèd arrows of light.
When I think of my own native land
    In a moment I seem to be there ;
But alas ! recollection at hand
    Soon hurries me back to despair.

—But the seafowl is gone to her nest,
    The beast is laid down in his lair ;
Even here is a season of rest,
    And I to my cabin repair.
There's mercy in every place,
    And mercy, encouraging thought !
Gives even affliction a grace,
    And reconciles man to his lot.

                                    W. Cowper

* 25 *

AT SEA

A WET sheet and a flowing sea,
    A wind that follows fast
And fills the white and rustling sail
    And bends the gallant mast ;
And bends the gallant mast, my boys,
    While like the eagle free
Away the good ship flies, and leaves
    Old England on the lee.

O for a soft and gentle wind !
    I heard a fair one cry ;
But give to me the snoring breeze
    And white waves heaving high ;

33 *glance*, thought 42 *lair*, den 44 *repair*, go 48 makes us content with life 1 *sheet*, sail ropes 8 *lee*, behind

    And white waves heaving high, my lads,
        The good ship tight and free :—
    The world of waters is our home,
        And merry men are we.

    There's tempest in yon hornéd moon,
        And lightning in yon cloud;
    But hark the music, mariners!
        The wind is piping loud;
    The wind is piping loud, my boys,
        The lightning flashes free—
    While the hollow oak our palace is,
        Our heritage the sea.
                        A. Cunningham

⁎ 26 ⁎

SPRING

SPRING, the sweet Spring, is the year's pleasant king;
Then blooms each thing, then maids dance in a ring,
Cold doth not sting, the pretty birds do sing,
    Cuckoo, jug-jug, pu-we, to-witta-woo!

The palm and may make country houses gay,
Lambs frisk and play, the shepherds pipe all day,
And we hear aye birds tune this merry lay,
    Cuckoo, jug-jug, pu-we, to-witta-woo.

The fields breathe sweet, the daisies kiss our feet,
Young lovers meet, old wives a-sunning sit,
In every street these tunes our ears do greet,
    Cuckoo, jug-jug, pu-we, to-witta-woo!
        Spring! the sweet Spring!
                        T. Nash

17 *hornéd*, new   23 *oak*, ship   24 *heritage*, proper home

* 27 *
COUNTRY SCENES IN OLD DAYS
Day-break

SEE the day begins to break,
And the light shoots like a streak
Of subtle fire; the wind blows cold
While the morning doth unfold;
Now the birds begin to rouse,
And the squirrel from the boughs
Leaps, to get him nuts and fruit;
The early lark, that erst was mute,
Carols to the rising day
Many a note and many a lay.

Unfolding the Flocks

Shepherds, rise, and shake off sleep—
See the blushing morn doth peep
Through the windows, while the sun
To the mountain-tops is run,
Gilding all the vales below
With his rising flames, which grow
Greater by his climbing still.—
Up! ye lazy swains! and fill
Bag and bottle for the field;
Clasp your cloaks fast, lest they yield
To the bitter north-east wind.
Call the maidens up, and find
Who lies longest, that she may
Be chidden for untimed delay.
Feed your faithful dogs, and pray
Heaven to keep you from decay;
So unfold, and then away.

Folding the Flocks

Shepherds all, and maidens fair,
Fold your flocks up; for the air
'Gins to thicken, and the sun
Already his great course hath run.

---

3 *subtle*, piercing   8 *erst*, before   10 *lay*, song   26 *decay*, harm
30 *'gins*, begins

See the dew-drops how they kiss
Every little flower that is;
Hanging on their velvet heads,
Like a rope of crystal beads.
See the heavy clouds low falling,
And bright Hesperus down calling
The dead Night from underground;
At whose rising, mists unsound,
Damps and vapours, fly apace,
Hovering o'er the wanton face
Of these pastures, where they come
Striking dead both bud and bloom:
Therefore from such danger lock
Every one his lovéd flock;
And let your dogs lie loose without,
Lest the wolf come as a scout
From the mountain, and ere day
Bear a lamb or kid away;
Or the crafty, thievish fox
Break upon your simple flocks.
To secure yourself from these
Be not too secure in case;
So shall you good shepherds prove,
And deserve your master's love.
Now, good night! may sweetest slumbers
And soft silence fall in numbers
On your eye-lids! so farewell;
—Thus I end my evening's knell.

J. Fletcher

* 28 *

THE COUNTRY LIFE

SWEET country life, to such unknown
Whose lives are others', not their own,
But, serving courts and cities, be
Less happy, less enjoying thee:—

---

7 *Hesperus*, the evening star   39 *unsound*, unhealthy   47 *scout*, spy   53 *secure*, careless   57 *in numbers*, musically, softly

--Thou never plough'st the ocean's foam
To seek and bring rough pepper home;
Nor to the Eastern Ind dost rove
To bring from thence the scorchéd clove;
Nor, with the loss of thy loved rest,
Bring'st home the ingot from the west:
No! thy ambition's masterpiece
Flies no thought higher than a fleece;
Or how to pay thy hinds, and clear
All scores, and so to end the year:
But walk'st about thine own dear bounds,
Not envying others' larger grounds;
For well thou know'st 'tis not the extent
Of land makes life, but sweet content.
When now the cock, the ploughman's horn,
Calls forth the lily-wristed morn,
Then to thy cornfields thou dost go,
Which though well soil'd, yet thou dost know
That the best compost for the lands
Is the wise master's feet and hands:
There at the plough thou find'st thy team,
With a hind whistling there to them;
And cheer'st them up, by singing how
The kingdom's portion is the plough:
This done, then to th' enamell'd meads
Thou go'st, and as thy foot there treads,
Thou seest a present God-like power
Imprinted in each herb and flower;
And smell'st the breath of great-eyed kine
Sweet as the blossoms of the vine:
Here thou behold'st thy large sleek neat
Unto the dew-laps up in meat;
And as thou look'st, the wanton steer,
The heifer, cow, and ox draw near,
To make a pleasing pastime there:—

10 *ingot*, gold or silver bars   11 thy highest wish   17 *extent*, size
20 *lily*, white   23 *compost*, manure   29 *enamell'd*, brightly-coloured

These seen, thou go'st to view thy flocks
Of sheep, safe from the wolf and fox,
And find'st their bellies there as full
Of short sweet grass, as backs with wool;
And leav'st them, as they feed and fill,
A shepherd piping on a hill.
For sports, for pageantry and plays,
Thou hast thy eves and holydays;
On which the young men and maids meet
To exercise their dancing feet,
Tripping the comely country round,
With daffodils and daisies crown'd.
Thy wakes, thy quintels, here thou hast,
Thy May-poles too with garlands graced.
Thy morris-dance, thy Whitsun-ale,
Thy shearing-feast, which never fail,
Thy harvest home, thy wassail bowl,
That's toss'd up after Fox'i'th'hole,
Thy mummeries, thy twelfth-tide kings
And queens, thy Christmas revellings, —
Thy nut-brown mirth, thy russet wit,
And no man pays too dear for it :—
To these, thou hast thy times to go
And trace the hare i'th'treacherous snow;
Thy witty wiles to draw, and get
The lark into the trammel net;
Thou hast thy cockrood and thy glade
To take the precious pheasant made;
Thy lime-twigs, snares, and pitfalls then
To catch the pilfering birds, not men.

O happy life! if that their good
The husbandmen but understood;

---

46 *pageantry*, shows   52 *quintels*, a game in which poles were run at a post   54 *morris*, mumming   56 *wassail-bowl*, cup of old ale   57 *Fox*, a game in which boys hopped and flogged each other   60 *russet*, homely   62 Besides   64 *witty*, clever   65 *trammel*, fowling   66 *cockrood*, see end

Who all the day themselves do please
And younglings, with such sports as these;
And, lying down, have nought t'affright
Sweet sleep, that makes more short the night.
R. Herrick

* 29 *

THE PASSIONATE SHEPHERD TO HIS LOVE

COME live with me and be my Love,
And we will all the pleasures prove
That hills and valleys, dale and field,
And all the craggy mountains yield.

There will we sit upon the rocks
And see the shepherds feed their flocks,
By shallow rivers, to whose falls
Melodious birds sing madrigals.

There will I make thee beds of roses
And a thousand fragrant posies,
A cap of flowers, and a kirtle
Embroider'd all with leaves of myrtle.

A gown made of the finest wool,
Which from our pretty lambs we pull,
Fair linéd slippers for the cold,
With buckles of the purest gold.

A belt of straw and ivy buds
With coral clasps and amber studs:
And if these pleasures may thee move,
Come live with me and be my Love.

Thy silver dishes for thy meat
As precious as the gods do eat,
Shall on an ivory table be
Prepared each day for thee and me.

8 *madrigals*, short songs   11 *kirtle*, jacket

The shepherd swains shall dance and sing
For thy delight each May-morning:
If these delights thy mind may move,
Then live with me and be my Love.
                              C. Marlowe

* 30 *

THE REAPER

BEHOLD her, single in the field,
Yon solitary Highland Lass!
Reaping and singing by herself;
Stop here, or gently pass!
Alone she cuts and binds the grain,
And sings a melancholy strain;
O listen! for the vale profound
Is overflowing with the sound.

No nightingale did ever chaunt
More welcome notes to weary bands
Of travellers, in some shady haunt
Among Arabian sands:
No sweeter voice was ever heard
In spring-time from the cuckoo-bird,
Breaking the silence of the seas
Among the farthest Hebrides.

Will no one tell me what she sings?
Perhaps the plaintive numbers flow
For old, unhappy, far-off things,
And battles long ago:
Or is it some more humble lay,
Familiar matter of to-day?
Some natural sorrow, loss, or pain,
That has been, and may be again?

Whate'er the theme, the maiden sang
As if her song could have no ending;
I saw her singing at her work,
And o'er the sickle bending;

       25 *theme*, subject of her song

I listen'd till I had my fill;
And as I mounted up the hill
The music in my heart I bore
Long after it was heard no more.

W. Wordsworth

* 31 *

NEW AND OLD

GLAD sight, wherever new with old
Is join'd through some dear homeborn tie;
The life of all that we behold
Depends upon that mystery.
Vain is the glory of the sky,
The beauty vain of field and grove,
Unless, while with admiring eye
We gaze, we also learn to love.

W. Wordsworth

* 32 *

AUTUMN

A Dirge

THE warm sun is failing, the bleak wind is wailing,
The bare boughs are sighing, the pale flowers are dying;
    And the year
On the earth her death-bed, in a shroud of leaves dead,
    Is lying.
    Come, Months, come away,
    From November to May,
    In your saddest array,
    Follow the bier
    Of the dead cold year,
And like dim shadows watch by her sepulchre.

8 *array*, dress   11 *sepulchre*, tomb

The chill rain is falling, the nipt worm is crawling,
The rivers are swelling, the thunder is knelling,
   For the year;
The blithe swallows are flown, and the lizards each gone
   To his dwelling.
  Come, Months, come away;
  Put on white, black, and gray;
  Let your light sisters play;
  Ye, follow the bier
  Of the dead cold year,
And make her grave green with tear on tear.
       P. B. Shelley

* 33 *

THE COUNTRYMAN

WHAT pleasures have great princes
 More dainty to their choice,
Than herdmen wild, who careless
 In quiet life rejoice;
And fortune's favours scorning,
Sing sweet in summer morning.

All day their flocks each tendeth;
 At night they take their rest;
More quiet than who sendeth
 His ship into the east,
Where gold and pearl are plenty,
But getting very dainty.

For lawyers and their pleading,
 They 'steem it not a straw :—
They think that honest meaning
 Is of itself a law :
Where conscience judgeth plainly,
They spend no money vainly.

    19 the summer months
  12 *dainty*, difficult   14 *'steem*, value

O happy who thus liveth,
  Not caring much for gold ;
With clothing, which sufficeth
  To keep him from the cold : -
Though poor and plain his diet,
Yet merry it is and quiet.
                           Unknown

* 34 *

TO A MOUNTAIN DAISY

WEE, modest, crimson-tippéd flower,
Thou's met me in an evil hour ;
For I maun crush amang the stour
      Thy slender stem ;
To spare thee now is past my power,
      Thou bonnie gem.

Alas ! it's no thy neebor sweet,
The bonnie lark, companion meet !
Bending thee 'mang the dewy weet
      Wi' spreckled breast,
When upward springing, blythe, to greet
      The purpling east.

Cauld blew the bitter-biting north
Upon thy early, humble, birth ;
Yet cheerfully thou glinted forth
      Amid the storm ;
Scarce rear'd above the parent earth
      Thy tender form.

The flaunting flowers our gardens yield
High sheltering woods and wa's maun shield,
But thou beneath the random bield
      O' clod or stane
Adorns the histie stibble-field,
      Unseen, alane.

3 *maun*, must : *stour*, dust   7 *no*, not : *neebor*, neighbour
8 *meet*, fit   9 *weet*, wet   10 *spreckled*, speckled
12 *purpling*, at dawn   15 *glinted*, glanced
20 *wa's*, walls   21 *bield*, shelter   23 *histie*, dry : *stibble*, stubble

There, in thy scanty mantle clad,
Thy snawy bosom sunward spread,
Thou lifts thy unassuming head
    In humble guise ;
But now the share uptears thy bed,
    And low thou lies !

R. Burns

* 35 *

THE WHIRL-BLAST

A WHIRL-BLAST from behind the hill
Rush'd o'er the wood with startling sound ;
Then—all at once the air was still,
And showers of hailstones patter'd round.
Where leafless oaks tower'd high above,
I sat within an undergrove
Of tallest hollies, tall and green ;
A fairer bower was never seen.
From year to year the spacious floor
With wither'd leaves is cover'd o'er,

And all the year the bower is green ;
But see ! where'er the hailstones drop
The wither'd leaves all skip and hop ;
There's not a breeze—no breath of air—
Yet here, and there, and every where
Along the floor, beneath the shade
By those embowering hollies made,
The leaves in myriads jump and spring,
As if with pipes and music rare
Some Robin Goodfellow were there,
And all those leaves, in festive glee,
Were dancing to the minstrelsy.

W. Wordsworth

27 *unassuming*, modest   28 *guise*, manner
20 *Robin Goodfellow*, a fairy   22 *minstrelsy*, music

* 36

WINTER

WHEN icicles hang by the wall,
   And Dick the shepherd blows his nail,
And Tom bears logs into the hall,
   And milk comes frozen home in pail;
When blood is nipt, and ways be foul,
Then nightly sings the staring owl
        Tuwhoo!
Tuwhit! tuwhoo! A merry note!
While greasy Joan doth keel the pot.

When all around the wind doth blow,
   And coughing drowns the parson's saw,
And birds sit brooding in the snow,
   And Marian's nose looks red and raw;
When roasted crabs hiss in the bowl —
Then nightly sings the staring owl
        Tuwhoo!
Tuwhit! tuwhoo! A merry note!
While greasy Joan doth keel the pot.
               W. Shakespeare

* 37 *

JOCK OF HAZELDEAN

'WHY weep ye by the tide, ladie?
   'Why weep ye by the tide?
'I'll wed ye to my youngest son,
   'And ye sall be his bride:
'And ye sall be his bride, ladie,
   'Sae comely to be seen'—
But aye she loot the tears down fa'
   For Jock of Hazeldean.

9 *keel*, skim   11 *saw*, speech   14 *crabs*, wild apples
       7 *loot*, let: *fa'* fall

'Now let this wilfu' grief be done,
  'And dry that cheek so pale ;
'Young Frank is chief of Errington,
  'And lord of Langley-dale ;
'His step is first in peaceful ha',
  'His sword in battle keen'—
But aye she loot the tears down fa'
  For Jock of Hazeldean.

'A chain of gold ye sall not lack,
  'Nor braid to bind your hair,
'Nor mettled hound, nor managed hawk,
  'Nor palfrey fresh and fair ;
'And you the foremost o' them a'
  'Sall ride our forest-queen'—
But aye she loot the tears down fa'
  For Jock of Hazeldean.

The kirk was deck'd at morning-tide,
  The tapers glimmer'd fair ;
The priest and bridegroom wait the bride,
  And dame and knight are there :
They sought her baith by bower and ha' ;
  The ladie was not seen !
She's o'er the Border, and awa'
  Wi' Jock of Hazeldean.
                                Sir W. Scott

· 38 ·

THE OUTLAW

O BRIGNALL banks are wild and fair,
  And Greta woods are green,
And you may gather garlands there
  Would grace a summer-queen.

13 *ha'*, hall, for house   19 *mettled*, spirited : *managed*, trained
25 *kirk*, church   29 *bower*, lady's own rown
    Outlaw, man driven out to live by himself, a robber

And as I rode by Dalton-Hall
  Beneath the turrets high,
A Maiden on the castle-wall
  Was singing merrily:
'O Brignall Banks are fresh and fair,
  'And Greta woods are green;
'I'd rather rove with Edmund there
  'Than reign our English queen.'

—'If, Maiden, thou wouldst wend with me,
  'To leave both tower and town,
'Thou first must guess what life lead we
  'That dwell by dale and down.
'And if thou canst that riddle read,
  'As read full well you may,
'Then to the greenwood shalt thou speed
  'As blithe as Queen of May.'
Yet sung she, 'Brignall banks are fair,
  'And Greta woods are green;
'I'd rather rove with Edmund there
  'Than reign our English queen.'

'I read you by your bugle-horn
  'And by your palfrey good,
'I read you for a ranger sworn
  'To keep the king's greenwood.'
—'A Ranger, lady, winds his horn,
  'And 'tis at peep of light;
'His blast is heard at merry morn,
  'And mine at dead of night.'
Yet sung she 'Brignall banks are fair,
  'And Greta woods are gay;
'I would I were with Edmund there
  'To reign his Queen of May!

---

13 *wend*, go 25 *read*, declare 26 *palfrey*, pony
27 *ranger*, forest-keeper 28 *keep*, guard 29 *winds*, blows

' With burnish'd brand and musketoon
' So gallantly you come.
' I read you for a bold Dragoon
  ' That lists the tuck of drum.'
—' I list no more the tuck of drum,
  ' No more the trumpet hear ;
' But when the beetle sounds his hum
  ' My comrades take the spear.
' And O ! though Brignall banks be fair
  ' And Greta woods be gay,
' Yet mickle must the maiden dare
  ' Would reign my Queen of May !

' Maiden ! a nameless life I lead,
  ' A nameless death I'll die !
' The fiend whose lantern lights the mead
  ' Were better mate than I !
' And when I'm with my comrades met
  ' Beneath the greenwood bough
' What once we were we all forget,
  ' Nor think what we are now.'

Chorus

Yet Brignall banks are fresh and fair,
  And Greta woods are green,
And you may gather garlands there
  Would grace a summer-queen.
                              Sir W. Scott

* 39 *

EDWIN AND ANGELINA

'TURN, gentle Hermit of the dale,
  ' And guide my lonely way
' To where yon taper cheers the vale
  ' With hospitable ray.

37 *brand*, sword : *musketoon*, blunderbuss   40 *tuck*, beat
47 *mickle*, much   51 Will o' the Wisp

' For here forlorn and lost I tread,
  ' With fainting steps and slow,
' Where wilds, immeasurably spread,
  ' Seem lengthening as I go.'

—' Forbear, my son,' the Hermit cries,
  ' To tempt the dangerous gloom,
' For yonder faithless phantom flies
  ' To lure thee to thy doom.

  Here to the houseless child of want
  ' My door is open still ;
' And though my portion is but scant
  ' I give it with goodwill.

' Then turn to-night, and freely share
  ' Whate'er my cell bestows ;
' My rushy couch and frugal fare,
  ' My blessing and repose.

' No flocks that range the valley free
  ' To slaughter I condemn ;
' Taught by that Power that pities me,
  ' I learn to pity them :

' But from the mountain's grassy side
  ' A guiltless feast I bring :
' A scrip with herbs and fruits supplied,
  ' And water from the spring.

' Then, pilgrim ! turn ; thy cares forego;
  ' All earth-born cares are wrong:
' Man wants but little here below,
  ' Nor wants that little long.'

---

7 *immeasurably*, without end   10 *tempt*, try
11 the Will-o'-the-Wisp   12 *lure*, tempt
19 bed of rushes   22 kill
27 *scrip*, little bag   29 *forego*, lay by

Soft as the dew from heaven descends
   His gentle accents fell :
The modest stranger lowly bends,
   And follows to the cell.

Far in a wilderness obscure
   The lonely mansion lay,
A refuge to the neighbouring poor,
   And strangers led astray.

No stores beneath its humble thatch
   Required a master's care,
The wicket, opening with a latch,
   Received the harmless pair.

And now, when busy crowds retire
   To take their evening rest,
The hermit trimm'd his little fire,
   And cheer'd his pensive guest:

And spread his vegetable store,
   And gaily press'd and smiled ;
And skill'd in legendary lore,
   The lingering hours beguiled.

Around, in sympathetic mirth,
   Its tricks the kitten tries ;
The cricket chirrups on the hearth,
   The crackling fagot flies.

But nothing could a charm impart
   To soothe the stranger's woe ;
For grief was heavy at his heart,
   And tears began to flow.

His rising cares the Hermit spied,
   With answering care oppress'd :
And 'Whence, unhappy youth,' he cried,
   'The sorrows of thy breast?

---

34 *accents*, voice   48 *pensive*, thoughtful
51 *legendary lore*, ancient stories   53 cheerful like the Hermit
57 *impart*, give   62 similar sadness

' From better habitations spurn'd
  ' Reluctant dost thou rove?
' Or grieve for friendship unreturn'd,
  ' Or unregarded love?

' Alas! the joys that fortune brings
  ' Are trifling, and decay;
' And those who prize the paltry things,
  ' More trifling still than they.

' And what is friendship but a name,
  ' A charm that lulls to sleep;
' A shade that follows wealth or fame,
  ' But leaves the wretch to weep?

' And love is still an emptier sound,
  ' The modern fair-one's jest;
' On earth unseen, or only found
  ' To warm the turtle's nest.

' For shame, fond youth! thy sorrows hush;
  ' And spurn the sex,' he said;
But while he spoke, a rising blush
  His love-lorn guest betray'd!

Surprised he sees new beauties rise,
  Swift mantling to the view;
Like colours o'er the morning skies,
  As bright, as transient too.

The bashful look, the rising breast,
  Alternate spread alarms:
The lovely stranger stands confess'd,
  A maid in all her charms.

And ' Ah! forgive a stranger rude,—
  ' A wretch forlorn,' she cried;
' Whose feet, unhallow'd, thus intrude
  ' Where Heaven and you reside!

---

65 *spurn'd*, driven 66 *reluctant*, unwilling 69 *fortune*, wealth
82 *the sex*, women   86 *mantling*, spreading
88 *transient*, soon passing 91 *confess'd*, revealed 95 *intrude*, push in

' But let a maid thy pity share,
    Whom love has taught to stray;
' Who seeks for rest, but finds despair
    ' Companion of her way.

' My father lived beside the Tyne,
    ' A wealthy lord was he;
' And all his wealth was mark'd as mine,
    ' He had but only me.

' To win me from his tender arms
    ' Unnumber'd suitors came,
' Who praised me for imputed charms,
    ' And felt or feign'd a flame.

' Each hour a mercenary crowd
    ' With richest proffers strove:
' Amongst the rest, young Edwin bow'd,
    ' But never talk'd of love.

' In humble, simple habit clad,
    ' No wealth nor power had he:
' Wisdom and worth were all he had,
    ' But these were all to me.

' And when, beside me in the dale,
    ' He caroll'd lays of love,
' His breath lent fragrance to the gale,
    ' And music to the grove.

' The blossom opening to the day,
    ' The dews of heaven refined,
' Could nought of purity display
    ' To emulate his mind.

' The dew, the blossom on the tree,
    ' With charms inconstant shine:
' Their charms were his; but, woe to me!
    ' Their constancy was mine.

107 *imputed*, which they said they saw   108 *flame*, love
109 *mercenary*, greedy of money   110 *proffers*, offers
124 *emulate*, rival   126 changeable beauties

'For still I tried each fickle art,
  'Importunate and vain ;
'And, while his passion touch'd my heart,
  'I triumph'd in his pain :

'Till, quite dejected with my scorn,
  'He left me to my pride ;
'And sought a solitude forlorn,
  'In secret, where he died.

'But mine the sorrow, mine the fault !
  'And well my life shall pay;
'I'll seek the solitude he sought,
  'And stretch me where he lay.

'And there, forlorn, despairing, hid,
  'I'll lay me down and die ;
''Twas so for me that Edwin did,
  'And so for him will I.'

—'Forbid it, Heaven !' the Hermit cried, 145
  And clasp'd her to his breast :
The wondering fair one turn'd to chide—
  'Twas Edwin's self that press'd !

'Turn, Angelina, ever dear,
  'My charmer, turn to see
'Thy own, thy long-lost Edwin here,
  'Restored to love and thee.

'Thus let me hold thee to my heart,
  'And every care resign :
'And shall we never, never part,
  'My life—my all that's mine ?

'No, never from this hour to part,
  'We'll live and love so true :
'The sigh that rends thy constant heart
  'Shall break thy Edwin's too.'
                               O. Goldsmith

132 *triumph'd*, rejoiced   133 *dejected*, grieved

40

THE LASS OF LOCHROYAN

'O WHO will shoe my bonny foot,
 'And who will glove my hand?
And who will lace my middle jimp
 'Wi' a long, long, linen band?

'Or who will kaim my yellow hair
 'Wi' a new-made silver kaim?
'O who will father my young son
 'Till Lord Gregory comes hame?

'O if I had a bonny ship,
 'And men to sail wi' me,
'It's I would gang to my true Love,
 'Since he winna come to me!'

Then she's gar'd build a bonny boat,
 To sail the salt, salt sea:
The sails were of the light-green silk,
 And the ropes of taffetie.

She had not been on the sea sailing
 About a month or more,
Till landed has she her bonny ship
 Near to her true Love's door.

She's ta'en her young-son in her arms
 And to the door she's gane;
And long she knock'd, and sair she call'd,
 But answer got she nane.

'O open the door, Lord Gregory!
 'O open, and let me in!
'For the wind blows through my yellow hair,
 'And the rain drops o'er my chin.'

---

3 *middle jimp*, slender waist   5 *kaim*, comb   12 *winna*, will not
13 *gar'd*, made   16 *taffetie*, thin silk   23 *sair*, sorely

Long stood she at Lord Gregory's door,
   And long she tirl'd the pin ;
At length up gat his false mother,
   Says, 'Who's that would be in?'

—'O it's Annie of Lochroyan,
   'Your Love, come o'er the sea,
'But and your young son in her arms ;
   'So open the door to me.'

—'Away, away, ye ill woman !
   'You're not come here for gude ;
'You're but a witch, or a vile warlock,
   'Or a mermaid o' the flood.'

—'I'm no a witch, nor vile warlock,
   'Nor mermaiden,' said she ;
'But I am Annie of Lochroyan,—
   'O open the door to me !'

—'If thou be Annie of Lochroyan
   '(As I trow ye binna she),
'Now tell me some of the love-tokens
   'That pass'd 'tween me and thee.'

—'O dinna ye mind, Lord Gregory,
   'As we sat at the wine,
'How we changed the rings from our fingers,
   'And I can show thee thine ?

'O yours was good, and good enough,
   'But not so good as mine ;
'For yours was o' the good red gold,
   'But mine of the diamond fine.

'So open the door, Love Gregory,
   'And open it with speed ;
'Or your young son that's in my arms,
   'For cold will soon be dead.'

          2 *tirl'd*, twisted the latch
35 *But and*, and also   39 *warlock*, wizard
46 *binna*, be not   49 *dinna*, do not

—' Away, away, ye ill woman!
　'Go from my door for shame!
'For I have gotten another Love,
　'So you may hie you hame.'

Fair Annie turn'd her round about;
　'Well! since that it be sae,
'May never a woman, that has borne a son,
　'Have a heart so full of wae!

'Take down, take down, the mast of gold,
　'Set up the mast o' tree:
'It ill becomes a forsaken lady
　'To sail so gallantlie.'

Lord Gregory started from his sleep,
　And to his mother did say,
'I dreamt a dream, this night, mother,
　'That makes my heart right wae.

'I dreamt that Annie of Lochroyan,
　'The flower of all her kin,
'E'en now was standing at my door,
　'But none would let her in.'

—'O there was a woman stood at the door,
　'With a bairn intill her arm;
'But I could not let her come within,
　'For fear she had done you harm.'

—'O wae betide ye, ill woman!
　'An ill death may ye dee!
'That wadna open the door to her,
　Nor yet would waken me!'

O, he's gone down to yon shore side
　As fast as he could fare;
He saw fair Annie in the boat,
　But the wind it toss'd her sair.

68 *wae*, woe　　70 *tree*, wood　　76 *wae*, sad
　82 *intill*, in　　87 *wadna*, would not

And 'hey, Annie!' and 'how, Annie!'
  'O Annie, winna ye bide?'
But aye the mair he cried 'Annie,'
  The broader grew the tide.

And 'hey, Annie!' and 'how, Annie!'
  'O Annie, speak to me!'
But aye the louder he cried 'Annie,'
  The louder roar'd the sea.

The wind blew loud, the sea grew rough,
  And the ship was rent in twain :
And soon he saw his fair Annie
  Come floating o'er the main.

He saw his young son in her arms,
  Both toss'd above the tide ;
He wrang his hands, and fast he ran
  And plunged in the sea sae wide.

He catch'd her by the yellow hair,
  And drew her up on the sand ;
But cold and stiff was every limb
  Before he reach'd the land.

And then he kiss'd her on the cheek,
  And kiss'd her on the chin ;
And sair he kiss'd her on the lips ;
  But there was no breath within.

'O wae betide my cruel mother !
  'An ill death may she dee !
'She turn'd fair Annie from my door,
  'Wha died for love of me!'

Unknown

94 *bide*, wait

* 41 *

CUMNOR HALL

The dews of summer night did fall ;
  The moon, sweet Regent of the sky,
Silver'd the walls of Cumnor Hall,
  And many an oak that grew thereby.

Now nought was heard beneath the skies ;
  The sounds of busy life were still,
Save an unhappy lady's sighs
  That issued from that lonely pile.

' Leicester !' she cried, ' is this thy love
  ' That thou so oft hast sworn to me,
' To leave me in this lonely grove,
  ' Immured in shameful privity ?

' No more thou com'st with lover's speed
  ' Thy once-belovéd bride to see ;
' But, be she alive, or be she dead,
  ' I fear, stern Earl, 's the same to thee.

' Not so the usage I received
  ' When happy in my father's hall :
' No faithless husband then me grieved ;
  ' No chilling fears did me appal.

' I rose up with the cheerful morn,
  ' No lark more blithe, no flower more gay :
' And like the bird that haunts the thorn,
  ' So merrily sung the live-long day.

' If that my beauty is but small,
  ' Among court-ladies all despised ;
' Why didst thou rend it from that hall
  ' Where, scornful Earl ! it well was prized ?

2 *regent*, ruler   8 *issued*, came forth : *pile*, building
12 *immured*, buried : *privity*, solitude
1 *usage*, treatment   20 *appal*, frighten   27 *rend*, take away

' But, Leicester, (or I much am wrong),
  ' Or 'tis not beauty lures thy vows ;
' Rather, ambition's gilded crown
  ' Makes thee forget thy humble spouse.

' Then, Leicester, why,—again I plead,
  ' The injured surely may repine.—
' Why didst thou wed a country maid,
  ' When some fair Princess might be thine ?

' Why didst thou praise my humble charms,
  ' And O ! then leave them to decay ?
' Why didst thou win me to thy arms,
  ' Then leave to mourn the live-long day ?

' The village maidens of the plain
  ' Salute me lowly as they go :
' Envious they mark my silken train,
  ' Nor think a Countess can have woe.

' How far less blest am I than them!
  ' Daily to pine and waste with care,
' Like the poor plant, that, from its stem
  ' Divided, feels the chilling air.

' My spirits flag ; my hopes decay :
  ' Still that dread death-bell smites my ear : 50
' And many a boding seems to say
  ' Countess, prepare ! thy end is near ! '

Thus sore and sad the Lady grieved
  In Cumnor Hall so lone and drear ;
And many a heartfelt sigh she heaved,
  And let fall many a bitter tear.

And ere the dawn of day appear'd,
  In Cumnor Hall so lone and drear,
Full many a piercing scream was heard,
  And many a cry of mortal fear.

---

    30 *lures*, tempts thy wishes   32 *spouse*, wife
34 *repine*, murmur   37 *charms*, beauties   42 bow to me
43 *train*, dress   49 *flag*, sink   51 *boding*, sign

The death-bell thrice was heard to ring ;
  An aerial voice was heard to call ;
And thrice the raven flapp'd its wing
  Around the towers of Cumnor Hall.

The mastiff howl'd at village door ;
  The oaks were shatter'd on the green ;
Woe was the hour ! for never more
  That hapless Countess e'er was seen.

And in that manor now no more
  Is cheerful feast and sprightly ball :
For ever since that dreary hour
  Have spirits haunted Cumnor Hall.

The village maids, with fearful glance,
  Avoid the ancient moss-grown wall,
Nor ever lead the merry dance
  Among the groves of Cumnor Hall.

Full many a traveller oft hath sigh'd,
  And pensive wept the Countess' fall,
As wandering onwards they've espied
  The haunted towers of Cumnor Hall.

W. J. Mickle

* 42 •

THE TRUE AND THE FALSE

WHERE shall the lover rest
  Whom the fates sever
From his true maiden's breast
  Parted for ever ?
Where, through groves deep and high
  Sounds the far billow,
Where early violets die
  Under the willow :—
    Eleu loro
  Soft shall be his pillow.

62 *aerial*, in the air   78 *pensive*, thoughtful

There, through the summer day
  Cool streams are laving :
There, while the tempests sway,
  Scarce are boughs waving ;
There thy rest shalt thou take,
  Parted for ever,
Never again to wake
  Never, O never !
    Eleu loro
  Never, O never !

—Where shall the traitor rest,
  He, the deceiver,
Who could win maiden's breast,
  Ruin, and leave her ?
In the lost battle,
  Borne down by the flying,
Where mingles war's rattle
  With groans of the dying ;
    Eleu loro
  There shall he be lying.

Her wing shall the eagle flap
  O'er the falsehearted ;
His warm blood the wolf shall lap
  Ere life be parted :
Shame and dishonour sit
  By his grave ever ;
Blessing shall hallow it
  Never, O never !
    Eleu loro
  Never, O never !

Sir W. Scott

· 43 ·

AULD ROBIN GRAY

WHEN the sheep are in the fauld, and the kye at hame,
And a' the warld to rest are gane,
The waes o' my heart fa' in showers frae my e'e,
While my gudeman lies sound by me.

Young Jamie lo'ed me weel, and sought me for his bride ;
But saving a croun he had naething else beside :
To make the croun a pund, young Jamie gaed to sea ;
And the croun and the pund were baith for me.

He hadna been awa' a week but only twa,
When my father brak his arm, and the cow was stown awa' ;
My mother she fell sick, and my Jamie at the sea –
And auld Robin Gray came a-courtin' me.

My father couldna work, and my mother couldna spin ;
I toil'd day and night, but their bread I couldna win ;
Auld Rob maintain'd them baith, and wi' tears in his e'e
'Said, Jennie, for their sakes, O, marry me !'

My heart it said nay ; I look'd for Jamie back ;
But the wind it blew high, and the ship it was a wrack ;
His ship it was a wrack—why didna Jamie dee ?
Or why do I live to cry, Wae's me ?

1 *fauld*, fold : *kye*, cattle   3 *fa'*, fall   7 *gaed*, went
9 *awa'*, away a fortnight   10 *stown*, stolen
13 *couldna*, could not   19 *dee*, die

My father urgit sair : my mother didna speak ;
But she look'd in my face till my heart was like to break :
They gi'ed him my hand, but my heart was at the sea :
Sae auld Robin Gray he was gudeman to me.

I hadna been a wife a week but only four,
When mournfu' as I sat on the stane at the door,
I saw my Jamie's wraith, for I couldna think it he—
Till he said, ' I'm come hame to marry thee.'

—O sair, sair did we greet, and muckle did we say ;
We took but ae kiss, and I bad him gang away :
I wish that I were dead, but I'm no like to dee ;
And why was I born to say, Wae's me !

I gang like a ghaist, and I carena to spin ;
I daurna think on Jamie, for that wad be a sin ;
But I'll do my best a gude wife aye to be,
For auld Robin Gray he is kind unto me.

Lady A. Lindsay

* 44 *

WILLY DROWNED IN YARROW

Down in yon garden sweet and gay
  Where bonnie grows the lily,
I heard a fair maid sighing say,
  ' My wish be wi' sweet Willie !

' Willie's rare, and Willie's fair,
  ' And Willie's wondrous bonny ;
' And Willie hecht to marry me
  ' Gin e'er he married ony.

21 *urgit*, pressed	24 *gudeman*, husband	27 *wraith*, ghost
29 *sair*, sorely : *greet*, cry : *muckle*, much		31 *like*, likely
34 *daurna*, dare not	7 *hecht*, promised	8 *gin*, if : *ony*, any

' O gentle wind, that bloweth south,
' From where my Love repaireth,
' Convey a kiss frae his dear mouth
' And tell me how he fareth !

' O tell sweet Willie to come doun
' And hear the mavis singing,
' And see the birds on ilka bush
' And leaves around them hinging.

' The lav'rock there, wi' her white breast
' And gentle throat sae narrow :
' There's sport eneuch for gentlemen
' On Leader-haughs and Yarrow.

' O Leader-haughs are wide and braid
' And Yarrow-haughs are bonny ;
' There Willie hecht to marry me
' If e'er he married ony.

' But Willie's gone, whom I thought on,
' And does not hear me weeping ;
' Draws many a tear frae true love's e'e
' When other maids are sleeping.

' O came ye by yon water-side ?
' Pou'd you the rose or lily ?
' Or came you by yon meadow green,
' Or saw you my sweet Willie ? '

She sought him up, she sought him down,
 She sought him braid and narrow ;
Syne, in the cleaving of a craig,
 She found him drown'd in Yarrow !
                                Unknown

10 *repaireth*, is going   14 *mavis*, thrush   15 *ilka*, every
17 *lav'rock*, lark   19 *eneuch*, enough   20 *haughs*, water-meadows
21 *braid*, broad   30 *pou'd*, pulled
34 through plain and valley   35 *syne*, then : *craig*, rock

* 45 *

LORD ULLIN'S DAUGHTER

A Chieftain to the Highlands b
Cries 'Boatman, do not tarry!
'And I'll give thee a silver pound
'   row us o'er the ferry!'

—' Now, who be ye, would cross Lochgyle
' This dark and stormy water?'
—' O I'm the chief of Ulva's isle,
' And this, Lord Ullin's daughter.

' And fast before her father's men
' Three days we've fled together,
' For should he find us in the glen,
' My blood would stain the heather.

' His horsemen hard behind us ride—
' Should they our steps discover,
' Then who will cheer my bonny bride
' When they have slain her lover?'

Out spoke the hardy Highland wight,
' I'll go, my chief, I'm ready:
' It is not for your silver bright,
' But for your winsome lady:—

' And by my word! the bonny bird
' In danger shall not tarry;
' So though the waves are raging white,
' I'll row you o'er the ferry.'

By this the storm grew loud apace,
The water-wraith was shrieking;
And in the scowl of heaven each face
Grew dark as they were speaking.

26 *water-wraith*, spirit of the lake   27 *scowl*, storminess

But still as wilder blew the wind,
And as the night grew drearer,
Adown the glen rode arméd men,
Their trampling sounded nearer.

' O haste thee, haste !' the lady cries,
' Though tempests round us gather ;
' I'll meet the raging of the skies,
' But not an angry father !'

The boat has left a stormy land,
A stormy sea before her,—
When, O ! too strong for human hand
The tempest gather'd o'er her.

And still they row'd amidst the roar
Of waters fast prevailing :
Lord Ullin reach'd that fatal shore,—
His wrath was changed to wailing.

For, sore dismay'd, through storm and shade
His child he did discover :—
One lovely hand she stretch'd for aid,
And one was round her lover.

' Come back ! come back !' he cried in grief
' Across this stormy water :
' And I'll forgive your Highland chief :—
' My daughter !—O my daughter !'

'Twas vain : the loud waves lash'd the shore,
Return or aid preventing :
The waters wild went o'er his child,
And he was left lamenting.

T. Campbell

※ 46 ※

THE DESTRUCTION OF SENNACHERIB

The Assyrian came down like the wolf on the fold,
And his cohorts were gleaming in purple and gold,
And the sheen of their spears was like stars on the sea,
When the blue wave rolls nightly on deep Galilee.

Like the leaves of the forest when summer is green,
That host with their banners at sunset were seen;
Like the leaves of the forest when autumn hath blown,
That host on the morrow lay wither'd and strown.

For the Angel of Death spread his wings on the blast,
And breathed in the face of the foe as he pass'd; 10
And the eyes of the sleepers wax'd deadly and chill,
And their hearts but once heaved, and for ever grew still.

And there lay the steed with his nostril all wide,
But through it there roll'd not the breath of his pride:
And the foam of his gasping lay white on the turf,
And cold as the spray of the rock-beating surf.

And there lay the rider, distorted and pale,
With the dew on his brow, and the rust on his mail;
And the tents were all silent, the banners alone,
The lances unlifted, the trumpet unblown.

2 *cohorts*, regiments   3 *sheen*, shining   11 *wax'd*, grew
13 *steed*, warhorse   16 *surf*, waves
1 *distorted*, twisted in death   18 *mail*, armour

And the widows of Ashur are loud in their wail,
And the idols are broke in the temple of Baal,
And the might of the Gentile, unsmote by the sword,
Hath melted like snow in the glance of the Lord!
Lord Byron

* 47 *

THE SPANISH ARMADA

ATTEND all ye who list to hear our noble England's praise,
I tell of the thrice famous deeds she wrought in ancient days,
When that great fleet invincible against her bore in vain
The richest spoils of Mexico, the stoutest hearts of Spain.

It was about the lovely close of a warm summer day,
There came a gallant merchant-ship full sail to Plymouth Bay;
Her crew hath seen Castile's black fleet beyond Aurigny's isle,
At earliest twilight, on the waves lie heaving many a mile;
At sunrise she escaped their van, by God's especial grace;
And the tall Pinta, till the noon, had held her close in chase.
Forthwith a guard at every gun was placed along the wall;
The beacon blazed upon the roof of Edgecumbe's lofty hall;

21 *Ashur*, Assyria 1 *list*, desire 7 *isle*, Alderney
9 *van*, foremost ships

Many a light fishing-bark put out to pry along the coast ;
And with loose rein and bloody spur rode inland many a post.
With his white hair unbonnet'd the stout old sheriff comes ;
Behind him march the halberdiers, before him sound the drums ;
His yeomen, round the market-cross, make clear an ample space,
For there behoves him to set up the standard of her Grace.
And haughtily the trumpets peal, and gaily dance the bells.
As slow upon the labouring wind the royal blazon swells.
Look how the Lion of the sea lifts up his ancient crown,
And underneath his deadly paw treads the gay Lilies down.
So stalk'd he when he turn'd to flight on that famed Picard field
Bohemia's plume, and Genoa's bow, and Cæsar's eagle shield :
So glared he when at Agincourt in wrath he turn'd to bay,
And crush'd and torn beneath his claws the princely hunters lay.
Ho ! strike the flag-staff deep, Sir Knight ; ho ! scatter flowers, fair maids :
Ho ! gunners, fire a loud salute : ho ! gallants, draw your blades ;

14 *post*, messenger 16 *halberdiers*, guards with axes
17 *yeomen*, stout followers
18 *standard*, great flag : *her Grace*, Queen Elizabeth
20 *blazon*, arms of England   22 *lilies*, old arms of France
23 *field*, Cressy   28 *salute*, volley : *blades*, swords

Thou sun, shine on her joyously—ye breezes waft her wide ;
Our glorious SEMPER EADEM—the banner of our pride.
The freshening breeze of eve unfurl'd that banner's massive fold,
The parting gleam of sunshine kiss'd that haughty scroll of gold ;
Night sank upon the dusky beach, and on the purple sea,—
Such night in England ne'er had been, nor e'er again shall be !
From Eddystone to Berwick bounds, from Lynn to Milford Bay,
That time of slumber was as bright and busy as the day ;
For swift to east and swift to west the ghastly war-flame spread ;
High on Saint Michael's Mount it shone—it shone on Beachy Head.
Far on the deep the Spaniard saw, along each southern shire,
Cape beyond cape, in endless range, those twinkling points of fire ;
The fisher left his skiff to rock on Tamar's glittering waves,
The rugged miners pour'd to war from Mendip's sunless caves.
O'er Longleat's towers, o'er Cranbourne's oaks, the fiery herald flew ;
He roused the shepherds of Stonehenge, the rangers of Beaulieu.
Right sharp and quick the bells all night rang out from Bristol town,
And ere the day three hundred horse had met on Clifton down ;

30 *Semper Eadem*, 'always the same': *banner*, flag   32 *scroll*, flag

The sentinel on Whitehall-gate look'd forth into the night,
And saw o'erhanging Richmond Hill, the streak of blood-red light.
Then bugle's note and cannon's roar the death-like silence broke,
And with one start, and with one cry, the royal city woke.
At once on all her stately gates arose the answering fires ;
At once the wild alarum clash'd from all her reeling spires ;
From all the batteries of the Tower peal'd loud the voice of fear ;
And all the thousand masts of Thames sent back a louder cheer :
And from the furthest wards was heard the rush of hurrying feet,
And the broad streams of pikes and flags rush'd down each roaring street :
And broader still became the blaze, and louder still the din,
As fast from every village round the horse came spurring in :
And eastward straight, from wild Blackheath, the warlike errand went,
And roused in many an ancient hall the gallant squires of Kent.
Southward, from Surrey's pleasant hills flew those bright couriers forth ;
High on bleak Hampstead's swarthy moor they star'ed for the North ;
And on, and on, without a pause, untired they bounded still.

50 *city*, London 52 *reeling*, trembling under the sound
55 *wards*, divisions of the city 56 *pikes*, spears 58 *horse*, soldiers
59 *errand*, the beacon-fires to rouse England : so
61 *couriers* 62 *swarthy*, dark 63 *pause*, stay

All night from tower to tower they sprang; they
  sprang from hill to hill:
Till the proud Peak unfurl'd the flag o'er Darwin's
  rocky dales,
Till like volcanoes flared to Heaven the stormy hills
  of Wales;
Till twelve fair counties saw the blaze on Malvern's
  lonely height,
Till stream'd in crimson on the wind the Wrekin's
  crest of light,
Till broad and fierce the star came forth on Ely's
  stately fane,
And tower and hamlet rose in arms o'er all the
  boundless plain;
Till Belvoir's lordly terraces the sign to Lincoln sent,
And Lincoln sped the message on o'er the wide vale
  of Trent;
Till Skiddaw saw the fire that burn'd on Gaunt's
  embattled pile,
And the red glare on Skiddaw roused the burghers
  of Carlisle.

Lord Macaulay

* 48

HOHENLINDEN

On Linden, when the sun was low,
All bloodless lay the untrodden snow;
And dark as winter was the flow
  Of Iser, rolling rapidly.

But Linden saw another sight,
When the drum beat at dead of night
Commanding fires of death to light
  The darkness of her scenery.

69 *fane*, cathedral   72 *sped*, sent quickly
   74 *burghers*, citizens

By torch and trumpet fast array'd
Each horseman drew his battle-blade,
And furious every charger neigh'd
    To join the dreadful revelry.

Then shook the hills with thunder riven;
Then rush'd the steed, to battle driven;
And louder than the bolts of Heaven
    Far flash'd the red artillery.

But redder yet that light shall glow
On Linden's hills of stainéd snow;
And bloodier yet the torrent flow
    Of Iser, rolling rapidly.

'Tis morn; but scarce yon level sun
Can pierce the war-clouds, rolling dun,
Where furious Frank and fiery Hun
    Shout in their sulphurous canopy.

The combat deepens. On, ye Brave
Who rush to glory, or the grave!
Wave, Munich, all thy banners wave,
    And charge with all thy chivalry!

Few, few shall part, where many meet!
The snow shall be their winding-sheet,
And every turf beneath their feet
    Shall be a soldier's sepulchre.
                      T. Campbell

· 49 ·
THE LAST CHARGE OF THE FRENCH AT WATERLOO

On came the whirlwind—like the last
But fiercest sweep of tempest-blast—
On came the whirlwind—steel-gleams broke
Like lightning through the rolling smoke;

9 *array'd*, dressed   11 *charger*, war-horse   15 than thunder
16 *artillery*, cannon   22 *dun*, gloomy
24 *sulphurous canopy*, overhanging smoke from guns
28 *chivalry*, horsemen   32 *sepulchre*, grave

The war was waked anew,
Three hundred cannon-mouths roar'd loud,
And from their throats, with flash and cloud,
　　Their showers of iron threw.
Beneath their fire, in full career,
Rush'd on the ponderous cuirassier,
The lancer couch'd his ruthless spear,
And hurrying as to havoc near,
　　The cohorts' eagles flew.
In one dark torrent, broad and strong,
The advancing onset roll'd along,
Forth harbinger'd by fierce acclaim,
That, from the shroud of smoke and flame,
Peal'd wildly the imperial name!

But on the British heart were lost
The terrors of the charging host;
For not an eye the storm that view'd
Changed its proud glance of fortitude;
Nor was one forward footstep stay'd,
As dropp'd the dying and the dead.
Fast as their ranks the thunders tear,
Fast they renew'd each serried square :
And on the wounded and the slain
Closed their diminish'd files again,
Till from their line scarce spears' lengths three,
Emerging from the smoke they see
Helmet, and plume, and panoply,—
　　Then waked their fire at once!
Each musketeer's revolving knell,
As fast, as regularly fell,
As when they practise to display
Their discipline on festal day.

　　　　10 *cuirassier*, heavily armed horseman
13 *cohort*, body of men　　16 *harbinger'd*, preceded
17 *shroud*, covering　　18 *name*, Napoleon Buonaparte
22 *fortitude*, bravery　　26 *serried*, closely drawn
31 *panoply*, armour　　33 firing in turn

Then down went helm and lance,
Down were the eagle-banners sent,
  Down reeling steeds and riders went,
Corslets were pierced, and pennons rent ;
  And to augment the fray,
Wheel'd full against their staggering flanks,
The English horsemen's foaming ranks
  Forced their resistless way.
Then to the musket-knell succeeds
The clash of swords—the neigh of steeds—
As plies the smith his clanging trade,
Against the cuirass rang the blade;
And while amid their close array
The well-served cannon rent their way,
And while amid their scatter'd band
Raged the fierce rider's bloody brand.
Recoil'd in common rout and fear
Lancer and guard and cuirassier,
Horsemen and foot,—a mingled host !
Their leaders fall'n,—their standards lost.

Sir W. Scott

· 50 ·

THE SOLDIER'S DREAM.

OUR bugles sang truce, for the night-cloud had
    lower'd,
  And the sentinel stars set their watch in the sky ;
And thousands had sunk on the ground overpower'd,
  The weary to sleep, and the wounded to die.

When reposing that night on my pallet of straw
  By the wolf-scaring faggot that guarded the slain,
At the dead of the night a sweet Vision I saw ;
  And thrice ere the morning I dreamt it again.

<small>38 the Eagle was borne by the French
40 *corslet*, body-armour   41 *augment*, increase
 1 *truce*, peace for the time : *lower'd*, descended
 5 *pallet*, couch   6 fire lighted to keep the wolves away</small>

Methought from the battlefield's dreadful array
  Far, far, I had roamed on a desolate track:
'Twas autumn,—and sunshine arose on the way
  To the home of my fathers, that welcomed me
    back.

I flew to the pleasant fields traversed so oft
  In life's morning march, when my bosom was
    young;
I heard my own mountain-goats bleating aloft,
  And knew the sweet strain that the corn-reapers
    sung.

Then pledged we the wine-cup, and fondly I swore
  From my home and my weeping friends never to
    part,
My little ones kissed me a thousand times o'er,
  And my wife sobbed aloud in her fulness of
    heart.

"Stay—stay with us,—rest,—thou art weary and
    worn,"—
  And fain was their war-broken soldier to stay;—
But sorrow returned with the dawning of morn,
  And the voice in my dreaming ear melted away.
                                         T. Campbell

= II =

BELISARIUS.

HEAVEN's gifts are unequal in this world awarded,
As the wise page of history to us has recorded;
Since the learn'd, great, and good of its frowns
    seldom scape any —
Witness brave Belisarius, who begg'd for a half-
    penny —
"Date obolum, Date obolum Belisario."

He whose fame from his valour and victories arose,
    sir,
Of his country the shield, and the scourge of her
    foes, sir;
By his poor faithful dog, blind and aged, was led
With one foot in the grave, thus to beg for his bread
When a young Roman knight, in the street passing
    by,
The veteran survey'd with a heart-rending sigh;
His purse in his helmet he dropp'd with a tear,
While the soldier's sad tale thus attracted his ear.

'I have fought, I have bled, I have conquer'd for
    Rome ;
'I have crown'd her with laurels, which for ages shall
    bloom ;
'I've enrich'd her with wealth, swell'd her pride and
    her power ;
'I espoused her for life,— and disgrace is my dower.
'Yet blood I ne'er wantonly wasted at random,
'Losing thousands their lives by a vain ambitious foe.
'But each conquest I gain'd, I made friend and foe
    know
'That my soul's only aim was *my country's* weal.
'Nor yet for my friends, for my kindred, or self,
'Has my glory been tarnish'd by base views of pelf;
'For such sordid designs I've so far been from
    carving,
'Old and blind, I've no choice, but of begging or
    starving
'Now if soldier or statesman, of what age or nation
'He hereafter may be, should hear this relation,
'And of eyesight bereft, should like me grow poor, straight,
'The bright sunbeams of virtue will turn night to
    day.'

'But if wanting that light, at the close of life's
    spark,
'He at length comes to take the great leap in the
    dark,
'He may wish, while his friends wring their hands
    round his bed,
'That, like poor Belisarius, he'd begg'd for his
    bread.
'But I to distress and to darkness inured,
'In this vile crust of clay when no longer im-
    mured,
'At death's welcome stroke my bright course shall
    begin, sir,
'And enjoy endless day from the sunshine within,
    sir :—
'*Date obolum, Date obolum, Date obolum, Belisario.*'
                                        J. Collins

* 52 *

THE FAIRY LIFE

I

WHERE the bee sucks, there suck I :
In a cowslip's bell I lie ;
There I couch, when owls do cry :
On the bat's back I do fly
After summer merrily.
    Merrily, merrily, shall I live now,
    Under the blossom that hangs on the bough.

II

COME unto these yellow sands,
    And then take hands :
Courtsied when you have and kiss'd
    The wild waves whist,

---

31 to die   34 *inured*, accustomed   35 *crust*, his body :
             immured, built up

Foot it featly here and there ; .
And, sweet sprites, the burthen bear.
    Hark, hark !
        Bow-wow.
    The watch-dog's bark :
        Bow-wow.
Hark, hark ! I hear
The strain of strutting chanticleer
Cry, Cock-a-diddle-dow !
              W. Shakespeare

* 53 *

THE FAIRIES

Up the airy mountain,
  Down the rushy glen,
We daren't go a-hunting
  For fear of little men ;
Wee folk, good folk,
  Trooping all together ;
Green jacket, red cap,
  And white owl's feather !

Down along the rocky shore
  Some make their home :
They live on crispy pancakes
  Of yellow tide-foam ;
Some in the reeds
  Of the black mountain lake,
With frogs for their watch-dogs,
  All night awake.

High on the hill-top
  The old King sits ;
He is now so old and gray,
  He's nigh lost his wits.
With a bridge of white mist
  Columbkill he crosses,

    5 *featly*, neatly   6 *sprites*, fairies

On his stately journeys
  From Slieveleague to Rosses :—
Or going up with music
  On cold starry nights,
To sup with the queen
  Of the gay Northern Lights.

They stole little Bridget
  For seven years long ;
When she came down again,
  Her friends were all gone.

They took her lightly back,
  Between the night and morrow ;
They thought that she was fast asleep,
  But she was dead with sorrow.
They have kept her ever since
  Deep within the lakes,
On a bed of flag-leaves,
  Watching till she wakes.

By the craggy hill-side,
  Through the mosses bare,
They have planted thorn-trees
  For pleasure here and there.
Is any man so daring
  As dig them up in spite,
He shall find their sharpest thorns
  In his bed at night.

Up the airy mountain,
  Down the rushy glen,
We daren't go a-hunting
  For fear of little men ;
Wee folk, good folk,
  Trooping all together ;
Green jacket, red cap,
  And white owl's feather !

W. Allingham

28 *Lights*, the Aurora

* 54 *

THE WIFE OF USHER'S WELL

THERE lived a wife at Usher's Well,
  And a wealthy wife was she:
She had three stout and stalwart sons,
  And sent them o'er the sea.

They had not been a week from her,
  A week but barely ane,
When word came to the carline wife
  That her three sons were gane.

They had not been a week from her,
  A week but barely three,
When word came to the carline wife
  That her sons she'd never see.

'I wish the wind may never cease,
  'Nor fishes in the flood,
'Till my three sons come hame to me,
  'In earthly flesh and blood!'

It fell about the Martinmas,
  When nights are lang and mirk,
The carline wife's three sons came home,
  And their hats were of the birk.

It neither grew in syke nor ditch,
  Nor yet in ony sheugh;
But at the gates of Paradise
  That birk grew fair eneugh.

'Blow up the fire, my maidens!
  'Bring water from the well!
'For all my house shall feast this night,
  'Since my three sons are well!'

---

7 *carline*, old peasant-woman 18 *mirk*, murky
20 *birk*, birch 21 *syke*, marsh 22 *sheugh*, trench

And she has made to them a bed,
　　She's made it large and wide ;
And she's ta'en her mantle her about ;
　　Sat down at the bed-side.

Up then crew the red, red cock,
　　And up and crew the gray :
The eldest to the youngest said,
　　' 'Tis time we were away !

' The cock doth craw, the day doth daw,
　　' The channerin' worm doth chide :
' If we be miss'd out of our place,
　　' A sore pain we must bide.

' Fare ye well, my mother dear !
　　' Farewell to barn and byre !
' And fare ye well, the bonny lass,
　　' That kindles my mother's fire !'

Unknown

* 55 *

ALICE BRAND

I

MERRY it is in the good greenwood,
　　When the mavis and merle are singing,
When the deer sweeps by, and the hounds are in
　　　cry,
　　And the hunter's horn is ringing.

' O Alice Brand, my native land
　　' Is lost for love of you ;
' And we must hold by wood and wold,
　　' As outlaws wont to do !

---

37 *daw*, dawn　　38 *channerin'*, scolding : probably here, impatient
42 *byre*, cattle-house　　　　2 *mavis*, thrush : *merle*, blackbird
　7 *hold*, live　　　8 *outlaws*, persons driven into wild places

'O Alice, 'twas all for thy locks so bright,
  'And 'twas all for thine eyes so blue,
'That on the night of our luckless flight,
  'Thy brother bold I slew.

'Now must I teach to hew the beech,
  'The hand that held the glaive,
'For leaves to spread our lowly bed,
  'And stakes to fence our cave.

'And for vest of pall, thy fingers small,
  'That wont on harp to stray,
'A cloak must shear from the slaughter'd deer,
  'To keep the cold away.'—

—'O Richard! if my brother died,
  ''Twas but a fatal chance:
'For darkling was the battle tried,
  'And fortune sped the lance.

'If pall and vair no more I wear,
  'Nor thou the crimson sheen,
'As warm, we'll say, is the russet gray;
  'As gay the forest-green.

'And, Richard, if our lot be hard,
  'And lost thy native land,
'Still Alice has her own Richárd,
  'And he his Alice Brand.'

II

'Tis merry, 'tis merry, in good greenwood,
  So blithe Lady Alice is singing;
On the beech's pride, and oak's brown side,
  Lord Richard's axe is ringing.

---

14 *glaive*, broad-sword   16 *pall*, fine cloth
24 *sped*, directed   25 *vair*, fur   35 the lofty beech

Up spoke the moody Elfin King,
    Who wonn'd within the hill,—
Like wind in the porch of a ruin'd church,
    His voice was ghostly shrill.

'Why sounds yon stroke on beech and oak,
    'Our moonlight circle's screen?
'Or who comes here to chase the deer,
    'Beloved of our Elfin Queen?
'Or who may dare on wold to wear
    'The fairies' fatal green?

'Up, Urgan, up! to yon mortal hie,
    'For thou wert christen'd man:
'For cross or sign thou wilt not fly,
    'For mutter'd word or ban.

'Lay on him the curse of the wither'd heart,
    'The curse of the sleepless eye;
'Till he wish and pray that his life would part,
    'Nor yet find leave to die!'

III

'Tis merry, 'tis merry, in good greenwood,
    Though the birds have still'd their singing:
The evening blaze doth Alice raise,
    And Richard is fagots bringing.

Up Urgan starts, that hideous dwarf,
    Before Lord Richard stands,
And as he cross'd and bless'd himself,
'I fear not sign,' quoth the grisly elf,
    'That is made with bloody hands.'

But out then spoke she, Alice Brand,
    That woman void of fear,—
'And if there's blood upon his hand,
    ''Tis but the blood of deer.'

---

37 *Elfin*, fairy 38 *wonn'd*, dwelt 47 *mortal*, man 50 *ban*, curse

—' Now loud thou liest, thou bold of mood !
 ' It cleaves unto his hand,
' The stain of thine own kindly blood,
 ' The blood of Ethert Brand.'

Then forward stepp'd she, Alice Brand,
 And made the holy sign,—
' And if there's blood on Richard's hand,
 ' A spotless hand is mine.

' And I conjure thee, Demon elf,
 ' By Him whom Demons fear,
' To show us whence thou art thyself,
 ' And what thine errand here ? '

IV

—' 'Tis merry, 'tis merry, in Fairy-land,
 ' When fairy birds are singing,
' When the court doth ride by their monarch's side,
 ' With bit and bridle ringing :

' And gaily shines the Fairy land—
 ' But all is glistening show,
' Like the idle gleam that December's beam
 ' Can dart on ice and snow.

' And fading, like that varied gleam,
 ' Is our inconstant shape,
' Who now like knight and lady seem,
 ' And now like dwarf and ape.

' It was between the night and day,
 ' When the Fairy King has power,
' That I sunk down in a sinful fray,
'And 'twixt life and death, was snatch'd away
 ' To the joyless Elfin bower.

76 *conjure*, order   89 *inconstant*, changeable   94 *fray*, quarrel

'But wist I of a woman bold,
  'Who thrice my brow durst sign,
'I might regain my mortal mould,
  'As fair a form as thine.'

She cross'd him once—she cross'd him twice—
  That lady was so brave;
The fouler grew his goblin hue,
  The darker grew the cave.

She cross'd him thrice, that lady bold!
  —He rose beneath her hand
The fairest knight on Scottish mould,
  Her brother, Ethert Brand!

— Merry it is in good greenwood,
  When the mavis and merle are singing;
But merrier were they in Dunfermline gray
  When all the bells were ringing.
                                     Sir W. Scott

* 56 *

KUBLA KHAN

A Vision in a Dream

In Xanadu did Kubla Khan
A stately pleasure-dome decree:
Where Alph, the sacred river, ran
Through caverns measureless to man
    Down to a sunless sea.
So twice five miles of fertile ground
With walls and towers were girdled round:
And there were gardens bright with sinuous rills
Where blossom'd many an incense-bearing tree;
And here were forests ancient as the hills,
Enfolding sunny spots of greenery.

97 *wist*, knew   2 *decree*, order to be built
        8 *sinuous*, winding

But oh! that deep romantic chasm which slanted
Down the green hill athwart a cedarn cover!
A savage place! as holy and enchanted
As e'er beneath a waning moon was haunted
By woman wailing for her demon-lover!
And from this chasm, with ceaseless turmoil seething,
As if this earth in fast thick pants were breathing,
A mighty fountain momently was forced:
Amid whose swift half-intermitted burst
Huge fragments vaulted like rebounding hail,
Or chaffy grain beneath the thresher's flail;
And 'mid these dancing rocks at once and ever
It flung up momently the sacred river.
Five miles meandering with a mazy motion
Through wood and dale the sacred river ran,
Then reach'd the caverns measureless to man,
And sank in tumult to a lifeless ocean:
And 'mid this tumult Kubla heard from far
Ancestral voices prophesying war!

 The shadow of the dome of pleasure
 Floated midway on the waves;
 Where was heard the mingled measure
 From the fountain and the caves.
It was a miracle of rare device,
A sunny pleasure-dome with caves of ice;
 A damsel with a dulcimer
 In a vision once I saw:
 It was an Abyssinian maid,
 And on her dulcimer she play'd,
 Singing of Mount Abora!
 Could I revive within me
 Her symphony and song,

12 *chasm*, sharp hollow
13 *cedarn*, of cedars 19 *momently*, every moment
20 *intermitted*, stopping 25 *meandering*, winding
30 voices of his forefathers 33 *measure*, song
37 *dulcimer*, guitar 43 *symphony*, accompaniment

To such a deep delight 'twould win me
That with music loud and long,
I would build that dome in air,
That sunny dome! Those caves of ice!
And all who heard should see them there,
And all should cry Beware! Beware!
His flashing eyes, his floating hair!
Weave a circle round him thrice,
And close your eyes with holy dread,
For he on honey-dew hath fed,
And drunk the milk of Paradise!

S. T. Coleridge

* 57 *

THE ECHOING GREEN

THE sun does arise
And make happy the skies;
The merry bells ring
To welcome the spring;
The skylark and thrush,
The birds of the bush,
Sing louder around
To the bells' cheerful sound;
While our sports shall be seen
On the echoing green.

Old John, with white hair,
Does laugh away care,
Sitting under the oak.
Among the old folk.
They laugh at our play.
And soon they all say,
' Such, such were the joys
' When we all girls and boys—
' In our youth-time were seen
' On the echoing green.'

Till the little ones, weary,
No more can be merry;
The sun does descend,
And our sports have an end.
Round the laps of their mothers
Many sisters and brothers,
Like birds in their nest,
Are ready for rest,
And sport no more seen
On the darkening green.
        W. Blake

* 58 *

A CRADLE SONG

Sleep, sleep, beauty bright,
Dreaming in the joys of night;
Sleep, sleep; in thy sleep
Little sorrows sit and weep.

Sweet babe, in thy face
Soft desires I can trace,
Secret joys and secret smiles,
Little pretty infant wiles.

As thy softest limbs I feel,
Smiles as of the morning steal
O'er thy cheek, and o'er thy breast
Where thy little heart doth rest.

Oh the cunning wiles that creep
In thy little heart asleep!
When thy little heart doth wake,
Then the dreadful light shall break.
        W. Blake

---

8 *wiles*, tricks   16 *light*, knowledge of life with its dangers and sufferings.

* 59 *
THE ORPHAN CHILDREN

I REACH'D the village on the plain,
    Just when the setting sun's last ray
Shone blazing on the golden vane
    Of the old church across the way.

Across the way alone I sped,
    And climb'd the stile, and sat me there,
To think in silence on the dead
    Who in the churchyard sleeping were.

There many a long, low grave I view'd
    Where toil and want in quiet lie;
And costly slabs amongst them stood
    That bore the names of rich and high.

One new made mound I saw close by,
    O'er which the grasses hardly crept,
Where, looking forth with listless eye,
    Two ragged children sat and wept.

A piece of bread between them lay,
    Which neither seem'd as it could take;
And yet so worn and white were they
    With want, it made my bosom ache.

I look'd a while, and said at last,
    ' Why in such sorrow sit you here?
' And why the food you leave and waste
    ' Which your own hunger well might cheer?'

The boy rose instant to his feet,
    And said with gentle, eager haste,
' Lady, we've not enough to eat:
    ' O if we had, we should not waste!

' But sister Mary's naughty grown,
    ' And will not eat, whate'er I say;
' Though sure I am the bread's her own,
    ' For she has tasted none to-day!'

' Indeed,' the poor starved Mary said,
　' Till Henry eats, I'll eat no more ;
' For yesterday I had some bread ;
　' He's had none since the day before.'

My heart with pity swell'd so high
　I could not speak a single word :
Yet the boy straightway made reply,
　As if my inward wish he heard.

' Before our father went away,
　' By bad men tempted o'er the sea,
' Sister and I did nought but play ;—
　' We lived beside yon great ash-tree.

' But then poor mother did so cry,
　' And look'd so changed, I cannot tell !
' She told us that she soon should die,
　' And bade us love each other well.

' She said that when the war was o'er,
　' Perhaps our father we might see :
' But if we never saw him more,
　' That God would then our father be.

' She kiss'd us both, and then she died,
　' And then they put her in the grave :
' There many a day we've sat and cried
　' That we no more a mother have.

' But when our father came not here,
　' I thought if we could find the sea
' We should be sure to meet him there,
　' And once again might happy be.

' So hand-in-hand for many a mile,
　' And many a long, long day we went :
' Some sigh'd to see, some turn'd to smile,
　' And fed us when our stock was spent.

‘ But when we reach'd the sea, and found
 ‘ 'Twas one great flood before us spread,
‘ We thought that father must be drown'd,
 ‘ And cried, and wish'd we too were dead.

‘ So we came back to mother's grave,
 ‘ And only long with her to be :
‘ For Goody, when this bread she gave,
 ‘ Said father died beyond the sea.

‘ So, since no parent we have here,
 ‘ We'll go and search for God around :—
‘ Pray, Lady, can you tell us where
 ‘ That God, our Father, may be found?

‘ He lives in heaven, mother said :
 ‘ And Goody says that mother's there :
‘ But though we've walk'd, and search'd, and pray'd,
 ‘ We cannot find them anywhere !'

I clasp'd the prattlers in my arms,
 I cried, ‘ Come, both, and live with me !
‘ I'll clothe and feed you, safe from harms —
 ‘ Your second mother I will be.

‘ Till you to your own mother's side
 ‘ He in his own good time may call,
‘ With Him for ever to abide
 ‘ Who is the Father of us all !'

         Unknown

✦ 60 ✦

THE CHILD AND THE MOWERS

Dorset Dialect

O, AYE ! they had woone chile bezide,
 An' a finer your eyes never met ;
'Twer a dear little fellow that died
 In the zummer that come wi' such het ;

1 *woone*, one   3 *'Twer*, it was   4 *het*, heat

By the mowers, too thoughtless in fun,
    He wer then a-zent off vrom our eyes,
Vrom the light ov the dew-dryèn zun,—
    Aye ! vrom days under blue-hollow'd skies.

He went out to the mowers in mead,
    When the zun wer a-rose to his height,
An' the men wer a-swingèn the snead,
    Wi' their eärms in white sleeves, left an' right :—
An' out there, as they rested at noon,
    O ! they drench'd en wi' cäle-horns too deep,
Till his thoughts wer a-drown'd in a swoon ;
    Aye ! his life wer a-smother'd in sleep.

Then they laid en there-right on the ground,
    On a grass-heap, a-zweltrèn wi' het,
Wi' his heäir all a-wetted around
    His young feäce, wi' the big drops o' zweat ;
In his little left palm he'd a-zet
    Wi' his right hand, his vore-vinger's tip,
As for zome'hat he woulden forget,—
    Aye ! zome thought that he woulden let slip.

Then they took en in hwome to his bed,
    An' he rose vrom his pillow noo mwore,
Vor the curls on his sleek little head
    To be blown by the wind out o' door.
Vor he died while the häy russled gray
    On the staddle so leätely begun,
Lik' the mown-grass a-dried by the day,—
    Aye ! the zwath-flow'r's a-kill'd by the zun.

                                 W. Barnes

  6 *a-zent*, sent   7 *dryèn*, drying   9 *in mead*, in the meadow
11 *snead*, handle of scythe   14 *en*, him ; *cäle-horns*, full of ale
18 *a-zweltrèn*, sweltering   21 *a-zet*, put
    23 *zome'hat*, something ; *woulden*, would not
    26 *noo mwore*, no more
    30 *staddle*, platform on which the rick stands
    32 *zwath-flow'r*, cut down with the swath

* 61 *

ELLEN BRINE OF ALLENBURN

Dorset dialect

Noo soul did hear her lips complain,
An' she's a-gone vrom all her païn,
An' others' loss to her is gaïn
For she do live in heaven's love;
Vull many a longsome day an' week
She bore her aïlèn, still, an' meek;
A-workèn while her strangth held on,
An' guidèn housework, when 'twer gone.
   Vor Ellen Brine of Allenburn
   Oh! there be souls to murn.

The last time I'd a-cast my zight
Upon her feäce, a-feäded white,
Wer in a zummer's mornèn light
In hall avore the smwold'rèn vire,
The while the childern beät the vloor
In plaÿ, wi' tiny shoes they wore,
An' call'd their mother's eyes to view
The feäts their little limbs could do.
   Oh! Ellen Brine of Allenburn,
   They childern now mus' murn.

Then woone, a-stoppèn vrom his reäce,
Went up, an' on her knee did pleäce
His hand, a-lookèn in her feäce,
An' wi' a smilèn mouth so small,
He zaid, 'You promised us to goo
'To Shroton feäir, an' teäke us two!'

---

2 *an'*, and: *vrom*, from: *v* used for *f* in Dorset
6 *ailen*, illness   7 *a-worken*, working   10 *murn*, mourn
12 *feaded*, faded   14 *avore*, before: *smwold'ren*, smouldering
21 *woone*, one: *reace*, running

She heärd it wi' her two white ears,
An' in her eyes there sprung two tears :
   Vor Ellen Brine of Allenburn
   Did veel that they mus' murn.

September come, wi' Shroton feäir,
But Ellen Brine wer never there !
A heavy heart wer on the meäre
Their father rod his hwomeward road.
'Tis true he brought some feärèns back,
Vor them two childern all in black ;
But they had now, wi' playthings new,
Noo mother vor to show em to :—
   Vor Ellen Brine of Allenburn
   Would never mwore return.
W. Barnes

* 62 *

HELVELLYN

I CLIMB'D the dark brow of the mighty Helvellyn,
   Lakes and mountains beneath me gleam'd misty and wide ;
All was still, save by fits, when the eagle was yelling,
   And starting around me the echoes replied.
On the right, Striden-edge round the Red-tarn was bending,
And Catchedicam its left verge was defending,
One huge nameless rock in the front was ascending,
   When I mark'd the sad spot where the wanderer had died.

Dark green was that spot 'mid the brown mountain heather,
   Where the Pilgrim of Nature lay stretch'd in decay,

---

33 *meäre*, mare   35 *feärèns*, fairings
  1 *brow*, mountain-side   3 *by fits*, now and then
     6 *verge*, edge : *defending*, sheltering
 10 *Pilgrim*, wanderer who admired the natural landscape

Like the corpse of an outcast abandon'd to weather
   Till the mountain-winds wasted the tenantless clay.
Nor yet quite deserted, though lonely extended,
For, faithful in death, his mute favourite attended,
The much-loved remains of her master defended,
   And chased the hill-fox and the raven away.

How long didst thou think that his silence was
      slumber?
   When the wind waved his garment, how oft didst
      thou start?
How many long days and long weeks didst thou
      number,
   Ere he faded before thee, the friend of thy
      heart?
And, oh! was it meet, that—no requiem read o'er
      him—
No mother to weep, and no friend to deplore him,
And thou, little guardian, alone stretch'd before
      him—
   Unhonour'd the Pilgrim from life should depart?

When a Prince to the fate of the Peasant has
      yielded,
   The tapestry waves dark round the dim-lighted
      hall;
With scutcheons of silver the coffin is shielded,
   And pages stand mute by the canopied pall:
Through the courts, at deep midnight, the torches
      are gleaming;
In the proudly-arch'd chapel the banners are beam-
      ing;
Far adown the long aisle sacred music is streaming,
   Lamenting a Chief of the People should fall.

<small>12 *tenantless clay*, body without soul   13 *extended*, stretched out
      14 *mute favourite*, speechless dog
21 *meet*, fit ; *requiem*, funeral service   25 has died
26 *tapestry*, rich hangings on walls   27 *scutcheons*, shields
      28 *pages*, servants ; *canopied*, covered</small>

But meeter for thee, gentle lover of nature,
   To lay down thy head like the meek mountain lamb,
When, wilder'd, he drops from some cliff huge in stature.
   And draws his last sob by the side of his dam.
And more stately thy couch by this desert lake lying,
Thy obsequies sung by the gray plover flying,
With one faithful friend but to witness thy dying,
   In the arms of Helvellyn and Catchedicam.
Sir W. Scott

· 63 ·
A REVERIE

WHEN, musing on companions gone,
We doubly feel ourselves alone,
Something, my Friend, we yet may gain;
There is a pleasure in this pain:
It soothes the love of lonely rest,
Deep in each gentler heart impress'd.
'Tis silent amid worldly toils,
And stifled soon by mental broils;
But, in a bosom thus prepared,
Its still small voice is often heard,
Whispering a mingled sentiment,
'Twixt resignation and content.

Oft in my mind such thoughts awake,
By lone Saint Mary's silent lake;
Thou know'st it well, nor fen, nor sedge,
Pollute the pure lake's crystal edge;
Abrupt and sheer, the mountains sink
At once upon the level brink;
And just a trace of silver sand
Marks where the water meets the land.

---

33 *meeter*, fitter   38 *obsequies*, funeral service   40 surrounded by   1 *musing*, thinking   6 *impressed*, stamped   8 by troubles of the mind   16 *pollute*, spoil   17 going straight up

Far in the mirror, bright and blue,
Each hill's huge outline you may view ;
Shaggy with heath, but lonely bare,
Nor tree, nor bush, nor brake, is there,
Save where, of land, yon slender line
Bears thwart the lake the scatter'd pine.
Yet even this nakeaness has power,
And aids the feeling of the hour :
Nor thicket, dell, nor copse you spy,
Where living thing conceal'd might lie ;
Nor point, retiring, hides a dell,
Where swain, or woodman lone, might dwell ;
There's nothing left to fancy's guess,
You see that all is loneliness :
And silence aids—though the steep hills
Send to the lake a thousand rills ;
In summer-tide, so soft they weep,
The sound but lulls the ear asleep ;
Your horse's hoof-tread sounds too rude,
So stilly is the solitude.

Sir W. Scott

* 64 *

SUCH IS LIFE

LIKE to the falling of a star,
Or as the flights of eagles are,
Or like the fresh Spring's gaudy hue,
Or silver drops of morning dew ;
Or like a wind that chafes the flood,
Or bubbles which on water stood ;—
E'en such is man, whose borrow'd light
Is straight call'd in and paid to-night.
The wind blows out, the bubble dies,
The Spring entomb'd in Autumn lies ;
The dew dries up, the star is shot,
The flight is past ;—and Man forgot.

Bishop King

26 *thwart*, crossing   36 *rills*, little streams   10 *entomb'd*, buried

* 65 *

JOHN ANDERSON

JOHN ANDERSON my jo, John,
When we were first acquent
Your locks were like the raven,
Your bonnie brow was brent;
But now your brow is bald, John,
Your locks are like the snow;
But blessings on your frosty pow,
John Anderson my jo.

John Anderson my jo, John,
We clamb the hill thegither,
And mony a canty day, John,
We've had wi' ane anither:
Now we maun totter down, John,
But hand in hand we'll go,
And sleep thegither at the foot,
John Anderson my jo.

R. Burns

* 66 *

A LESSON

THERE is a flower, the Lesser Celandine,
That shrinks like many more from cold and rain,
And the first moment that the sun may shine,
Bright as the sun himself, 'tis out again!

When hailstones have been falling, swarm on swarm,
Or blasts the green field and the trees distrest,
Oft have I seen it muffled up from harm
In close self-shelter, like a thing at rest.

---

1 *jo*, love 2 *acquent*, acquainted 4 *brent*, smooth
7 *pow*, head 10 *thegither*, together 11 *canty*, cheerful
13 *maun*, must

But lately, one rough day, this flower I past,
And recognized it, though an alter'd form,
Now standing forth an offering to the blast,
And buffeted at will by rain and storm.

I stopp'd and said, with inly-mutter'd voice,
' It doth not love the shower, nor seek the cold ;
' This neither is its courage nor its choice,
' But its necessity in being old.

' The sunshine may not cheer it, nor the dew ;
' It cannot help itself in its decay ;
' Stiff in its members, wither'd, changed of hue,'
And, in my spleen, I smiled that it was gray.

To be a prodigal's favourite—then, worse truth,
A miser's pensioner — behold our lot !
O Man ! that from thy fair and shining youth
Age might but take the things Youth needed not !
W. Wordsworth

* 67 *

TRUE GROWTH

    It is not growing like a tree
    In bulk, doth make Man better be ;
Or standing long an oak, three hundred year,
To fall a log at last, dry, bald, and sere :
        A lily of a day
        Is fairer far in May,
    Although it fall and die that night—
    It was the plant and flower of Light !
In small proportions we just beauties see ;
And in short measures life may perfect be.
B. Jonson

    21 *a prodigal's favourite*, wasting the many gifts of Youth
    22 *a miser's pensioner*, getting the little we can from Age
        9 *just*, true

* 68 *

FLOWERS WITHOUT FRUIT

PRUNE thou thy words ; the thoughts control
    That o'er thee swell and throng :—
They will condense within thy soul,
    And change to purpose strong.

But he who lets his feelings run
    In soft luxurious flow,
Shrinks when hard service must be done,
    And faints at every woe.

Faith's meanest deed more favour bears,
    Where hearts and wills are weigh'd,
Than brightest transports, choicest prayers,
    Which bloom their hour, and fade.
                            J. H. Newman

* 69 *

CONTENTMENT

My mind to me a kingdom is ;
    Such perfect joy therein I find,
As far exceeds all earthly bliss
    That world affords, or grows by kind :
Though much I want what most men have,
Yet doth my mind forbid me crave.

Content I live—this is my stay ;
    I seek no more than may suffice :
I press to bear no haughty sway ;
    Look—what I lack, my mind supplies !
Lo ! thus I triumph like a king,
Content with that my mind doth bring.

---

3 *condense*, grow close and strong
4 *by kind*, naturally   6 *crave*, desire
7 *stay*, support   8 *suffice*, be enough   9 *press*, strive

I see how plenty surfeits oft,
   And hasty climbers soonest fall;
I see how those that sit aloft
   Mishap doth threaten most of all;
These get with toil, and keep with fear:
Such cares my mind could never bear.

I laugh not at another's loss;
   I grudge not at another's gain;
No worldly wave my mind can toss;
   I brook that is another's pain.
I fear no foe: I scorn no friend:
I dread no death: I fear no end.

Some have too much, yet still they crave;
   I little have, yet seek no more:
They are but poor, though much they have,
   And I am rich, with little store.
They poor, I rich: they beg, I give:
They lack, I lend: they pine, I live.

I wish but what I have at will:
   I wander not to seek for more:
I like the plain; I climb no hill:
   In greatest storm I sit on shore,
And laugh at those that toil in vain,
To get what must be lost again.
—This is my choice; for why?—I find
No wealth is like a quiet mind.
Unknown

* 70 *

THE SEARCH FOR PEACE

Sweet Peace, where dost thou dwell? I humbly crave,
   Let me once know.
  I sought thee in a secret cave,
   And ask'd, if Peace were there?

---

13 *surfeits*, sickens   22 *brook that*, bear easily what
31 *at will*, at command   1 *crave*, beg to know

A hollow wind did seem to answer, 'No:—
    'Go seek elsewhere.'

I did; and going did a rainbow note:
    Surely, thought I,
This is the lace of Peace's coat:
    I will search out the matter.
But while I look'd, the clouds immediately
    Did break and scatter.

Then went I to a garden, and did spy
    A gallant flower,
The Crown Imperial: Sure, said I,
    Peace at the root must dwell.
But when I digg'd, I saw a worm devour
    What show'd so well.

At length I met a reverend good old man:
    Whom when for Peace
I did demand, he thus began:
    'There was a Prince of old
'At Salem dwelt, who liv'd with good increase
    'Of flock and fold.

'He sweetly lived; yet sweetness did not save
    'His life from foes.
'But after death, out of his grave
    'There sprang twelve stalks of wheat:
'Which many wondering at, got some of those
    'To plant and set.

'It prosper'd strangely, and did soon disperse
    'Through all the earth:
'For they that taste it do rehearse,
    'That virtue lies therein;
'A secret virtue, bringing peace and mirth
    'By flight of sin.

    31 *it*, the Gospel   33 *rehearse*, say   35 *virtue*, power

Take of this grain, which in my garden grows,
'And grows for you;
'Make bread of it:—and that repose
'And peace, which everywhere
With so much earnestness you do pursue,
'Is only there.'

G. Herbert

* 71 *

THE KITTEN AND FALLING LEAVES.

That way look, my Infant, lo!
What a pretty baby-show!
See the Kitten on the wall,
Sporting with the leaves that fall,
Wither'd leaves—one—two—and three—
From the lofty elder-tree!
Through the calm and frosty air
Of this morning bright and fair,
Eddying round and round they sink
Softly, slowly: one might think,
From the motions that are made,
Every little leaf convey'd
Sylph or Faery hither tending,—
To this lower world descending,
Each invisible and mute,
In his wavering parachute.
——But the Kitten, how she starts,
Crouches, stretches, paws, and darts!
First at one, and then its fellow
Just as light and just as yellow;
There are many now—now one—
Now they stop, and there are none:
What intenseness of desire
In her upward eye of fire!

9 *eddying*, turning   13 *Sylph*, learned name for fairy
16 *parachute*, machine to float slowly down in the air
23 *intenseness*, strength

With a tiger-leap half way
Now she meets the coming prey,
Lets it go as fast, and then
Has it in her power again :
Now she works with three or four,
Like an Indian conjuror ;
Quick as he in feats of art,
Far beyond in joy of heart.
Were her antics play'd in th' eye
Of a thousand standers-by,
Clapping hands with shout and stare,
What would little Tabby care
For the plaudits of the crowd?
Over happy to be proud,
Over wealthy in the treasure
Of her own exceeding pleasure!
   'Tis a pretty baby-treat ;
Nor, I deem, for me unmeet ;
Here, for neither Babe nor me,
Other play-mate can I see.
Of the countless living things,
That with stir of feet and wings
(In the sun or under shade,
Upon bough or grassy blade)
And with busy revellings,
Chirp and song, and murmurings,
Made this orchard's narrow space
And this vale so blithe a place,—
Multitudes are swept away
Never more to breathe the day :
Some are sleeping : some in bands
Travell'd into distant lands ;
Others slunk to moor and wood,
Far from human neighbourhood ;
And, among the Kinds that keep
With us closer fellowship,

31 *feats*, tricks   37 *plaudits*, shouts   42 *unmeet*, unfit

With us openly abide,
All have laid their mirth aside.
  Where is he that giddy Sprite,
Blue-cap, with his colours bright,
Who was blest as bird could be,
Feeding in the apple-tree ;
Made such wanton spoil and rout,
Turning blossoms inside out ;
Hung—head pointing towards the ground—
Flutter'd, perch'd, into a round
Bound himself, and then unbound ;
Lithest, gaudiest Harlequin !
Prettiest Tumbler ever seen !
Light of heart and light of limb ;
What is now become of Him ?
Lambs, that through the mountains went
Frisking, bleating merriment,
When the year was in its prime,
They are sober'd by this time.
If you look to vale or hill,
If you listen, all is still,
Save a little neighbouring rill,
That from out the rocky ground
Strikes a solitary sound.
Vainly glitter hill and plain,
And the air is calm in vain :
Vainly Morning spreads the lure
Of a sky serene and pure ;
Creature none can she decoy
Into open sign of joy :
Is it that they have a fear
Of the dreary season near ?
Or that other pleasures be
Sweeter e'en than gaiety ?
  Yet, whate'er enjoyments dwell

87 Morning in vain tempts   89 *decoy*, tempt

In the impenetrable cell
Of the silent heart which Nature
Furnishes to every creature ;
Whatsoe'er we feel and know
Too sedate for outward show,
Such a light of gladness breaks,
Pretty Kitten ! from thy freaks, —
Spreads with such a living grace
O'er my little Dora's face ;
Yes, the sight so stirs and charms
Thee, Baby, laughing in my arms,
That almost I could repine
That your transports are not mine,
That I do not wholly fare
Even as ye do, thoughtless pair !
And I will have my careless season,
Spite of melancholy reason ;
Will walk through life in such a way
That, when time brings on decay,
Now and then I may possess
Hours of perfect gladsomeness.
—Pleased by any random toy ;
By a kitten's busy joy,
Or an infant's laughing eye
Sharing in the ecstasy ;
I would fare like that or this,
Find my wisdom in my bliss ;
Keep the sprightly soul awake ;
And have faculties to take.
Even from things by sorrow wrought,
Matter for a jocund thought ;
Spite of care, and spite of grief,
To gambol with Life's falling Leaf.
W. Wordsworth

6, 97 We cannot look into the hearts of living creatures
   100 *sedate*, saddening   117 *repine*, regret
   108 *transports*, delights   124 *faculties*, powers

A SONG OF PRAISE

To God, ye choir above, begin
    A hymn so loud and strong
That all the universe may hear
    And join the grateful song.

Praise Him, thou sun, Who dwells unseen
    Amidst transcendent light,
Where thy refulgent orb would seem
    A spot, as dark as night.

Thou silver moon, ye host of stars,
    The universal song
Through the serene and silent night
    To listening worlds prolong.

Sing Him, ye distant worlds and suns,
    From whence no travelling ray
Hath yet to us, through ages past,
    Had time to make its way.

Assist, ye raging storms, and bear
    On rapid wings His praise,
From north to south, from east to west,
    Through heaven, and earth, and seas.

Exert your voice, ye furious fires
    That rend the watery cloud,
And thunder to this nether world
    Your Maker's words aloud.

Ye works of God, that dwell unknown
    Beneath the rolling main;
Ye birds, that sing among the groves,
    And sweep the azure plain;

---

1 *choir*, all Nature   6 *transcendent*, surpassingly bright
7 *refulgent*, shining   11 *serene*, clear
13 stars so distant that their light has not yet reached us
21 *fires*, lightnings   23 *nether*, lower   28 the sky

Ye stately hills, that rear your heads,
  And towering pierce the sky;
Ye clouds, that with an awful pace
  Majestic roll on high;

Ye insects small, to which one leaf
  Within its narrow sides
A vast extended world displays,
  And spacious realms provides;

Ye race, still less than these, with which
  The stagnant water teems,
To which one drop, however small,
  A boundless ocean seems;

Whate'er ye are, where'er ye dwell,
  Ye creatures great or small.
Adore the wisdom, praise the power,
  That made and governs all.
                    P. Skelton

* 73 *

THE SONG OF DAVID

HE sang of God, the mighty source
Of all things, the stupendous force
  On which all strength depends;
From whose right arm, beneath whose eyes,
All period, power, and enterprize
  Commences, reigns, and ends.

The world, the clustering spheres he made,
The glorious light, the soothing shade,
  Dale, champaign, grove, and hill:
The multitudinous abyss,
Where secresy remains in bliss,
  And wisdom hides her skill.

7 *spheres*, stars   9 *champaign*, level country
              10 *abyss*, space

Tell them, I AM, Jehovah said
To Moses : while Earth heard in dread,
   And, smitten to the heart,
At once, above, beneath, around,
All Nature, without voice, or sound,
   Replied, 'O Lord, THOU ART.'
C. Smart

• 74 •

THE TRAVELLER

How are thy servants blest, O Lord !
   How sure is their defence !
Eternal wisdom is their guide,
   Their help, Omnipotence.

In foreign realms, and lands remote,
   Supported by Thy care,
Through burning climes I pass'd unhurt,
   And breathed in tainted air.

Thy mercy sweeten'd every soil,
   Made every region please ;
The hoary Alpine hills it warm'd,
   And smoothed the Tyrrhene seas.

Think, O my soul, devoutly think,
   How, with affrighted eyes,
Thou saw'st the wide-extended deep
   In all its horrors rise.

Confusion dwelt in every face,
   And fear in every heart ;
When waves on waves, and gulfs on gulfs,
   O'ercame the pilot's art.

---

4 *Omnipotence*, all powerfulness   5 *realms*, kingdoms
11 Switzerland   12 North western coast of Italy
    17 No one knew what to do

Yet then from all my griefs, O Lord,
    Thy mercy set me free;
Whilst, in the confidence of prayer,
    My soul took hold on Thee.

For though in dreadful whirls we hung
    High on the broken wave,
I knew Thou wert not slow to hear,
    Nor impotent to save.

—The storm was laid; the winds retired,
    Obedient to Thy will;
The sea that roar'd at Thy command,
    At Thy command was still.

J. Addison

· 75 ·

WRITTEN IN EARLY SPRING.

I HEARD a thousand blended notes
While in a grove I sat reclined,
In that sweet mood when pleasant thoughts
Bring sad thoughts to the mind.

To her fair works did Nature link
The human soul that through me ran;
And much it grieved my heart to think
What Man has made of Man.

Through primrose tufts, in that sweet bower,
The periwinkle trail'd its wreaths;
And 'tis my faith that every flower
Enjoys the air it breathes.

28 *impotent*, unable   29 *laid*, stilled
1 *blended*, mixed together   2 *reclined*, resting
3 *mood*, humour   11 *faith*, belief

The birds around me hopp'd and play'd ;
Their thoughts I cannot measure —
But the least motion which they made
It seem'd a thrill of pleasure.

The budding twigs spread out their fan
To catch the breezy air ;
And I must think, do all I can,
That there was pleasure there.

If this belief from Heaven be sent,
If such be Nature's holy plan,
Have I not reason to lament
What Man has made of Man?

W. Wordsworth

* 76 *

THE RAINBOW

Triumphal arch, that fill'st the sky
   When storms prepare to part,
I ask not proud Philosophy
   To teach me what thou art.

Still seem, as to my childhood's sight,
   A midway station given,
For happy spirits to alight,
   Betwixt the earth and heaven.

Can all that optics teach, unfold
   Thy form to please me so,
As when I dreamt of gems and gold
   Hid in thy radiant bow?

When science from creation's face
   Enchantment's veil withdraws,
What lovely visions yield their place
   To cold material laws!

1 arch in remembrance of victory   2 *part*, clear off
9 *optics*, laws of sight : *unfold*, explain
13 *enchantment*, the poetry of youth   16 laws of matter

And yet, fair bow, no fabling dreams,
   But words of the Most High,
Have told why first thy robe of beams
   Was woven in the sky.

When o'er the green undeluged earth
   Heaven's covenant thou didst shine,
How came the world's gray fathers forth
   To watch thy sacred sign!

And when its yellow lustre smiled
   O'er mountains yet untrod,
Each mother held aloft her child
   To bless the bow of God.

The earth to thee her incense yields,
   The lark thy welcome sings,
When, glittering in the freshen'd fields,
   The snowy mushroom springs.

How glorious is thy girdle, cast
   O'er mountain, tower, and town,
Or mirror'd in the ocean vast
   A thousand fathoms down!

As fresh in yon horizon dark,
   As young thy beauties seem,
As when the eagle from the ark
   First sported in thy beam.

For, faithful to its sacred page,
   Heaven still rebuilds thy span;
Nor lets the type grow pale with age
   That first spoke peace to man.
                              T. Campbell

22 *covenant*, sign of peace   23 *gray fathers*, Noah and his family
25 *lustre*, light   29 *incense*, sweetness
32 the mushroom springs up after rain   33 *girdle*, arch, bow
35 *mirror'd*, reflected   42 *span*, arch   43 *type*, sign

TO THE CUCKOO.

Hail, beauteous stranger of the grove!
    Thou messenger of spring!
Now Heaven repairs thy rural seat,
    And woods thy welcome sing.

What time the daisy decks the green,
    Thy certain voice we hear;
Hast thou a star to guide thy path,
    Or mark the rolling year?

Delightful visitant, with thee
    I hail the time of flowers,
And hear the sound of music sweet
    From birds among the bowers.

The schoolboy wandering through the wood
    To pull the primrose gay,
Starts the new voice of spring to hear,
    And imitates thy lay.

What time the pea puts on the bloom
    Thou fliest thy vocal vale,
An annual guest in other lands,
    Another spring to hail.

Sweet bird! thy bower is ever green,
    Thy sky is ever clear;
Thou hast no sorrow in thy song,
    No winter in thy year!

O could I fly, I'd fly with thee!
    We'd make, with joyful wing,
Our annual visit o'er the globe,
    Companions of the spring.

J. Logan

3 the trees are in leaf   6 *certain*, sure to come   16 *lay*, song
18 *vocal vale*, valley where you have sung
19 a guest who comes every year

78

TO THE CUCKOO

O BLITHE new-comer! I have heard,
   I hear thee and rejoice:
O Cuckoo! shall I call thee bird,
   Or but a wandering Voice?

While I am lying on the grass
   Thy twofold shout I hear;
From hill to hill it seems to pass,
   At once far off and near.

Though babbling only to the vale
   Of sunshine and of flowers,
Thou bringest unto me a tale
   Of visionary hours.

Thrice welcome, darling of the Spring!
   Even yet thou art to me
No bird, but an invisible thing —
   A voice, a mystery;

The same whom in my schoolboy days
   I listen'd to; that Cry
Which made me look a thousand ways
   In bush, and tree, and sky.

To seek thee did I often rove
   Through woods and on the green;
And thou wert still a hope, a love;
   Still long'd for, never seen!

And I can listen to thee yet;
   Can lie upon the plain
And listen, till I do beget
   That golden time again.

_{27, 28} *till*, until I fancy myself young again

O blessèd bird ! the earth we pace
Again appears to be
An unsubstantial fairy place
That is fit home for Thee !

W. Wordsworth

* 79 *

TO A WATERFOWL

WHITHER, 'midst falling dew,
While glow the heavens with the last steps of day,
Far through their rosy depths, dost thou pursue
    Thy solitary way?

Vainly the fowler's eye
Might mark thy distant flight to do thee wrong,
As, darkly painted on the crimson sky,
    Thy figure floats along.

Seek'st thou the plashy brink
Of weedy lake, or marge of river wide,
Or where the rocking billows rise and sink
    On the chafed ocean side?

There is a Power whose care
Teaches thy way along that pathless coast,—
The desert and illimitable air,—
    Lone wandering, but not lost.

All day thy wings have fann'd,
At that far height, the cold, thin atmosphere ;
Yet stoop not, weary, to the welcome land,
    Though the dark night is near.

And soon that toil shall end ;
Soon shalt thou find a summer home, and rest
And scream among thy fellows ; reeds shall bend
    Soon o'er thy shelter'd nest.

3 *pursue*, follow   5 to shoot thee   10 *marge*, edge
15 *illimitable*, without bounds   18 *atmosphere*, air

Thou'rt gone—the abyss of heaven
Hath swallow'd up thy form—yet on my heart
Deeply hath sunk the lesson thou hast given,
    And shall not soon depart.

He, who from zone to zone
Guides through the boundless sky thy certain flight,
In the long way that I must tread alone,
    Will lead my steps aright.
W. C. Bryant

* 80 *

SIGNS OF EVENING

THE sun upon the lake is low,
    The wild birds hush their song;
The hills have evening's deepest glow,
    Yet Leonard tarries long.
Now all whom varied toil and care
    From home and love divide,
In the calm sunset may repair
    Each to the loved one's side.

The noble dame on turret high,
    Who waits her gallant knight,
Looks to the western beam to spy
    The flash of armour bright.
The village maid, with hand on brow
    The level ray to shade,
Upon the footpath watches now
    For Colin's darkening plaid.

Now to their mates the wild swans row,
    By day they swam apart;
And to the thicket wanders slow
    The hind beside the hart.

---

25 *abyss*, depths   29 *zone*, region of the world   31 through life
    9 *turret*, little tower   14 *level*, setting

The woodlark at his partner's side
Twitters his closing song—
All meet whom day and care divide,—
But Leonard tarries long!

Sir W. Scott

* 81 *

ARETHUSA

ARETHUSA arose
From her couch of snows
In the Acroceraunian mountains,—
From cloud and from crag
With many a jag,
Shepherding her bright fountains.
She leapt down the rocks
With her rainbow locks
Streaming among the streams ;—
Her steps paved with green
The downward ravine
Which slopes to the western gleams :
And gliding and springing,
She went, ever singing,
In murmurs as soft as sleep ;
The Earth seem'd to love her,
And Heaven smiled above her,
As she linger'd towards the deep.

Then Alphéus bold,
On his glacier cold,
With his trident the mountains strook ;
And open'd a chasm
In the rocks ; with the spasm
All Erymanthus shook.

3 *Acroceraunian*, see end   6 *shepherding*, leading
8 little rainbows appear in the spray
11 *ravine*, mountain-valley   21 *trident*, fork with three prongs
22 *chasm*, rent   23 *spasm*, shock

And the black south wind
It conceal'd behind
The urns of the silent snow,
    And earthquake and thunder
    Did rend in sunder
The bars of the springs below:
    The beard and the hair
    Of the river God were
Seen through the torrent's sweep,
    As he follow'd the light
    Of the fleet nymph's flight
To the brink of the Dorian deep.

'Oh, save me! Oh, guide me!
'And bid the deep hide me,
'For he grasps me now by the hair!'
    The loud Ocean heard,
    To its blue depth stirr'd,
And divided at her prayer;
    And under the water
    The Earth's white daughter
Fled like a sunny beam;
    Behind her descended
    Her billows, unblended
With the brackish Dorian stream:
    Like a gloomy stain
    On the emerald main
Alphéus rush'd behind,—
    As an eagle pursuing
    A dove to its ruin
Down the streams of the cloudy wind.

    Under the bowers
    Where the Ocean Powers
Sit on their pearlèd thrones:

---

35 *nymph*, girl-goddess   44 Arethusa   47 *unblended*, not mixed
48 *brackish*, saltish   50 *emerald*, ear green   56 *Powers*, gods

Through the coral woods
Of the weltering floods,
Over heaps of unvalued stones;
Through the dim beams
Which amid the streams
Weave a net-work of colour'd light;
And under the caves,
Where the shadowy waves
Are as green as the forest's night :—
Outspeeding the shark
And the sword-fish dark,
Under the ocean foam,
And up through the rifts
Of the mountain clifts;
They pass'd to their Dorian home.

And now from their fountains
In Enna's mountains,
Down one vale where the morning basks,
Like friends once parted
Grown single-hearted,
They ply their watery tasks.
At sunrise they leap
From their cradles steep
In the cave of the shelving hill;
At noon-tide they flow
Through the woods below
And the meadows of Asphodel;
And at night they sleep
In the rocking deep
Beneath the Ortygian shore ;—
Like spirits that lie
In the azure sky
When they love but live no more.

P. B. Shelley

58 *woods*, coral grows like a tree beneath the water
59 *weltering*, rolling   72 *Dorian*, in Sicily
84 *Asphodel*, probably meadow-narcissus

* 82 *

L'ALLEGRO

Hence, loathéd Melancholy,
  Of Cerberus and blackest Midnight born
In Stygian cave forlorn
  'Mongst horrid shapes, and shrieks, and sights unholy!
Find out some uncouth cell
  Where brooding Darkness spreads his jealous wings
And the night-raven sings;
  There under ebon shades, and low-brow'd rocks
As ragged as thy locks,
  In dark Cimmerian desert ever dwell.

    But come, thou Goddess fair and free,
    In heaven yclept Euphrosyné,
    And by men, heart-easing Mirth,
    Whom lovely Venus at a birth
    With two sister Graces more
    To ivy-crownéd Bacchus bore:
    Or whether (as some sager sing)
    The frolic wind that breathes the spring
    Zephyr, with Aurora playing,
    As he met her once a-Maying—
    There on beds of violets blue
    And fresh-blown roses wash'd in dew
    Fill'd her with thee, a daughter fair,
    So buxom, blithe, and debonair.

    Haste thee, Nymph, and bring with thee
    Jest, and youthful jollity,
    Quips, and cranks, and wanton wiles,

L'Allegro, the Cheerful man; pronounce *Alaygro*
2 *Cerberus*, the fabled Dog of the dead   3 *Stygian*, gloomy
8 *ebon*, black   10 *Cimmerian*, Northern, gloomy
12 *yclept*, called   24 *debonair*, handsome
25 *Nymph*, maiden   27 smart and odd turns of speech

Nods, and becks, and wreathéd smiles
Such as hang on Hebe's cheek,
And love to live in dimple sleek ;
Sport that wrinkled Care derides,
And Laughter holding both his sides :—
Come, and trip it as you go
On the light fantastic toe ;
And in thy right hand lead with thee
The mountain nymph, sweet Liberty ;
And if I give thee honour due
Mirth, admit me of thy crew,
To live with her, and live with thee
In unreprovéd pleasures free ;
To hear the lark begin his flight
And singing startle the dull night
From his watch-tower in the skies,
Till the dappled dawn doth rise ;
Then to come, in spite of sorrow,
And at my window bid good-morrow
Through the sweetbriar, or the vine,
Or the twisted eglantine :
While the cock with lively din
Scatters the rear of darkness thin,
And to the stack, or the barn-door,
Stoutly struts his dames before :
Oft listening how the hounds and horn
Cheerly rouse the slumbering morn:
From the side of some hoar hill,
Through the high wood echoing shrill.
Sometime walking, not unseen,
By hedge-row elms, on hillocks green,
Right against the eastern gate
Where the great Sun begins his state

---

29 *Hebe*, Youth   36 see end   40 *unreprovéd*, innocent
45 *eglantine*, dog-rose   52 *dames*, hens
54 seem to waken the day   60 *state*, progress

Robed in flames and amber light ;
The clouds in thousand liveries dight ;
While the ploughman, near at hand,
Whistles o'er the furrow'd land,
And the milkmaid singeth blithe,
And the mower whets his scythe,
And every shepherd tells his tale
Under the hawthorn in the dale.
   Straight mine eye hath caught new pleasures
Whilst the landscape round it measures ;
Russet lawns, and fallows gray,
Where the nibbling flocks do stray ;
Mountains, on whose barren breast
The labouring clouds do often rest ;
Meadows trim with daisies pied,
Shallow brooks, and rivers wide ;
Towers and battlements it sees
Bosom'd high in tufted trees,
Where perhaps some Beauty lies,
The Cynosure of neighbouring eyes.
   Hard by, a cottage chimney smokes
From betwixt two agéd oaks,
Where Corydon and Thyrsis, met,
Are at their savoury dinner set
Of herbs, and other country messes
Which the neat-handed Phillis dresses ;
And then in haste her bower she leaves
With Thestylis to bind the sheaves ;
Or, if the earlier season lead,
To the tann'd haycock in the mead.
   Sometimes with secure delight
The upland hamlets will invite,

---

62 *dight*, dressed   67 *tells his tale*, counts his flock
71 *lawns*, open grass or moorside   75 *pied*, variegated
80 *Cynosure*, Pole-star, to which every one looks up
83 *Corydon, &c.*, poetical names for country-people
90 *tann'd*, turned brown   91 *secure*, free from care

When the merry bells ring round,
And the jocund rebecks sound
To many a youth and many a maid,
Dancing in the chequer'd shade ;
And young and old come forth to play
On a sun-shine holy-day,
Till the live-long daylight fail :
Then to the spicy nut-brown ale,
With stories told of many a feat,
How faery Mab the junkets eat ;
She was pinch'd, and pull'd, she said ;
And he, by friar's lantern led ;
Tells how the drudging Goblin sweat
To earn his cream-bowl duly set,
When in one night, ere glimpse of morn,
His shadowy flail hath thresh'd the corn
That ten day-labourers could not end ;
Then lies him down the lubber fiend,
And, stretch'd out all the chimney's length,
Basks at the fire his hairy strength ;
And crop-full out of doors he flings,
Ere the first cock his matin rings.
   Thus done the tales, to bed they creep,
By whispering winds soon lull'd asleep.
   Tower'd cities please us then
And the busy hum of men,
Where throngs of knights and barons bold,
In weeds of peace high triumphs hold,
With store of ladies, whose bright eyes
Rain influence, and judge the prize
Of wit or arms, while both contend
To win her grace, whom all commend.
There let Hymen oft appear
In saffron robe, with taper clear,

94 *rebecks*, small fiddles   102 *junkets*, milk-dainties
104 *friar's lantern*, Will o' the wisp   105 *Goblin*, Robin Goodfellow
110 *lubber*, lubberly   120 *weeds*, dress : *triumphs*, splendid entertainments   125 *Hymen*, fabled God of Marriage

And pomp, and feast, and revelry,
With mask, and antique pageantry ;
Such sights as youthful poets dream
On summer eves by haunted stream.
Then to the well-trod stage anon,
If Jonson's learned sock be on,
Or sweetest Shakspeare, Fancy's child,
Warble his native wood-notes wild.
   And ever against eating cares
Lap me in soft Lydian airs
Married to immortal verse,
Such as the meeting soul may pierce
In notes, with many a winding bout
Of linkéd sweetness long drawn out ;
With wanton heed and giddy cunning,
The melting voice through mazes running,
Untwisting all the chains that tie
The hidden soul of harmony ;
That Orpheus' self may heave his head
From golden slumber, on a bed
Of heap'd Elysian flowers, and hear
Such strains as would have won the ear
Of Pluto, to have quite set free
His half-regain'd Eurydice.
   These delights if thou canst give,
Mirth, with thee I mean to live.
J. Milton

* 83 *

IL PENSEROSO

HENCE, vain deluding Joys,
  The brood of Folly without father bred !
    How little you bestead
    Or fill the fixéd mind with all your toys !

---

128 *mask*, sort of play   132 *sock*, Ben Jonson's comedies
136 *Lydian*, light and festive   139 *bout*, turn or strain
145 *Orpheus*, see end   *Il Penseroso*, the Pensive or Thoughtful man
  3 *bestead*, avail   4 *toys*, trifles

Dwell in some idle brain,
   And fancies fond with gaudy shapes possess
As thick and numberless
   As the gay motes that people the sunbeams,
Or likest hovering dreams
   The fickle pensioners of Morpheus' train.
   But hail, thou goddess sage and holy,
Hail, divinest Melancholy!
Whose saintly visage is too bright
To hit the sense of human sight,
And therefore to our weaker view
O'erlaid with black, staid Wisdom's hue;
Black, but such as in esteem
Prince Memnon's sister might beseem,
Or that starr'd Ethiop queen that strove
To set her beauty's praise above
The sea nymphs, and their powers offended:
Yet thou art higher far descended:
Thee bright-hair'd Vesta, long of yore,
To solitary Saturn bore;
His daughter she; in Saturn's reign
Such mixture was not held a stain:
Oft in glimmering bowers and glades
He met her, and in secret shades
Of woody Ida's inmost grove,
While yet there was no fear of Jove.
   Come, pensive nun, devout and pure,
Sober, steadfast, and demure,
All in a robe of darkest grain
Flowing with majestic train,
And sable stole of cypres lawn
Over thy decent shoulders drawn:

6 *fond*, foolish: *possess*, fill   9 *likest*, most like
10 *pensioners*, followers: *Morpheus*, sleep   14 to be visible
16 *staid*, sober   18 an African prince   19 *Queen*, Cassiopea
31 *nun*, person retired from the world   33 *grain*, dyed stuff
           35 *cypres*, crape

Come, but keep thy wonted state,
With even step, and musing gait,
And looks commercing with the skies,
Thy rapt soul sitting in thine eyes :
There, held in holy passion still,
Forget thyself to marble, till,
With a sad leaden downward cast,
Thou fix them on the earth as fast :
And join with thee, calm Peace, and Quiet ;
Spare Fast, that oft with gods doth diet,
And hears the Muses in a ring
Aye round about Jove's altar sing :
And add to these retired Leisure,
That in trim gardens takes his pleasure :—
But first, and chiefest, with thee bring
Him that yon soars on golden wing,
Guiding the fiery-wheeled throne,
The cherub Contemplation ;
And the mute Silence hist along,
'Less Philomel will deign a song
In her sweetest, saddest plight,
Smoothing the rugged brow of Night,
While Cynthia checks her dragon yoke
Gently o'er the accustom'd oak.
—Sweet bird, that shunn'st the noise of folly,
Most musical, most melancholy !
Thee, chauntress, oft, the woods among
I woo, to hear thy even-song ;
And missing thee, I walk unseen
On the dry, smooth-shaven green,
To behold the wandering Moon
Riding near her highest noon,

38 *musing gait*, thoughtful pace   39 *commercing*, holding speech
40 *rapt*, tranced   41 *passion*, ecstasy   46 see end
55 *hist*, go quietly   56 *'less*, unless : *Philomel*, nightingale
57 *plight*, state   58 softening the gloom
59 *Cynthia*, Moon : Milton fancies her in a chariot drawn by two dragons   63 *chauntress*, singer   64 *woo*, walk and look for

Like one that had been led astray
Through the heaven's wide pathless way
And oft, as if her head she bow'd,
Stooping through a fleecy cloud.
 Oft, on a plat of rising ground
I hear the far-off curfeu sound
Over some wide-water'd shore,
Swinging slow with sullen roar:
Or, if the air will not permit,
Some still removéd place will fit,
Where glowing embers through the room
Teach light to counterfeit a gloom;
Far from all resort of mirth,
Save the cricket on the hearth,
Or the bellman's drowsy charm
To bless the doors from nightly harm.
 Or let my lamp at midnight hour
Be seen in some high lonely tower,
Where I may oft out-watch the Bear
With thrice-great Hermes, or unsphere
The spirit of Plato, to unfold
What worlds or what vast regions hold
The immortal mind, that hath forsook
Her mansion in this fleshly nook:
And of those demons that are found
In fire, air, flood, or under ground,
Whose power hath a true consent
With planet, or with element.
Sometime let gorgeous Tragedy
In scepter'd pall come sweeping by,
Presenting Thebes, or Pelops' line,
Or the tale of Troy divine;

---

74 *curfeu*, evening bell   80 serve to show the darkness
87 sit up all night   88-9, *Hermes*, *Plato*, ancient philo-
sophers: *unsphere*, bring down upon earth   92 *nook*, the body
95 *consent*, agreement   96 with the stars and the forces of **Nature**
       98 see end

Or what (though rare) of later age
Ennobled hath the buskin'd stage.
 But, O sad Virgin, that thy power
Might raise Musaeus from his bower,
Or bid the soul of Orpheus sing
Such notes as, warbled to the string,
Drew iron tears down Pluto's cheek
And made Hell grant what Love did seek!
Or call up him that left half-told
The story of Cambuscan bold,
Of Camball, and of Algarsife,
And who had Canacé to wife
That own'd the virtuous ring and glass;
And of the wondrous horse of brass
On which the Tartar king did ride:
And if aught else great bards beside
In sage and solemn tunes have sung
Of turneys, and of trophies hung,
Of forests, and enchantments drear,
Where more is meant than meets the ear.
 Thus, Night, oft see me in thy pale career,
Till civil-suited Morn appear,
Not trick'd and frounced as she was wont
With the Attic Boy to hunt,
But kercheft in a comely cloud
While rocking winds are piping loud,
Or usher'd with a shower still,
When the gust hath blown his fill,
Ending on the rustling leaves
With minute-drops from off the eaves.
And when the sun begins to fling
His flaring beams, me, Goddess, bring

104 *Musaeus*, a fabled poet   109 *him*, Chaucer, in his unfinished Squire's Tale   118 *turneys*, solemn fights: *trophies*, armour and weapons of defeated enemies   121 *career*, course
122 *civil-suited*, peacefully dressed   123 *frounced*, curled
124 *Boy*, Cephalus supposed 'husband to the Dawning
125 *kercheft*, hooded   127 *ushered*, led in

To archéd walks of twilight groves,
And shadows brown, that Sylvan loves,
Of pine, or monumental oak,
Where the rude axe, with heavéd stroke,
Was never heard the nymphs to daunt
Or fright them from their hallow'd haunt.
There in close covert by some brook
Where no profaner eye may look,
Hide me from day's garish eye,
While the bee with honey'd thigh
That at her flowery work doth sing,
And the waters murmuring,
With such concert as they keep
Entice the dewy-feather'd Sleep ;
And let some strange mysterious dream
Wave at his wings in aery stream
Of lively portraiture display'd,
Softly on my eyelids laid :
And, as I wake, sweet music breathe
Above, about, or underneath,
Sent by some spirit to mortals good,
Or the unseen Genius of the wood.
  But let my due feet never fail
To walk the studious cloister's pale,
And love the high-embowéd roof,
With antique pillars massy proof,
And storied windows richly dight,
Casting a dim religious light :
There let the pealing organ blow
To the full-voiced quire below
In service high and anthems clear,
As may with sweetness, through mine ear,

---

134 *Sylvan*, fabled God of the woods   137 *nymphs*, wood-fairies
   141 *garish*, staring   154 *Genius*, Spirit
   156 *pale*, enclosure   157 Gothic vaulting
   158 *massy*, massive   159 *dight*, adorned

Dissolve me into ecstasies,
And bring all Heaven before mine eyes.
　And may at last my weary age
Find out the peaceful hermitage,
The hairy gown and mossy cell,
Where I may sit and rightly spell
Of every star that heaven doth show,
And every herb that sips the dew ;
Till old experience do attain
To something like prophetic strain.
　These pleasures, Melancholy, give,
And I with thee will choose to live.
　　　　　　　　　　　J. Milton

* 84 *

A HAPPY OLD AGE

HAPPY were he could finish forth his fate
In some unhaunted desert, where, obscure
From all society, from love and hate
Of worldly folk, there should he sleep secure ;

Then wake again, and yield God ever praise ;
Content with hip, with haws, and brambleberry ;
In contemplation passing still his days.
And change of holy thoughts to make him merry :

Who, when he dies, his tomb might be the bush
Where harmless robin resteth with the thrush :
　—Happy were he !
　　　　　　　　　　　Unknown

　　170 *spell*, study　　　1 *he could*, he who could end his life
　　　　2 *unhaunted*, unpeopled : *obscure*, hidden
　　　　　　8 *merry*, cheer him up

End of First Part

The Children's Treasury

SECOND PART

* I *

THE BATTLE OF AGINCOURT

Agincourt, Agincourt! know ye not Agincourt?
  Where the English slew and hurt
    All the French foemen.
  With our guns and bills brown,
  O! the French were beat down,
    Morris-pikes and bowmen!

T. Heywood

* * * * *

Fair stood the wind for France
When we our sails advance,
Nor now to prove our chance
  Longer will tarry;
But putting to the main,
At Kaux, the mouth of Seine,
With all his martial train,
  Landed King Harry.

And taking many a fort,
Furnish'd in warlike sort,
Marcheth towards Agincourt
  In happy hour;

4 *bills*, pikes
3 *prove*, try 5 sailing forth
9 *fort*, castle
6 *Morris*-pikes, large-sized
7 *martial*, warlike
10 supplied for war

Skirmishing day by day
With those that stopp'd his way,
Where the French general lay
   With all his power.

Which in his height of pride,
King Henry to deride,
His ransom to provide
   To the King sending;
Which he neglects the while,
As from a nation vile,
Yet with an angry smile,
   Their fall portending.

And turning to his men,
Quoth our brave Henry then,
'Though they to one be ten,
   'Be not amazéd!
'Yet have well begun,
'Battles so bravely won
'Have ever to the sun
   'By fame been raiséd.

'And for myself,' quoth he,
'This my full rest shall be;
'England, ne'er mourn for me,
   'Nor more esteem me:—
'Victor I will remain,
'Or on this earth lie slain;
'Never shall she sustain
   'Loss to redeem me.

'Poictiers and Cressy tell,
'When most their pride did swell,
'Under our swords they fell:—
   'No less our skill is

13 *skirmishing*, irregular fighting
21 *which*, insult: *he*, Henry
26 *quoth*, spoke
37 *victor*, conqueror
17 *his*, the French general's
24 *portending*, prophesying
36 if I am beaten
40 pay ransom for

'Than when our grandsire great,
'Claiming the regal seat,
'By many a warlike feat
  'Lopp'd the French lilies.'

The Duke of York so dread,
The eager vaward led;
With the main Henry sped,
  Amongst his henchmen.
Exeter had the rear,
A braver man not there;
Heavens! how hot they were
  On the false Frenchmen!

They now to fight are gone:
Armour on armour shone,
Drum now to drum did groan;
  To hear was wonder;
That with the cries they make
The very earth did shake;
Trumpet to trumpet spake;
  Thunder to thunder.

Well it thine age became,
O noble Erpingham,
Which did the signal aim
  To our hid forces;
When from a meadow by,
Like a storm suddenly,
The English archery
  Stuck the French horses,

With Spanish yew so strong,
Arrows a cloth-yard long,
That like to serpents stung,
  Piercing the weather;

---

47 *feat*, deed   48 see end   50 *vaward*, foremost men
52 *henchmen*, attendants   71 *archery*, bowmen
73 *yew*, used for bows   76 *weather*, air

None from his fellow starts,
But playing manly parts,
And like true English hearts,
   Stuck close together.

When down their bows they threw,
And forth their bilbows drew,
And on the French they flew;
   Not one was tardy;
Arms were from shoulders sent;
Scalps to the teeth were rent,
Down the French peasants went;
   Our men were hardy.

This while our noble King,
His broad sword brandishing,
Down the French host did ding,
   As to o'erwhelm it;
And many a deep-wound lent,
His arms with blood besprent;
And many a cruel dent
   Bruiséd his helmet.

Gloucester, that duke so good,
Next of the royal blood,
For famous England stood,
   With his brave brother,
Clarence, in steel so bright,
Though but a maiden knight,
Yet in that furious fight
   Scarce such another.

Warwick in blood did wade,
Oxford the foe invade,
And cruel slaughter made,
   Still as they ran up;

---

82 *bilbows*, swords   91 *ding*, cut down violently
94 *besprent*, sprinkled   102 *maiden*, untried

Suffolk his axe did ply,
Beaumont and Willoughby
Bare them right doughtily—
Ferrers and Fanhope.

Upon Saint Crispin's day
Fought was this noble fray,
Which fame did not delay
  To England to carry.
O when shall Englishmen
With such acts fill a pen,
Or England breed again
  Such a King Harry!

M. Drayton

* 2 *

AFTER BLENHEIM

It was a summer evening;
  Old Kaspar's work was done,
And he before his cottage door
  Was sitting in the sun;
And by him sported on the green
His little grandchild Wilhelmine.

She saw her brother Peterkin
  Roll something large and round
Which he beside the rivulet
  In playing there had found;
He came to ask what he had found
That was so large and smooth and round.

Old Kaspar took it from the boy,
  Who stood expectant by;
And then the old man shook his head,
  And with a natural sigh
''Tis some poor fellow's skull,' said he,
'Who fell in the great victory.'

111 *doughtily*, bravely 113 October 25
115 *fame*, report 118 give writers such a fine subject

'I find them in the garden,
　'For there's many here about;
'And often when I go to plough
　'The ploughshare turns them out.
'For many thousand men,' said he,
'Were slain in that great victory.'

'Now tell us what 'twas all about,'
　Young Peterkin he cries;
And little Wilhelmine looks up
　With wonder-waiting eyes;
'Now tell us all about the war,
'And what they fought each other for?'

'It was the English,' Kaspar cried,
　'Who put the French to rout;
'But what they fought each other for
　'I could not well make out.
'But everybody said,' quoth he,
'That 'twas a famous victory.

'My father lived at Blenheim then,
　'Yon little stream hard by;
'They burnt his dwelling to the ground,
　'And he was forced to fly:
'So with his wife and child he fled,
'Nor had he where to rest his head.

'With fire and sword the country round
　'Was wasted far and wide,
'And many a childing mother then
　'And newborn baby died:
'But things like that, you know, must be
'At every famous victory.

'They say it was a shocking sight
　'After the field was won;
'For many thousand bodies here
　'Lay rotting in the sun:

'But things like that, you know, must be
'After a famous victory.

'Great praise the Duke of Marlbro' won
   'And our good Prince Eugene;'
—'Why 'twas a very wicked thing!'
   Said little Wilhelmine;
'Nay .. nay .. my little girl,' quoth he,
'It was a famous victory!

'And everybody praised the Duke
   'Who this great fight did win.'·
—'But what good came of it at last?'
   Quoth little Peterkin :—
'Why that I cannot tell,' said he,
'But 'twas a famous victory.'
R. Southey

* 3 ·

LUCY GRAY

OFT I had heard of Lucy Gray:
   And, when I cross'd the wild,
I chanced to see at break of day
   The solitary child.

No mate, no comrade Lucy knew;
   She dwelt on a wide moor,
—The sweetest thing that ever grew
   Beside a human door!

You yet may spy the fawn at play,
   The hare upon the green;
But the sweet face of Lucy Gray
   Will never more be seen.

'To-night will be a stormy night—
   'You to the town must go;
'And take a lantern, Child, to light
   'Your mother through the snow.'

'That, Father, will I gladly do :
'"Tis scarcely afternoon—
'The minster-clock has just struck two,
'And yonder is the moon!'

At this the father raised his hook,
And snapp'd a faggot band ;
He plied his work ;—and Lucy took
The lantern in her hand.

Not blither is the mountain roe :
With many a wanton stroke
Her feet disperse the powdery snow,
That rises up like smoke.

The storm came on before its time :
She wander'd up and down ;
And many a hill did Lucy climb :
But never reach'd the town.

The wretched parents all that night
Went shouting far and wide ;
But there was neither sound nor sight
To serve them for a guide.

At daybreak on a hill they stood
That overlook'd the moor ;
And thence they saw the bridge of wood,
A furlong from their door.

They wept—and, turning homeward, cried,
'In heaven we all shall meet!'
—When in the snow the mother spied
The print of Lucy's feet.

Then downwards from the steep hill's edge
They track'd the footmarks small ;
And through the broken hawthorn hedge,
And by the long stone-wall :

And then an open field they cross'd :
  The marks were still the same ;
They track'd them on, nor ever lost ;
  And to the bridge they came.

They follow'd from the snowy bank
  Those footmarks, one by one,
Into the middle of the plank ;
  And further there were none !

—Yet some maintain that to this day
  She is a living child ;
That you may see sweet Lucy Gray
  Upon the lonesome wild.

O'er rough and smooth she trips along,
  And never looks behind ;
And sings a solitary song
  That whistles in the wind.

W. Wordsworth

* 4 *

NURSE'S SONG

WHEN the voices of children are heard on the green,
  And laughing is heard on the hill,
My heart is at rest within my breast,
  And everything else is still.
Then come home, my children, the sun is gone
    down,
  And the dews of night arise ;
Come, come, leave off play, and let us away
  Till the morning appears in the skies.

' No, no, let us play, for it is yet day,
  ' And we cannot go to sleep ;
' Besides in the sky the little birds fly,
  ' And the hills are all cover'd with sheep.'

—Well, well, go and play till the light fades away,
  And then go home to bed.——
The little ones leap'd, and shouted, and laugh'd ;
  And all the hills echoéd.

W. Blake

* 5 *

INFANT JOY,
OR, THE BABY

'I HAVE no name;
'I am but two days old.'
—'What shall I call thee?'
  —'I happy am ;
  'Joy is my name.'
—Sweet joy befall thee !

Pretty joy !
Sweet joy, but two days old.
Sweet joy I call thee :
  Thou dost smile :
  I sing the while,
Sweet joy befall thee !

W. Blake

* 6 *

THE BLIND LASSIE

O HARK to the strain that sae sweetly is ringin',
  And echoing clearly o'er lake and o'er lea,
Like some fairy bird in the wilderness singin' ;
  It thrills to my heart, yet nae minstrel I see.
Round yonder rock knittin', a dear child is sittin',
  Sae toilin' her pitifu' pittance is won,
Hersel' tho' we see nae, 'tis mitherless Jeanie,—
  The bonnie blind lassie that sits 'i' the sun.

---

1 *strain*, music 4 *minstrel*, singer
6 *pitifu' pittance*, small livelihood 7 *mither*, mother

Five years syne come autumn she cam' wi' her mither,
   A sodger's puir widow, sair wasted an' gane;
As brown fell the leaves, sae wi' them did she wither,
   And left the sweet child on the wide world her lane.
She left Jeanie weepin', in His holy keepin'
   Wha shelters the lamb frae the cauld wintry win';
We had little siller, yet a' were good till her,
   The bonnie blind lassie that sits i' the sun.

An' blythe now an' cheerfu', frae mornin' to e'enin
   She sits thro' the simmer, an' gladdens ilk ear,
Baith auld and young daut her, sae gentle and winnin';
   To a' the folks round the wee lassie is dear.
Braw leddies caress her, wi' bounties would press her;
   The modest bit darlin' their notice would shun;
For though she has naething, proud-hearted this wee thing,
   The bonnie blind lassie that sits i' the sun.

T. C. Latto

* 7 *

NIGHT

The sun descending in the west,
   The evening star does shine;
The birds are silent in their nest,
   And I must seek for mine.
     The moon, like a flower
     In heaven's high bower,
     With silent delight
     Sits and smiles on the night.

---

9 *syne*, since   10 *sair*, sorely   12 *her lane*, alone
15 *siller*, money: *till*, to   18 *simmer*, summer: *ilk*, every
19 *daut*, dote on   20 *a'*, all   21 *braw leddies*, fine ladies
               22 *bit*, little

Farewell, green fields and happy groves,
  Where flocks have ta'en delight ;
Where lambs have nibbled, silent moves
  The feet of angels bright ;
    Unseen, they pour blessing,
    And joy without ceasing,
    On each bud and blossom,
    And each sleeping bosom.

They look in every thoughtless nest,
  Where birds are cover'd warm,
They visit caves of every beast,
  To keep them all from harm :—
    If they see any weeping
    That should have been sleeping,
    They pour sleep on their head,
    And sit down by their bed.

W. Blake

* 8 *

SIMON LEE THE OLD HUNTSMAN

IN the sweet shire of Cardigan,
Not far from pleasant Ivor Hall,
An old man dwells, a little man,
I've heard he once was tall.
Full five-and-thirty years he lived
A running huntsman merry ;
And still the centre of his cheek
Is red as a ripe cherry.

No man like him the horn could sound,
And hill and valley rang with glee,
When Echo bandied round and round
The halloo of Simon Lee.
In those proud days he little cared
For husbandry or tillage ;
To blither tasks did Simon rouse
The sleepers of the village.

11 *bandied*, sent

He all the country could outrun,
Could leave both man and horse behind;
And often, ere the chase was done,
He reel'd and was stone-blind.
And still there's something in the world
At which his heart rejoices;
For when the chiming hounds are out,
He dearly loves their voices.

But O the heavy change!—bereft
Of health, strength, friends and kindred, see
Old Simon to the world is left
In liveried poverty:
His master's dead, and no one now
Dwells in the Hall of Ivor;
Men, dogs, and horses, all are dead;
He is the sole survivor.

And he is lean and he is sick:
His body, dwindled and awry,
Rests upon ankles swoln and thick;
His legs are thin and dry.
He has no son, he has no child;
His wife, an agéd woman,
Lives with him, near the waterfall,
Upon the village common.

Beside their moss-grown hut of clay,
Not twenty paces from the door,
A scrap of land they have, but they
Are poorest of the poor.
This scrap of land he from the heath
Enclosed when he was stronger;
But what avails the land to them
Which he can till no longer?

25 *bereft*, cut off from 28 in a huntsman's dress
32 only one left alive 47 what use is

Oft, working by her husband's side,
Ruth does what Simon cannot do ;
For she, with scanty cause for pride,
Is stouter of the two.
And, though you with your utmost skill
From labour could not wean them,
'Tis little, very little, all
That they can do between them.

Few months of life has he in store,
As he to you will tell,
For still, the more he works, the more
Do his weak ankles swell.
—My gentle reader, I perceive
How patiently you've waited,
And now I fear that you expect
Some tale will be related.

O reader ! had you in your mind
Such stores as silent thought can bring,
O gentle reader ! you would find
A tale in everything.
What more I have to say is short,
And you must kindly take it :
It is no tale ; but, should you think,
Perhaps a tale you'll make it.—

One summer-day I chanced to see
This old man doing all he could
To unearth the root of an old tree,
A stump of rotten wood.
The mattock totter'd in his hand ;
So vain was his endeavour
That at the root of the old tree
He might have work'd for ever.

64 *related*, told

'You're overtask'd, good Simon Lee,
'Give me your tool,' to him I said ;
And at the word right gladly he
Received my proffer'd aid.
I struck, and with a single blow
The tangled root I sever'd,
At which the poor old man so long
And vainly had endeavour'd.

The tears into his eyes were brought,
And thanks and praises seem'd to run
So fast out of his heart, I thought
They never would have done.
—I've heard of hearts unkind, kind deeds
With coldness still returning ;
Alas ! the gratitude of men
Has oftener left me mourning.

W. Wordsworth

* 9 *

LULLABY FOR TITANIA

First Fairy

YOU spotted snakes with double tongue,
  Thorny hedgehogs, be not seen ;
Newts, and blind-worms, do no wrong ;
  Come not near our Fairy Queen.

Chorus

  Philomel with melody
  Sing in our sweet lullaby :
Lulla, lulla, lullaby ; lulla, lulla, lullaby
Never harm, nor spell, nor charm,
  Come our lovely lady nigh !
  So good-night, with lullaby.

<hr>

8 4 *proffer'd*, offered

4 *Queen*, Titania   5 *Philomel*, nightingale

Second Fairy

Weaving spiders, come not here ;
  Hence, you long-legg'd spinners, hence ;
Beetles black, approach not near ;
  Worm, nor snail, do no offence.

Chorus

  Philomel with melody
  Sing in our sweet lullaby ;
Lulla, lulla, lullaby ; lulla, lulla, lullaby !
Never harm, nor spell, nor charm,
  Come our lovely lady nigh !
  So good-night, with lullaby.
                              W. Shakespeare

* 10 *

ROBIN GOODFELLOW

FROM Oberon, in fairy land,
The king of ghosts and shadows there,
Mad Robin I, at his command,
Am sent to view the night-sports here.
      What revel rout
      Is kept about,
  In every corner where I go,
      I will o'ersee,
      And merry be,
  And make good sport, with ho, ho, ho !

More swift than lightning can I fly
About this airy welkin soon,
And, in a minute's space, descry
Each thing that's done below the moon.

5, 6 whatever sport goes on   12 *welkin*, sky
             13 *descry*, see

There's not a hag
Or ghost shall wag,
Or cry 'ware goblins! where I go;
But, Robin, I
Their feats will spy,
And send them home with ho, ho, ho!

Whene'er such wanderers I meet,
As from their night-sports they trudge home,
With counterfeiting voice I greet,
And call them on with me to roam;
Through woods, through lakes,
Through bogs, through brakes,
Or else, unseen, with them I go,
All in the nick
To play some trick,
And frolic it, with ho, ho, ho!

Sometimes I meet them like a man,
Sometimes an ox, sometimes a hound;
And to a horse I turn me can,
To trip and trot about them round.
But if to ride,
My back they stride,
More swift than wind away I go,
O'er hedge and lands,
Through pools and ponds,
I hurry, laughing, ho, ho, ho!

By wells and rills, in meadows green,
We nightly dance our heyday guise;
And to our fairy King and Queen,
We chant our moonlight minstrelsies.

---

16 *wag*, stir   17 *'ware*, beware of   19 *feats*, doings
23 *counterfeiting*, mimicking   28 *in the nick*, at the right moment
42 *heyday guise*, frolicsome game   44 *minstrelsies*, songs

When larks 'gin sing,
Away we fling;
And babes new born steal as we go;
And elf in bed,
We leave instead,
And wend us laughing, ho, ho, ho!

From hag-bred Merlin's time have I
Thus nightly revell'd to and fro;
And for my pranks men call me by
The name of Robin Good-fellow.
Fiends, ghosts, and sprites,
Who haunt the nights,
The hags and goblins do me know;
And beldames old
My feats have told,
So *valé, valé!* ho, ho, ho!

Unknown

* I I *

THE FAIRY PRINCE

It was intill a pleasant time,
Upon a summer's day,
The noble Earl Mar's daughter
Went forth to sport and play.

And as she play'd and sported
Below a green oak tree,
There she saw a sprightly doo
Set on a branch so hie.

'O Coo-my-doo, my Love so true,
' If ye'll come down to me,
' Ye'll have a cage of good red gold
' Instead of simple tree.'

50 *wend*, go 51 *hag-bred*, witch-born: *Merlin*, a magician
60 *valé*, farewell   1 *intill*, in   7 *do*. dove   8 *hie*, high
12 *tree*, wood

And she had not these words well spoke,
    Nor yet these words well said,
'Till Coo-my-doo flew from the branch,
    And lighted on her head.

Then she has brought this pretty bird
    Home to her bower and hall,
And made him shine as fair a bird
    As any of them all.

When day was gone and night was come,
    About the evening-tide,
This lady spied a sprightly youth
    Stand straight up by her side.

'O who are ye, young man?' she said,
    'What country come ye frae?'
—'I flew across the sea,' he said,
    ''Twas but this very day.

'My mother is a queen,' he says,
    'Likewise of magic skill;
''Twas she that turn'd me in a doo,
    'To fly where'er I will.

'And it was but this very day
    'That I came o'er the sea:
'I loved you at a single look;
    'With you I'll live and dee.'

—'O Coo-my-doo, my Love so true,
    'No more from me ye'll gae.'
—'That's never my intent, my Love;
    'As ye said, it shall be sae.'

Thus he has stay'd in bower with her
    For twenty years and three;
Till there came a lord of high renown
    To court this fair ladye.

    31 *in*, to   38 *gae*, go

But still his proffer she refused,
    And all his presents too;
Says, 'I'm content to live alone
    'With my bird Coo-my-doo.'

Her father sware a solemn oath,
    Among the nobles all,
'To-morrow, ere I eat or drink,
    'That bird I'll surely kill.'

The bird was sitting in his cage,
    And heard what he did say;
He jump'd upon the window-sill:
    '"Tis time I was away.'

Then Coo-my-doo took flight and flew
    Beyond the raging sea,
And lighted at his mother's castle,
    On a tower of gold so hie.

The Queen his mother was walking out,
    To see what she could see,
And there she saw her darling son
    Set on the tower so hie.

'Get dancers here to dance,' she said,
    'And minstrels for to play;
'For here's my dear son Florentine
    'Come back with me to stay.'

—'Instead of dancers to dance, mother,
    'Or minstrels for to play,
'Turn four-and-twenty well-wight men
    'Like storks, in feathers gray;

'My seven sons in seven swans,
    'Above their heads to flee;
'And I myself a gay goshawk,
    'A bird of high degree.'

---

45 *proffer*, offer   71 *well-wight*, stalwart
    75 *goshawk*, large hawk

This flock of birds took flight and flew
  Beyond the raging sea ;
They landed near the Earl Mar's castle,
  Took shelter in every tree.

These birds flew up from bush and tree,
  And lighted on the hall ;
And when the wedding-train came forth
  Flew down among them all.

The storks they seized the boldest men,
  That they could not fight or flee ;
The swans they bound the bridegroom fast
  Unto a green oak tree.

They flew around the bride-maidens,
  Then on the bride's own head ;
And with the twinkling of an eye,
  The bride and they were fled !
                                Unknown

* 12 *

THE ANCIENT MARINER

PART I

IT is an ancient Mariner,
And he stoppeth one of three.
—' By thy long gray beard and glittering eye,
' Now wherefore stopp'st thou me ?

' The Bridegroom's doors are open'd wide,
' And I am next of kin ;
' The guests are met, the feast is set :
' May'st hear the merry din !'

He holds him with his skinny hand,
' There was a ship,' quoth he.
—' Hold off ! unhand me, gray-beard loon !'
Eftsoons his hand dropt he.

12 *eftsoons*, at once

He holds him with his glittering eye :—
The wedding-guest stood still,
And listens like a three years' child :
The Mariner hath his will.

The Wedding-Guest sat on a stone :
He cannot choose but hear ;
And thus spake on that ancient man,
The bright-eyed Mariner :—

' The ship was cheer'd, the harbour clear'd ;
' Merrily did we drop
' Below the kirk, below the hill,
' Below the light-house top.

' The sun came up upon the left,
' Out of the sea came he !
' And he shone bright, and on the right
' Went down into the sea.

' Higher and higher every day,
' Till over the mast at noon '—
The Wedding-Guest here beat his breast,
For he heard the loud bassoon.

The bride hath paced into the hall,
Red as rose is she ;
Nodding their heads before her goes
The merry minstrelsy.

The Wedding-Guest he beat his breast,
Yet he cannot choose but hear ;
And thus spake on that ancient man,
The bright-eyed Mariner : —

' And now the storm-blast came, and he
Was tyrannous and strong :
He struck with his o'ertaking wings,
And chased us South along.

23 *kirk*, church 25 *left*, East, as they were going South
32 *bassoon*, wind-instrument 36 *minstrelsy*, musicians

With sloping masts and dipping prow,
As who pursued with yell and blow
Still treads the shadow of his foe,
And forward bends his head,
The ship drove fast, loud roar'd the blast,
And southward aye we fled.

And now there came both mist and snow,
And it grew wondrous cold :
And ice, mast-high, came floating by,
As green as emerald.

And through the drifts the snowy clifts
Did send a dismal sheen :
Nor shapes of men nor beasts we ken—
The ice was all between.

The ice was here, the ice was there,
The ice was all around :
It crack'd and growl'd, and roar'd and howl'd,
Like noises in a swound !

At length did cross an Albatross,
Thorough the fog it came ;
As if it had been a Christian soul,
We hail'd it in God's name.

It ate the food it ne'er had ate,
And round and round it flew :—
The ice did split with a thunder-fit ;
The helmsman steer'd us through !

And a good south wind sprung up behind ;
The Albatross did follow,
And every day, for food or play,
Came to the mariners' hollo !

53 glaciers 56 *sheen*, shining 57 *ken*, see
62 *swound*, swoon 63 *Albatross*, great sea-bird

In mist or cloud, on mast or shroud,
It perch'd for vespers nine;
Whiles all the night, through fog-smoke white,
Glimmer'd the white moon-shine.

'God save thee, ancient Mariner!
'From the fiends, that plague thee thus!—
'Why look'st thou so?'—'With my cross-bow
I shot the Albatross.'

PART II

'The sun now rose upon the right:
Out of the sea came he
Still hid in mist,—and on the left
Went down into the sea.

And the good south wind still blew behind,
But no sweet bird did follow,
Nor any day for food or play
Came to the mariners' hollo!

And I had done a hellish thing,
And it would work 'em woe:
For all averr'd, I had kill'd the bird
That made the breeze to blow.
Ah wretch! said they, the bird to slay,
That made the breeze to blow!

Nor dim nor red, like God's own head,
The glorious Sun uprist:
Then all averr'd, I had kill'd the bird
That brought the fog and mist:—
'Twas right, said they, such birds to slay,
That bring the fog and mist.

75 *shroud*, rigging   76 *vespers*, evenings
93 *averr'd*, declared

The fair breeze blew, the white foam flew,
The furrow follow'd free ;
We were the first that ever burst
Into that silent sea.

Down dropt the breeze, the sails dropt down,
'Twas sad as sad could be ;
And we did speak only to break
The silence of the sea !

All in a hot and copper sky,
The bloody Sun, at noon,
Right up above the mast did stand,
No bigger than the Moon.

Day after day, day after day,
We stuck, nor breath nor motion ;
As idle as a painted ship
Upon a painted ocean.

Water, water, everywhere,
And all the boards did shrink ;
Water, water, everywhere,
Nor any drop to drink.

The very deep did rot : O Heaven !
That ever this should be !
Yea, slimy things did crawl with legs
Upon the slimy sea.

About, about, in reel and rout
The death-fires danced at night ;
The water, like a witch's oils,
Burnt green, and blue, and white.

And some in dreams assuréd were
Of the spirit that plagued us so ;
Nine fathom deep he had follow'd us
From the land of mist and snow.

And every tongue, through utter drought,
Was wither'd at the root ;
We could not speak, no more than if
We had been choked with soot.

Ah ! well a-day ! what evil looks
Had I from old and young !
Instead of the cross, the Albatross
About my neck was hung.

PART III

' There pass'd a weary time. Each throat
Was parch'd, and glazed each eye.
A weary time ! a weary time !
How glazed each weary eye !
When looking westward, I beheld
A something in the sky.

At first it seem'd a little speck,
And then it seem'd a mist ;
It moved and moved, and took at last
A certain shape, I wist.
A speck, a mist, a shape, I wist !
And still it near'd and near'd :
As if it dodged a water-sprite,
It plunged and tack'd and veer'd.

With throats unslaked, with black lips baked,
We could nor laugh nor wail ;
Through utter drought all dumb we stood !
I bit my arm, I suck'd the blood,
And cried, A sail- a sail !

With throats unslaked, with black lips baked,
Agape they heard me call :
Gramercy ! they for joy did grin,
And all at once their breath drew in,
As they were drinking all.

_{152 *wist*, perceived}

See! see! (I cried) she tacks no more!
Hither to work us weal;
Without a breeze, without a tide,
She steadies with upright keel!

The western wave was all a-flame,
The day was wellnigh done!
Almost upon the western wave
Rested the broad bright Sun;
When that strange shape drove suddenly
Betwixt us and the Sun.

And straight the Sun was fleck'd with bars,
(Heaven's Mother send us grace!)
As if through a dungeon-grate he peer'd
With broad and burning face.

Alas! (thought I. and my heart beat loud)
How fast she nears and nears!
Are those her sails that glance in the Sun,
Like restless gossameres?

Are those her ribs through which the Sun
Did peer, as through a grate?
And is that woman all her crew?
Is that a Death? and are there two?
Is Death that woman's mate?

Her lips were red, her looks were free,
Her locks were yellow as gold:
Her skin was as white as leprosy.
The Night-mare Life-in-Death was she,
Who thicks man's blood with cold.

The naked hulk alongside came,
And the twain were casting dice;
'The game is done! I've ... I've won!'
Quoth she, and whistles thrice.

<small>168 do us good   175 *hulk*, body of the ship</small>

The Sun's rim dips; the stars rush out:
At one stride comes the dark;
With far-heard whisper, o'er the sea,
Off shot the spectre-bark.

We listen'd and look'd sideways up!
Fear at my heart, as at a cup,
My life-blood seem'd to sip!
The stars were dim, and thick the night;
The steersman's face by his lamp gleam'd white;
From the sails the dew did drip—
Till clomb above the eastern bar
The hornéd Moon, with one bright star
Within the nether tip.

One after one, by the star-dogg'd Moon,
Too quick for groan or sigh,
Each turn'd his face with a ghastly pang,
And cursed me with his eye.

Four times fifty living men,
(And I heard nor sigh nor groan,)
With heavy thump, a lifeless lump,
They dropt down one by one.

The souls did from their bodies fly,—
They fled to bliss or woe!
And every soul, it pass'd me by
Like the whizz of my cross-bow.'

PART IV.

' I fear thee, ancient Mariner!
' I fear thy skinny hand!
' And thou art long, and lank, and brown,
' As is the ribb'd sea-sand.

200 Near the Equator there is hardly any twilight
212 *dogg'd*, followed closely by

'I fear thee and thy glittering eye,
'And thy skinny hand, so brown.'
—'Fear not, fear not, thou Wedding-Guest!
This body dropt not down.

Alone, alone ; all, all alone,
Alone on a wide, wide sea !
And never a saint took pity on
My soul in agony.

The many men, so beautiful !
And they all dead did lie :
And a thousand thousand slimy things
Lived on ; and so did I.

I look'd upon the rotting sea,
And drew my eyes away ;
I look'd upon the rotting deck,
And there the dead men lay.

I look'd to heaven, and tried to pray ;
But or ever a prayer had gusht,
A wicked whisper came, and made
My heart as dry as dust.

I closed my lids, and kept them close,
And the balls like pulses beat ;
For the sky and the sea, and the sea and the sky
Lay like a load on my weary eye,
And the dead were at my feet.

The cold sweat melted from their limbs,
Nor rot nor reek did they :
The look with which they look'd on me
Had never pass'd away.

An orphan's curse would drag to hell
A spirit from on high ;
But, oh ! more horrible than that
Is the curse in a dead man's eye !
Seven days, seven nights, I saw that curse,
And yet I could not die.

The moving Moon went up the sky,
And nowhere did abide :
Softly she was going up,
And a star or two beside :

Her beams bemock'd the sultry main,
Like April hoar-frost spread ;
But where the ship's huge shadow lay,
The charmèd water burnt alway
A still and awful red.

Beyond the shadow of the ship,
I watch'd the water snakes :
They moved in tracks of shining white,
And when they rear'd, the elfish light
Fell off in hoary flakes.

Within the shadow of the ship
I watch'd their rich attire :
Blue, glossy green, and velvet black,
They coil'd and swam ; and every track
Was a flash of golden fire.

O happy living things ! no tongue
Their beauty might declare :
A spring of love gush'd from my heart,
And I bless'd them unaware :
Sure my kind saint took pity on me,
And I bless'd them unaware.

The self-same moment I could pray ;
And from my neck so free
The Albatross fell off, and sank
Like lead into the sea.

PART V

'O sleep ! it is a gentle thing,
Beloved from pole to pole !
To Mary Queen the praise be given !
She sent the gentle sleep from Heaven
That slid into my soul.

The silly buckets on the deck
That had so long remain'd,
I dreamt that they were fill'd with dew ;
And when I awoke, it rain'd.

My lips were wet, my throat was cold,
My garments all were dank ;
Sure I had drunken in my dreams,
And still my body drank.

I moved, and could not feel my limbs :
I was so light ; almost
I thought that I had died in sleep
And was a blessèd ghost.

And soon I heard a roaring wind ;
It did not come anear ;
But with its sound it shook the sails,
That were so thin and sere.

The upper air burst into life !
And a hundred fire-flags sheen,
To and fro, they were hurried about !
And to and fro, and in and out,
The wan stars danced between.

And the coming wind did roar more loud,
And the sails did sigh like sedge ;
And the rain pour'd down from one black
    cloud ;
The Moon was at its edge.

The thick black cloud was cleft, and still
The Moon was at its side :
Like waters shot from some high crag,
The lightning fell with never a jag,
A river steep and wide.

The loud wind never reach'd the ship,
Yet now the ship moved on !
Beneath the lightning and the Moon
The dead men gave a groan.

312 *sere*, withered and dry   317 *wan*, pale

They groan'd, they stirr'd, they all uprose,
Nor spake, nor moved their eyes;
It had been strange, e'en in a dream,
To have seen those dead men rise.

The helmsman steer'd; the ship moved on;
Yet never a breeze up blew;
The mariners all 'gan work the ropes
Where they were wont to do;
They raised their limbs like lifeless tools—
We were a ghastly crew!

The body of my brother's son
Stood by me, knee to knee:
The body and I pull'd at one rope,
But he said nought to me.'

'—I fear thee, ancient mariner!'
'—Be calm, thou Wedding Guest!
'Twas not those souls that fled in pain,
Which to their corses came again,
But a troop of spirits blest—

For when it dawn'd they dropp'd their arms,
And cluster'd round the mast;
Sweet sounds rose slowly through their mouths,
And from their bodies pass'd.

Around, around, flew each sweet sound,
Then darted to the Sun:
Slowly the sounds came back again,
Now mix'd, now one by one.

Sometimes a-dropping from the sky
I heard the skylark sing;
Sometimes all little birds that are,
How they seem'd to fill the sea and air
With their sweet jargoning!

348 *corses*, dead bodies   361 *jargoning*, chattering

And now 'twas like all instruments,
Now like a lonely flute;
And now it is an angel's song,
That makes the heavens be mute.

It ceased; yet still the sails made on
A pleasant noise till noon,
A noise like of a hidden brook
In the leafy month of June,
That to the sleeping woods all night
Singeth a quiet tune.

Till noon we quietly sail'd on,
Yet never a breeze did breathe:
Slowly and smoothly went the ship,
Moved onward from beneath.

Under the keel nine fathom deep,
From the land of mist and snow,
The spirit slid; and it was he
That made the ship to go.
The sails at noon left off their tune,
And the ship stood still also.

The sun, right up above the mast,
Had fix'd her to the ocean:
But in a minute she 'gan stir,
With a short uneasy motion —
Backwards and forwards half her length,
With a short uneasy motion.

Then like a pawing horse let go,
She made a sudden bound:
It flung the blood into my head,
And I fell down in a swound.

How long in that same fit I lay,
I have not to declare;
But ere my living life return'd,
I heard, and in my soul discern'd
Two voices in the air.

396 *discerned*, heard

'Is it he?' quoth one, 'is this the man?
'By Him who died on cross,
'With his cruel bow he laid full low
'The harmless albatross.

'The spirit who bideth by himself
'In the land of mist and snow,
'He loved the bird that loved the man
'Who shot him with his bow.'

The other was a softer voice,
As soft as honey-dew :
Quoth he, 'The man hath penance done,
'And penance more will do.'

PART VI
First Voice

'But tell me, tell me! speak again,
'Thy soft response renewing—
'What makes that ship drive on so fast?
'What is the ocean doing?'

Second Voice

'Still as a slave before his lord,
'The ocean hath no blast!
'His great bright eye most silently
'Up to the Moon is cast—

'If he may know which way to go :
'For she guides him smooth or grim :
'See, brother, see! how graciously
'She looketh down on him !'

First Voice

'But why drives on that ship so fast,
'Without or wave or wind?'

Second Voice

'The air is cut away before,
'And closes from behind.

'Fly, brother, fly! more high, more high!
'Or we shall be belated:
'For slow and slow that ship will go,
'When the Mariner's trance is abated.'

I woke; and we were sailing on
As in a gentle weather:
'Twas night, calm night, the moon was high;
The dead men stood together.

All stood together on the deck,
For a charnel-dungeon fitter:
All fix'd on me their stony eyes,
That in the moon did glitter.

The pang, the curse with which they died,
Had never pass'd away:—
I could not draw my eyes from theirs,
Nor turn them up to pray.

And now this spell was snapt once more:—
I view'd the ocean green,
And look'd far forth, yet little saw
Of what had else been seen:—

Like one, that on a lonesome road
Doth walk in fear and dread,
And having once turn'd round, walks on,
And turns no more his head;
Because he knows a frightful fiend
Doth close behind him tread.

But soon there breathed a wind on me,
Nor sound nor motion made:
Its path was not upon the sea,
In ripple or in shade.

427 *belated*, too late   429 *abated*, over

It raised my hair, it fann'd my cheek
Like a meadow-gale of spring :—
It mingled strangely with my fears,—
Yet it felt like a welcoming.

Swiftly, swiftly flew the ship,
Yet she sail'd softly, too ;
Sweetly, sweetly blew the breeze—
On me alone it blew.

Oh ! dream of joy ! is this indeed
The light-house top I see?
Is this the hill ? is this the kirk ?
Is this mine own countree?

We drifted o'er the harbour-bar,
And I with sobs did pray—
O let me be awake, my God !
Or let me sleep alway.

The harbour-bay was clear as glass,
So smoothly it was strewn :
And on the bay the moonlight lay,
And the shadow of the moon.

The rock shone bright, the kirk no less
That stands above the rock :
The moonlight steep'd in silentness
The steady weather-cock.

And the bay was white with silent light :
Till, rising from the same,
Full many shapes, that shadows were,
In crimson colours came.

A little distance from the prow
Those crimson shadows were :
I turn'd my eyes upon the deck —
Oh, Heaven ! —what saw I there !

Each corse lay flat, lifeless and flat,
And, by the holy rood !
A man all light, a seraph-man,
On every corse there stood.

This seraph-band, each waved his hand:
It was a heavenly sight !
They stood as signals to the land,
Each one a lovely light.

This seraph-band, each waved his hand,
No voice did they impart—
No voice ; but oh ! the silence sank
Like music on my heart.

But soon I heard the dash of oars :
I heard the pilot's cheer ;
My head was turn'd perforce away,
And I saw a boat appear.

The Pilot and the Pilot's boy,
I heard them coming fast :
Dear Lord in Heaven ! it was a joy
The dead men could not blast.

I saw a third—I heard his voice :
It is the Hermit good !
He singeth loud his godly hymns
That he makes in the wood.
He'll shrieve my soul, he'll wash away
The Albatross's blood.

PART VII

'This Hermit good lives in that wood
Which slopes down to the sea :—
How loudly his sweet voice he rears !
He loves to talk with marineres
That come from a far countree.

497 *impart*, utter   507 *blast*, spoil   512 *shrieve*, cleanse from sin

He kneels at morn, and noon, and eve
He hath a cushion plump :
It is the moss that wholly hides
The rotted old oak-stump.

The skiff-boat near'd : I heard them talk,
' Why, this is strange, I trow !
' Where are those lights so many and fair,
' That signal made but now ?'

' Strange, by my faith,' the Hermit said—
' And they answer'd not our cheer !
' The planks look'd warp'd ! and see those sails,
' How thin they are and sere !
' I never saw aught like to them,
' Unless perchance it were

' Brown skeletons of leaves that lag
' My forest-brook along ;
' When the ivy-tod is heavy with snow,
' And the owlet whoops to the wolf below,
' That eats the she-wolf's young.'

' Dear Lord ! it hath a fiendish look '
(The Pilot made reply)
' I am a-fear'd.' 'Push on, push on !'
Said the Hermit cheerily.

The boat came closer to the ship,
But I nor spake nor stirr'd ;
The boat came close beneath the ship,
And straight a sound was heard :—

Under the water it rumbled on,
Still louder and more dread :
It reach'd the ship, it split the bay ;
The ship went down like lead.

524 *trow*, think   **530** *sere*, withered   **535** *tod*, bush

Stunn'd by that loud and dreadful sound,
Which sky and ocean smote,
Like one that hath been seven days drown'd
My body lay afloat ;
But swift as dreams, myself I found
Within the Pilot's boat.

Upon the whirl, where sank the ship,
The boat spun round and round :
And all was still, save that the hill
Was telling of the sound.

I moved my lips--the Pilot shriek'd
And fell down in a fit :
The holy Hermit raised his eyes,
And pray'd where he did sit.

And now, all in my own countree,
I stood on the firm land !
The Hermit stepp'd forth from the boat,
And scarcely he could stand.

'O shrieve me, shrieve me, holy man !'
The Hermit cross'd his brow,
'Say quick,' quoth he, 'I bid thee say—
'What manner of man art thou ?'

Forthwith this frame of mine was wrench'd
With a woful agony,
Which forced me to begin my tale ;
And then it left me free.

Since then, at an uncertain hour,
That agony returns :
And till my ghastly tale is told,
This heart within me burns.

I pass, like night, from land to land ;
I have strange power of speech :
That moment that his face I see,
I know the man that must hear me :
To him my tale I teach.

—What loud uproar bursts from that door !
The wedding guests are there :
But in the garden-bower the bride
And bridemaids singing are :
And hark the little vesper bell,
Which biddeth me to prayer !

O wedding-guest ! this soul hath been
Alone on a wide, wide sea :
So lonely 'twas, that God Himself
Scarce seeméd there to be.

O sweeter than the marriage-feast,
'Tis sweeter far to me,
To walk together to the kirk
With a goodly company !
To walk together to the kirk,
And all together pray,
While each to his Great Father bends,
Old men, and babes, and loving friends,
And youths and maidens gay !

—Farewell, farewell ! but this I tell
To thee, thou Wedding-guest !
He prayeth well who loveth well
Both man and bird and beast.

He prayeth best who loveth best
All things both great and small ;
For the dear God who loveth us,
He made and loveth all.'

— The Mariner, whose eye is bright,
Whose beard with age is hoar,
Is gone : and now the wedding-guest
Turn'd from the bridegroom's door.

He went like one that hath been stunn'd,
And is of sense forlorn :—
A sadder and a wiser man,
He rose the morrow morn.

S. T. Coleridge

* 13 *

THE FEARFUL STORY

'O WHERE have ye been, my long-lost lover,
   'This long seven years and mair?'
'—O, I'm come again to seek your love,
   'And the vows that ye did swear.'

'Now haud your tongue of my love and vows,
   'For they can breed but strife;
'Now haud your tongue of my former vows,
   'For I am another man's wife.'

'—Had I kenn'd that ere I came here,
   'I ne'er had come to thee;
'For I might ha'e married the king's daughter,
   'Were it not for the love of thee.

'I despised the crown of gold,
   'And the fair ladye also;
'And I am come back to my own true Love,
   'But with me she'll not go.

'Ye may leave your husband to himself,
   'And your little son also,
'And sail with me across the sea
   'Where the stormy winds do blow.'

'—O, what have you to keep me with,
   'If I with you should go
'If I should forsake my good husband,
   'My little young son also?'

'—See ye not yon seven pretty ships—
   'The eighth brought me to land—
'With merchandise and mariners,
   'And wealth in every hand?'

7 *haud*, hold

She turn'd her round upon the shore,
   Her Love's ships to behold ;
Their mainyards and their topmasts high
   Were cover'd o'er with gold.

And she has gone to her little young son,
   Kiss'd him both cheek and chin :
'O fare ye well, my little son !
   'For I'll never see you again.'

She has drawn the slippers on her feet,
   Well wrought with threads o' gold,
And he's wrapt her round with the soft velvet
   To hold her from the cold.

She had not sail'd a league from land,
   A league but barely three,
Till she minded on her dear husband,
   And her little young son tee.

'O if I were on shore again,
   'On shore where I would be,
'No living man should flatter me
   'To sail upon the sea !'

—'O haud your tongue of weeping,' says he,
'Let all your mourning be ;
'I'll show ye how the lilies grow
   'On the banks of Italie.'

'—O, what hills are yon, yon pleasant hills,
   'That the sun shines sweetly on ?'
'—O, yon are the hills o' Heaven,' he said,
   'Where you will never win.'

'—O, whatna mountain is yon,' she said,
   'Sae dreary with frost and snow ?'
'—O, yon is the mountain of Hell,' he cried,
   'Where you and I must go !'

43 *minded on*, remembered   44 *tee*, too

And aye when she turn'd her round about,
  Aye taller he seem'd for to be :
Until that the tops of that gallant ship
  No taller were than he !

He strack the mainmast with his hand,
  The foremast with his knee :
The gallant ship was broken in twain,
  And sank into the sea !

Unknown

* 14 *

THE WRECK OF THE HESPERUS

It was the schooner *Hesperus*,
  That sail'd the wintry sea ;
And the skipper had taken his little daughter,
  To bear him company.

Blue were her eyes as the fairy flax,
  Her cheeks like the dawn of day,
And her bosom white as the hawthorn buds,
  That ope in the month of May.

The skipper he stood beside the helm,
  With his pipe in his mouth,
And watch'd how the veering flaw did blow
  The smoke now West, now South.

Then up and spake an old Sailor,
  Had sail'd the Spanish Main,
' I pray thee, put into yonder port,
  ' For I fear a hurricane.

' Last night, the moon had a golden ring,
  ' And to-night no moon we see !'
The skipper, he blew a whiff from his pipe,
  And a scornful laugh laugh'd he.

3 *skipper*, captain   11 *veering flaw*, changeable gusts of wind
16 *hurricane*, sudden storm   17 *ring*, halo

Colder and louder blew the wind,
    A gale from the North-east;
The snow fell hissing in the brine,
    And the billows froth'd like yeast.

Down came the storm, and smote amain
    The vessel in its strength;
She shudder'd and paused, like a frighted steed,
    Then leap'd her cable's length.

' Come hither! come hither! my little daughter,
    ' And do not tremble so!
' For I can weather the roughest gale,
    ' That ever wind did blow.'

He wrapp'd her warm in his seaman's coat
    Against the stinging blast;
He cut a rope from a broken spar,
    And bound her to the mast.

' O father! I hear the church-bells ring,
    ' O say, what may it be?'
' —'Tis a fog-bell on a rock-bound coast!'—
    And he steer'd for the open sea.

' O father! I hear the sound of guns,
    ' O say, what may it be?'
' —Some ship in distress that cannot live
    ' In such an angry sea!'

' O father! I see a gleaming light,
    ' O say what may it be?'
But the father answer'd never a word,—
    A frozen corpse was he.

Lash'd to the helm, all stiff and stark,
    With his face to the skies,
The lantern gleam'd through the gleaming snow
    On his fix'd and glassy eyes.

---

39 *fog-bell*, rung in thick weather to warn ships

Then the maiden clasp'd her hands and pray'd
    That savéd she might be;
And she thought of Christ, who still'd the waves
    On the Lake of Galilee.

And fast through the midnight dark and drear,
    Through the whistling sleet and snow,
Like a sheeted ghost, the vessel swept
    Towards the reef of Norman's Woe.

And ever the fitful gusts between
    A sound came from the land;
It was the sound of the trampling surf.
    On the rocks and the hard sea-sand.

The breakers were right beneath her bows,
    She drifted a dreary wreck,
And a whooping billow swept the crew
    Like icicles from her deck.

She struck where the white and fleecy waves
    Look'd soft as carded wool,
But the cruel rocks they gored her sides
    Like the horns of an angry bull.

Her rattling shrouds all sheathed in ice,
    With the masts went by the board;
Like a vessel of glass she stove and sank,
    Ho! ho! the breakers roar'd.

At day-break on the bleak sea-beach
    A fisherman stood aghast,
To see the form of a maiden fair
    Lash'd close to a drifting mast.

60 *reef*, bank of half-covered rock   61 *fitful*, rising and falling
65 *bows*, forepart   70 *carded*, combed fine
73 *shrouds*, mast-ropes   74 went clean over the deck
75 *stove*, was broken in   78 *aghast*, horrified

The salt sea was frozen on her breast,
  The salt tears in her eyes ;
And he saw her hair like the brown sea-weed
  On the billows fall and rise.
                              H. W. Longfellow

* 15 *

ROSABELLE

O LISTEN, listen, ladies gay !
  No haughty feat of arms I tell;
Soft is the note, and sad the lay
  That mourns the lovely Rosabelle.

' Moor, moor the barge, ye gallant crew,
  ' And, gentle lady, deign to stay !
' Rest thee in Castle Ravensheuch,
  ' Nor tempt the stormy firth to-day.

' The blackening wave is edged with white ;
  ' To inch and rock the sea-mews fly ;
' The fishers have heard the Water-Sprite,
  ' Whose screams forebode that wreck is nigh.

' Last night the gifted Seer did view
  ' A wet shroud swathed round lady gay ;
' Then stay thee, Fair, in Ravensheuch ;
  ' Why cross the gloomy firth to-day ?'

—' 'Tis not because Lord Lindesay's heir
  ' To-night at Roslin leads the ball ;
' But that my lady-mother there
  ' Sits lonely in her castle-hall.

' 'Tis not because the ring they ride,
  ' And Lindesay at the ring rides well,
' But that my sire the wine will chide
  ' If 'tis not fill'd by Rosabelle.'

2 *feat*, deed   6 *deign*, be kind enough
8 *firth*, strait   10 *inch*, island   13 *seer*, prophet
22 *ring*, a game in which riders drove through a ring

O'er Roslin all that weary night
    A wondrous blaze was seen to gleam ;
'Twas broader than the watch-fire's light,
    And redder than the bright moonbeam.

It glared on Roslin's castled rock,
    It ruddied all the copse-wood glen ;
'Twas seen from Dryden's groves of oak,
    And seen from cavern'd Hawthornden.

Seem'd all on fire that chapel proud,
    Where Roslin's chiefs uncoffin'd lie,
Each Baron, for a sable shroud,
    Sheathed in his iron panoply.

Seem'd all on fire within, around,
    Deep sacristy and altar's pale ;
Shone every pillar foliage-bound,
    And glimmer'd all the dead men's mail.

Blazed battlement and pinnet high,
    Blazed every rose-carved buttress fair —
So still they blaze, when fate is nigh
    The lordly line of high Saint Clair.

There are twenty of Roslin's barons bold
    Lie buried within that proud chapelle ;
Each one the holy vault doth hold,—
    But the sea holds lovely Rosabelle !

And each Saint Clair was buried there
    With candle, with book, and with knell ;
But the sea-caves rung, and the wild winds sung
    The dirge of lovely Rosabelle.

Sir W. Scott

36 *panoply*, complete coat of armour
38 *sacristy*, vestry : *pale*, space round altar
39 *foliage-bound*, carved with leaves   40 *mail*, chain-armour
41 *pinnet*, pinnacle   43 *fate*, death
50 with the old funeral service   52 *dirge*, funeral chant

16

GLENCOE

' O TELL me, Harper, wherefore flow
Thy wayward notes of wail and woe
Far down the desert of Glencoe,
   Where none may list their melody?
Say, harp'st thou to the mists that fly,
Or to the dun-deer glancing by,
Or to the eagle that from high
   Screams chorus to thy minstrelsy?'

—' No, not to these, for they have rest :—
The mist-wreath has the mountain-crest,
The stag his lair, the erne her nest,
   Abode of lone security.
But those for whom I pour the lay,
Not wild-wood deep, nor mountain gray,
Not this deep dell, that shrouds from day,
   Could screen from treach'rous cruelty.

' Their flag was furl'd, and mute their drum :
The very household dogs were dumb,
Unwont to bay at guests that come
   In guise of hospitality.
His blithest notes the piper plied,
Her gayest snood the maiden tied,
The dame her distaff flung aside,
   To tend her kindly housewifery.

' The hand that mingled in the meal,
At midnight drew the felon steel,
And gave the host's kind breast to feel
   Meed, for his hospitality !

  3 see end   8 screams in answer   11 *erne*, eagle
15 *shrouds*, hides   17 *mute*, silent   19 *unwont*, not accustomed
20 *guise*, look   22 *snood*, hair-ribbon worn by girls
26 *felon*, base, treacherous   28 *meed*, reward

The friendly hearth which warm'd that hand,
At midnight arm'd it with the brand,
That bade destruction's flames expand
   Their red and fearful blazonry.
' Then woman's shriek was heard in vain,—
Nor infancy's unpitied plain
More than the warrior's groan, could gain
   Respite from ruthless butchery!
The winter wind that whistled shrill,
The snows that night that cloked the hill,
Though wild and pitiless, had still
   Far more than Southron clemency.
' Long have my harp's best notes been gone,
Few are its strings, and faint their tone;
They can but sound in desert lone
   Their gray-hair'd master's misery.
Were each gray hair a minstrel string,
Each chord should imprecations fling,
Till startled Scotland loud should ring,
   ' Revenge for blood and treachery!'

                          Sir W. Scott

* 17 *

SONG OF THE EMIGRANTS IN BERMUDA

WHERE the remote Bermudas ride
In the ocean's bosom unespied,
From a small boat that row'd along
The listening winds received this song :
' What should we do but sing His praise
That led us through the watery maze
Where He the huge sea monsters wracks
That lift the deep upon their backs,
Unto an isle so long unknown,
And yet far kinder than our own?

30 *brand*, torch   34 *plain*, crying   35 *gain respite*, save itself
   40 *clemency*, mercy   41 *chord*, string
1 *ride*, lie   2 *unespied*, hidden   6 *maze*, pathless sea

He lands us on a grassy stage,
Safe from the storms, and prelate's rage :
He gave us this eternal spring
Which here enamels everything,
And sends the fowls to us in care
On daily visits through the air.
He hangs in shades the orange bright
Like golden lamps in a green night,
And does in the pomegranates close
Jewels more rich than Ormus shows .
He makes the figs our mouths to meet,
And throws the melons at our feet ;
But apples plants of such a price,
No tree could ever bear them twice !
With cedars chosen by his hand
From Lebanon he stores the land ;
And makes the hollow seas that roar
Proclaim the ambergris on shore.
He cast (of which we rather boast)
The Gospel's pearl upon our coast ;
And in these rocks for us did frame
A temple where to sound His name.
O let our voice His praise exalt
Till it arrive at Heaven's vault,
Which then perhaps rebounding may
Echo beyond the Mexique bay !'
—Thus sung they in the English boat
A holy and a cheerful note :
And all the way, to guide their chime,
With falling oars they kept the time.

A. Marvell

---

11 *stage*, plain   12 see end   14 *enamels*, colours brightly
19 the pomegranate seeds are like rubies
20 *Ormus*, island in the Persian Gulf   23 *price*, value
   28 *proclaim*, give notice of ; *ambergris*, fragrant gum floating on the sea

* 18 *
THE PILGRIM
Who would true valour see
  Let him come hither !
One here will constant be,
  Come wind, come weather :
There's no discouragement
Shall make him once relent
His first-avow'd intent
  To be a Pilgrim.

Whoso beset him round
  With dismal stories,
Do but themselves confound ;
  His strength the more is.
No lion can him fright ;
He'll with a giant fight ;
But he will have a right
  To be a Pilgrim.

Nor enemy, nor fiend,
  Can daunt his spirit ;
He knows he at the end
  Shall Life inherit :—
Then, fancies, fly away :
He'll not fear what men say ;
He'll labour, night and day,
  To be a Pilgrim.
              J. Bunyan

* 19 *
TRUE GREATNESS
The fairest action of our human life
  Is scorning to revenge an injury :
For who forgives without a further strife
  His adversary's heart to him doth tie :
And 'tis a firmer conquest truly said
To win the heart, than overthrow the head.

6 *relent*, slacken   7 *avow'd*, proclaimed   17 *daunt*, frighten
                  5 *said*, called

If we a worthy enemy do find,
  To yield to worth, it must be nobly done :—
But if of baser metal be his mind,
  In base revenge there is no honour won.
Who would a worthy courage overthrow?
And who would wrestle with a worthless foe?

We say our hearts are great, and cannot yield ;
  Because they cannot yield, it proves them poor:
Great hearts are task'd beyond their power but seld :
  The weakest lion will the loudest roar.
Truth's school for certain does this same allow,
High-heartedness doth sometimes teach to bow.
Lady E. Carew

* 20 *

CHARACTER OF A HAPPY LIFE

How happy is he born and taught
That serveth not another's will ;
Whose armour is his honest thought,
And simple truth his utmost skill !

Whose passions not his masters are,
Whose soul is still prepared for death,
Not tied unto the world with care
Of public fame, or private breath ;

Who envies none that chance doth raise
Or vice ; who never understood
How deepest wounds are given by praise ;
Nor rules of state, but rules of good :

---

8 it must be a noble thing to yield to a worthy enemy
9 *metal*, quality   11 *courage*, enemy   15 *seld*, seldom
Character, description   8 *private breath*, what his neighbours say
    12 *state*, policy, craft

Who hath his life from rumours freed ;
Whose conscience is his strong retreat ;
Whose state can neither flatterers feed,
Nor ruin make accusers great ;

Who God doth late and early pray
More of His grace than gifts to lend ;
And entertains the harmless day
With a well-chosen book or friend ;

—This man is freed from servile bands
Of hope to rise, or fear to fall ;
Lord of himself, though not of lands ;
And having nothing, yet hath all.
Sir H. Wotton

* 21 *

THE CHIMNEY SWEEPER

WHEN my mother died I was very young,
And my father sold me while yet my tongue
Could scarcely cry, *'weep! 'weep!' 'weep! 'weep!*
So your chimneys I sweep, and in soot I sleep.

There's little Tom Dacre, who cried when his head,
That curl'd like a lamb's back, was shaved ; so I said,
'Hush, Tom ! never mind it, for when your head's bare,
'You know that the soot cannot spoil your white hair.'

And so he was quiet : and that very night,
As Tom was a-sleeping, he had such a sight,
That thousands of sweepers, Dick, Joe, Ned, and Jack,
Were all of them lock'd up in coffins of black.

  13 *rumours*, I suppose, vain alarms
  15 not rich enough to invite flatterers or enemies
  21 *servile bands*, from being bound like a slave

And by came an angel, who had a bright key,
And he open'd the coffins, and set them all free ;
Then down a green plain, leaping, laughing they run,
And wash in a river, and shine in the sun.

Then naked and white, all their bags left behind,
They rise upon clouds, and sport in the wind ;
And the angel told Tom, if he'd be a good boy,
He'd have God for his father, and never want joy.

And so Tom awoke ; and we rose in the dark,
And got with our bags and our brushes to work ;
Though the morning was cold, Tom was happy and warm :
So, if all do their duty, they need not fear harm.

W. Blake

* 22 *

DEATH THE LEVELLER

THE glories of our blood and state
   Are shadows, not substantial things ;
There is no armour against fate ;
   Death lays his icy hand on kings :
      Sceptre and Crown
      Must tumble down,
And in the dust be equal made
With the poor crookèd scythe and spade.

Some men with swords may reap the field,
   And plant fresh laurels where they kill :
But their strong nerves at last must yield ;
   They tame but one another still :
      Early or late
      They stoop to fate,
And must give up their murmuring breath
When they, pale captives, creep to death.

1 *blood and state*, life and condition must die   9 *field*, of glory   5 kings and labourers, all 10 and gain fresh fame
12 *tame*, conquer

The garlands wither on your brow ;
Then boast no more your mighty deeds ;
Upon Death's purple altar now
See where the victor-victim bleeds !
    Your heads must come
    To the cold tomb :—
Only the actions of the just
Smell sweet, and blossom in their dust.
                           J. Shirley

* 23 *

READEN OV A HEAD-STWONE

Dorset dialect

As I wer readèn ov a stwone,
In Grenley church-yard, all alwone,
A little maïd ran up, wi' pride
To zee me there ; an' push'd azide
A bunch o' bennets, that did hide
    A verse her father, as she zaid,
    Put up above her mother's head
To tell how much he loved her.

The verse wer short, but very good,
I stood an' learn'd en where I stood,
'Mid God, dear Meäry, gi'e me greäce
'To vind, like thee, a better pleäce,
'Where I, oonce mwore, mid zee thy feäce ;
    'An' bring thy childern up, to know
    'His word, that they mid come an' show
'Thy soul how much I loved thee.'

'Where's father, then,' I zaid, 'my chile ?'
'Dead, too,' she answer'd wi' a smile :
'An' I an' brother Jem do bide
'At Betty White's, o' tother zide

---

17 *garlands*, crowns of glory   20 *victor-victim*, the dying conqueror
                      23 *just*, good
Head-stwone, stone at head of a grave   5 *bennets*, bent-grass
   11 *mid*, might   12 *vind*, find   19 *bide*, live

'O' road.'—'Mid He, my chile,' I cried,
'That's father to the fatherless,
'Become thy father now, an' bless
'An' keep, an' lead, an' love thee.'
—Though she've a-lost, I thought, so much,
Still He don't let the thoughts o't touch
Her litsome heart, by day or night;
An' zoo, if we could teäke it right,
Do show He'll meake his burdens light
  To weaker souls; an' that his smile,
  Is sweet upon a little chile,
    When they be dead that loved it.

W. Barnes

* 24 *

THE BURIAL OF SIR JOHN MOORE AT CORUNNA

Not a drum was heard, not a funeral note,
  As his corpse to the rampart we hurried;
Not a soldier discharged his farewell shot
  O'er the grave where our hero we buried.

We buried him darkly at dead of night,
  The sods with our bayonets turning;
By the struggling moonbeam's misty light
  And the lantern dimly burning.

No useless coffin inclosed his breast,
  Not in sheet nor in shroud we wound him;
But he lay like a warrior taking his rest
  With his martial cloak around him.

Few and short were the prayers we said,
  And we spoke not a word of sorrow;
But we steadfastly gazed on the face that was dead,
  And we bitterly thought of the morrow.

27 *litsome*, light
2 *rampart*, wall or line of fortification
4 *hero*, noble and loved one
12 *martial*, soldier's

1 *note*, sound
3 *discharged*, fired
11 *warrior*, soldier

We thought as we hollow'd his narrow bed
  And smoothed down his lonely pillow,
That the foe and the stranger would tread o'er his
    head,
  And we far away on the billow !

Lightly they'll talk of the spirit that's gone
  And o'er his cold ashes upbraid him,—
But little he'll reck, if they let him sleep on
  In the grave where a Briton has laid him.

But half of our heavy task was done
  When the clock struck the hour for retiring ;
And we heard the distant and random gun
  That the foe was sullenly firing.

Slowly and sadly we laid him down,
  From the field of his fame fresh and gory ;
We carved not a line, and we raised not a stone—
  But we left him alone with his glory.
                                            C. Wolfe

* 25 *

THE BRITISH SOLDIER IN CHINA

LAST night among his fellow-roughs
  He jested, quaff'd, and swore :
A drunken private of the Buffs,
  Who never look'd before.
To-day, beneath the foeman's frown,
  He stands in Elgin's place,
Ambassador from Britain's crown,
  And type of all her race.

22 *ashes*, body : *upbraid*, blame   23 *reck*, care
 6 Lord Elgin was then our ambassador in China : see end
 7 *ambassador*, person sent to represent the Queen
 8 *type*, example

Poor, reckless, rude, low-born, untaught,
  Bewilder'd, and alone,
A heart, with English instinct fraught,
  He yet can call his own.
Ay! tear his body limb from limb;
  Bring cord, or axe, or flame!—
He only knows, that not through him
  Shall England come to shame.

Far Kentish hopfields round him seem'd
  Like dreams to come and go;
Bright leagues of cherry-blossom gleam'd,
  One sheet of living snow:
The smoke above his father's door
  In gray soft eddyings hung:—
Must he then watch it rise no more,
  Doom'd by himself, so young?

Yes, Honour calls!—with strength like steel
  He put the vision by:
Let dusky Indians whine and kneel;
  An English lad must die!
And thus, with eyes that would not shrink,
  With knee to man unbent,
Unfaltering on its dreadful brink
  To his red grave he went.

—Vain, mightiest fleets of iron framed;
  Vain, those all-shattering guns;
Unless proud England keep, untamed,
  The strong heart of her sons!
So, let his name through Europe ring—
  A man of mean estate
Who died, as firm as Sparta's king,
  Because his soul was great.

Sir F. H. Doyle

10 *bewildered*, puzzled   11 full of true English feeling
17 The Buffs are the East Kent Regiment   19 *leagues*, miles
26 *vision*, thought of home   32 *red*, bloody
39 Leonidas, who died at Thermopylæ

* 26 *
YOUNG LOCHINVAR

O, YOUNG Lochinvar is come out of the West!
Through all the wide Border his steed is the best;
And save his good broadsword he weapons had none;
He rode all unarm'd and he rode all alone.
So faithful in love, and so dauntless in war,
There never was knight like the young Lochinvar!

He stay'd not for brake and he stopp'd not for stone;
He swam the Eske river where ford there was none;
But ere he alighted at Netherby gate,
The bride had consented; the gallant came late;
For a laggard in love and a dastard in war,
Was to wed the fair Ellen of brave Lochinvar.

So boldly he enter'd the Netherby Hall,
Among bridesmen and kinsmen and brothers and all;—
Then spoke the bride's father, his hand on his sword,
For the poor craven bridegroom said never a word,
'O come ye in peace here, or come ye in war,
'Or to dance at our bridal, young Lord Lochinvar?'

—'I long woo'd your daughter, my suit you denied;
'Love swells like the Solway, but ebbs like its tide;
'And now am I come with this lost Love of mine
'To lead but one measure, drink one cup of wine.
'There are maidens in Scotland more lovely by far,
'That would gladly be bride to the young Lochinvar!'

The bride kiss'd the goblet, the knight took it up,
He quaff'd off the wine and he threw down the cup;

5 *dauntless,* bold   19 *suit,* courtship

She look'd down to blush, and she look'd up to sigh,
With a smile on her lips and a tear in her eye :—
He took her soft hand ere her mother could bar ;
'Now tread we a measure!' said young Lochinvar.

So stately his form, and so lovely her face,
That never a hall such a galliard did grace :
While her mother did fret and her father did fume,
And the bridegroom stood dangling his bonnet and
   plume ;
And the bride-maidens whispered, '"Twere better
   by far
'To have match'd our fair cousin with young Lochin-
   var !'

One touch to her hand and one word in her ear,
When they reach'd the hall door; and the charger
   stood near ;
So light to the croupe the fair lady he swung,
So light to the saddle before her he sprung !
'She is won ! we are gone, over bank, bush and
   scaur,
'They'll have fleet steeds that follow !' quoth young
   Lochinvar.

There was mounting 'mong Græmes of the Netherby
   clan ;
Forsters, Fenwicks, and Musgraves, they rode and
   they ran :
There was racing and chasing on Cannobie lea ;
But the lost bride of Netherby ne'er did they see :—
So daring in love, and so dauntless in war,
Have ye e'er heard of gallant like young Lochinvar?
                                            Sir W. Scott

30 *measure*, dance   32 *galliard*, lively dance
38 *charger*, war-horse   39 *croupe*, hind-pa t
41 *scaur*, broken cliff-side   43 *clan*, family

* 27 *
THE MAID OF NEIDPATH

O LOVERS' eyes are sharp to see,
   And lovers' ears in hearing;
And love, in life's extremity,
   Can lend an hour of cheering.
Disease had been in Mary's bower
   And slow decay from mourning,
Though now she sits on Neidpath's tower
   To watch her Love's returning.

All sunk and dim her eyes so bright,
   Her form decay'd by pining,
Till through her wasted hand, at night,
   You saw the taper shining.
By fits a sultry hectic hue
   Across her cheek was flying;
By fits so ashy pale she grew
   Her maidens thought her dying.

Yet keenest powers to see and hear
   Seem'd in her frame residing;
Before the watch-dog prick'd his ear
   She heard her lover's riding;
Ere scarce a distant form was kenn'd
   She knew and waved to greet him,
And o'er the battlement did bend
   As on the wing to meet him.

He came—he pass'd—a heedless gaze
   As o'er some stranger glancing;
Her welcome, spoke in faltering phrase,
   Lost in his courser's prancing:
The castle-arch, whose hollow tone
   Returns each whisper spoken,
Could scarcely catch the feeble moan
   Which told her heart was broken
                        Sir W. Scott

13 *hectic*, fitful colour of consumption

* 28 *

ANNAN WATER

'ANNAN Water's wading deep,
  'And my Love Annie's wondrous bonny;
'And I am loath she should wet her feet,
  'Because I love her best of ony.'

He's loupen on his bonny gray,
  He rode the right gate and the ready;
For all the storm he wadna stay,
  For seeking of his bonny lady.

And he has ridden o'er field and fell,
  Through moor, and moss, and many a mire; 10
His spurs of steel were sair to bide,
  And from her four feet flew the fire.

'My bonny gray, now play your part!
  'If ye be the steed that wins my dearie,
'With corn and hay ye'll be fed for aye,
  'And never spur shall make you wearie.'

The gray was a mare, and a right gude mare;
  But when she wan the Annan Water,
She could not have ridden the ford that night
  Had a thousand merks been wadded at her.

'O boatman, boatman, put off your boat,
  'Put off your boat for golden money!'
But for all the gold in fair Scotland,
  He dared not take him through to Annie.

'O I was sworn so late yestreen,
  'Not by a single oath, but mony!
'I'll cross the drumly stream to-night,
  'Or never could I face my honey.'

          5 *loupen*, leaped
6 *gate*, way   11 *sair*, hard   18 *wan*, reached
20 *merks*, old coin: *wadded at*, betted upon   27 *drumly*, muddy

The side was stey, and the bottom deep,
 From bank to brae the water pouring ;
The bonny gray mare she swat for fear,
 For she heard the water-kelpy roaring.

He spurr'd her forth into the flood,
 I wot she swam both strong and steady ;
But the stream was broad, and her strength did fail,
 And he never saw his bonny lady !
Unknown

* 29 *

THE ROVER

'A WEARY lot is thine, fair maid,
 ' A weary lot is thine !
' To pull the thorn thy brow to braid,
 ' And press the rue for wine.
' A lightsome eye, a soldier's mien,
 ' A feather of the blue,
' A doublet of the Lincoln green—
 ' No more of me you knew
    ' My Love !
' No more of me you knew.

' The morn is merry June, I trow,
 ' The rose is budding fain ;
' But she shall bloom in winter snow
 ' Ere we two meet again.'
He turn'd his charger as he spake
 Upon the river shore,
He gave the bridle-reins a shake,
 Said ' Adieu for evermore
    ' My Love !
 ' And adieu for evermore.'
Sir W. Scott

29 *stey*, steep   30 *brae*, slope   32 *kelpy*, spirit
 5 *mien*, face, air   12 *fain*, gaily

* 30 *

A MORNING SONG

PACK, clouds, away, and welcome day:
  With night we banish sorrow;
Sweet air blow soft, mount larks aloft,
  To give my Love good-morrow!
Wings from the wind to please her mind,
  Notes from the lark I'll borrow;
Bird prune thy wing, nightingale sing,
  To give my Love good-morrow;
    To give my Love good-morrow
    Notes from them both I'll borrow.

Wake from thy nest, Robin-red-breast,
  Sing birds in every furrow;
And from each hill, let music shrill
  Give my fair Love good-morrow!
Blackbird and thrush in every bush,
  Stare, linnet, and cock-sparrow!
You pretty elves, amongst yourselves
  Sing my fair Love good-morrow;
    To give my Love good-morrow
    Sing birds in every furrow!
              T. Heywood

* 31 *

A HAPPY LIFE

UNDER the greenwood tree
  Who loves to lie with me,
  And tune his merry note
  Unto the sweet bird's throat—
Come hither, come hither, come hither!
      Here shall he see
      No enemy
  But winter and rough weather.

2 *banish*, send away   16 *stare*, starling
    17 *elves*, little live things

Who doth ambition shun,
And loves to live i' the sun.
Seeking the food he eats
And pleased with what he gets—
Come hither, come hither, come hither!
    Here shall he see
    No enemy
But winter and rough weather.
W. Shakespeare

* 32 *

TO BLOSSOMS

FAIR pledges of a fruitful tree,
    Why do ye fall so fast?
    Your date is not so past,
But you may stay yet here a while
    To blush and gently smile,
        And go at last.

What, were ye born to be
    An hour or half's delight,
    And so to bid good-night?
'Twas pity Nature brought ye forth
    Merely to show your worth,
        And lose you quite.

But you are lovely leaves, where we
    May read how soon things have
    Their end, though ne'er so brave:
And after they have shown their pride
    Like you, a while, they glide
        Into the grave.
R. Herrick

---

9 *ambition*, struggle to get on   1 promises of fruit
3 *date*, time   15 *brave*, brilliant   16 *pride*, beauty

* 33 *
THE DAFFODILS

I WANDER'D lonely as a cloud
That floats on high o'er vales and hills,
When all at once I saw a crowd,
A host of golden daffodils,
Beside the lake beneath the trees
Fluttering and dancing in the breeze.

Continuous as the stars that shine
And twinkle on the milky-way,
They stretch'd in never-ending line
Along the margin of a bay :
Ten thousand saw I at a glance
Tossing their heads in sprightly dance.

The waves beside them danced, but they
Out-did the sparkling waves in glee :—
A Poet could not but be gay
In such a jocund company !
I gazed—and gazed—but little thought
What wealth the show to me had brought;

For oft, when on my couch I lie
In vacant or in pensive mood,
They flash upon that inward eye
Which is the bliss of solitude ;
And then my heart with pleasure fills,
And dances with the daffodils.
W. Wordsworth

· 34 *
A THANKSGIVING TO GOD, FOR HIS HOUSE

LORD, thou hast given me a cell,
    Wherein to dwell ;
A little house, whose humble roof
    Is weather-proof;

7 *continuous*, close together   10 *margin*, edge
18 *wealth*, benefit   20 idle or thoughtful   21 *inward eye*, thought

Under the spars of which I lie
    Both soft and dry ;
Where thou, my chamber for to ward,
    Hast set a guard
Of harmless thoughts, to watch and keep
    Me, while I sleep.
Low is my porch, as is my fate :
    Both void of state ;
And yet the threshold of my door
    Is worn by th' poor,
Who thither come, and freely get
    Good words, or meat.
Like as my parlour, so my hall
    And kitchen's small ;
A little buttery, and therein
    A little bin,
Which keeps my little loaf of bread
    Unchipt, unflead ;
Some brittle sticks of thorn or briar
    Make me a fire,
Close by whose living coal I sit,
    And glow like it.
Lord, I confess too, when I dine,
    The pulse is thine,
And all those other bits that be
    There placed by thee ;
The worts, the purslain, and the mess
    Of water-cress,
Which of thy kindness thou hast sent ;
    And my content
Makes those, and my beloved beet,
    To be more sweet.
'Tis thou that crown'st my glittering hearth
    With guiltless mirth,

---

5 *spars*, timbers   7 *ward*, protect   11 *fate*, place in life
  12 *state*, grandeur   22 *unflead*, unpared
  28 *pulse*, pottage   31 *purslain*, a salad

And giv'st me wassail-bowls to drink,
    Spiced to the brink.
Lord, 'tis thy plenty-dropping hand
    That soils my land,
And giv'st me, for my bushel sown,
    Twice ten for one;
Thou mak'st my teeming hen to lay
    Her egg each day;
Besides my healthful ewes to bear
    Me twins each year;
The while the conduits of my kine
    Run cream, for wine:
All these, and better, thou dost send
    Me,—to this end,
That I should render, for my part,
    A thankful heart.
R. Herrick

* 35 *

SUNSHINE AFTER A SHOWER

Ever after summer shower,
When the bright sun's returning power
With laughing beam has chased the storm,
And cheer'd reviving Nature's form,
By sweet-briar hedges bathed in dew,
Let me my wholesome path pursue;
There, issuing forth, the frequent snail
Wears the dank way with slimy trail;
While as I walk, from pearlèd bush
The sunny, sparkling drop I brush;
And all the landscape fair I view
Clad in robe of fresher hue;
And so loud the blackbird sings,
That far and near the valley rings.

39 *wassail-bowls*, cups of old ale   42 *soils*, manures
4) *conduits*, udders   8 *dank*, moist; *trail*, track

From shelter deep of shaggy rock
The shepherd drives his joyful flock;
From bowering beech the mower blithe
With new-born vigour grasps the scythe;
While o'er the smooth unbounded meads
His last faint gleam the rainbow spreads.
T. Warton

* 36 *

THE HOCK-CART, OR HARVEST-HOME

COME, sons of summer, by whose toil
We are the lords of wine and oil;
By whose tough labours and rough hands,
We rip up first, then reap our lands.
Crown'd with the ears of corn, now come,
And, to the pipe, sing Harvest Home!
Come forth, my lord, and see the cart
Drest up with all the country art:
See, here a maukin, there a sheet,
As spotless pure as it is sweet;
The horses, mares, and frisking fillies,
Clad all in linen white as lilies:—
The harvest swains and wenches bound
For joy, to see the hock-cart crown'd.

About the cart hear how the rout
Of rural younglings raise the shout,
Pressing before, some coming after,
Those with a shout, and these with laughter.
Some bless the cart, some kiss the sheaves,
Some prank them up with oaken leaves;
Some cross the fill-horse, some with great
Devotion stroke the home-borne wheat;
While other rustics, less attent

---

18 *vigour*, strength
9 *maukin*, coarse cloth
21 *fill*, shaft-horse
7 *lord*, the Earl of Westmorland
14 *hock-cart*, last from harvest-field
23 *attent*, eager

To prayers than to merriment,
Run after with their breeches rent.
  Well, on, brave boys, to your lord's hearth,
Glitt'ring with fire, where, for your mirth,
Ye shall see first the large and chief
Foundation of your feast, fat beef!
With upper stories, mutton, veal,
And bacon, which makes full the meal;
With sev'ral dishes standing by,
As, here a custard, there a pie,
And here all-tempting frumenty.
And for to make the merry cheer,
If smirking wine be wanting here,
There's that, which drowns all care, stout beer;
Which freely drink to your lord's health,
Then to the plough, the commonwealth,
Next to your flails, your fanes, your fatts;
Then to the maids with wheaten hats;
To the rough sickle, and crook't scythe,
Drink, frolick, boys, till all be blythe.
Feed and grow fat, and as ye eat,
Be mindful that the lab'ring neat,
As you, may have their fill of meat;
And know, besides, ye must revoke
The patient ox unto the yoke,
And all go back unto the plough
And harrow, though they're hanged up now.
And, you must know, your lord's word's true,
Feed him ye must, whose food fills you:
And that this pleasure is like rain,
Not sent ye for to drown your pain,
But for to make it spring again.
R. Herrick

40 *fanes*, apparently weathercocks: *fatts*, casks
41 *wheaten*, straw   45 *neat*, oxen   47 *revoke*, call back

* 37 *
THE FIRST SWALLOW
THE gorse is yellow on the heath ;
The banks with speedwell flowers are gay ;
The oaks are budding, and beneath,
The hawthorn soon will bear the wreath,
    The silver wreath of May.

The welcome guest of settled spring,
The swallow, too, is come at last ;
Just at sunset, when thrushes sing,
I saw her dash with rapid wing,
    And hail'd her as she past.

Come, summer visitant, attach
To my reed roof your nest of clay,
And let my ear your music catch,
Low twittering underneath the thatch,
    At the gray dawn of day.

                              C. Smith

* 38 *
TO A REDBREAST
LITTLE bird, with bosom red,
Welcome to my humble shed !
Courtly domes of high degree
Have no room for thee and me ;
Pride and pleasure's fickle throng
Nothing mind an idle song.

    Daily near my table steal,
While I pick my scanty meal :—
Doubt not little though there be,
But I'll cast a crumb to thee ;
Well rewarded, if I spy
Pleasure in thy glancing eye ;
See thee, when thou'st eat thy fill,
Plume thy breast, and wipe thy bill.

---

3 *domes*, houses   5 the changeable crowd of proud and idle people
                    14 *plume*, trim

Come, my feather'd friend, again!
Well thou know'st the broken pane:—
Ask of me thy daily store;
Go not near Avaro's door;
Once within his iron hall,
Woful end shall thee befall.
Savage!—he would soon divest
Of its rosy plumes thy breast;
Then, with solitary joy,
Eat thee, bones and all, my boy!

J. Langhorne

* 39 *

TO THE SKYLARK

ETHEREAL minstrel! pilgrim of the sky!
Dost thou despise the earth where cares abound?
Or while the wings aspire, are heart and eye
Both with thy rest upon the dewy ground?
Thy nest which thou canst drop into at will,
Those quivering wings composed, that music still!

To the last point of vision, and beyond,
Mount, daring warbler!—that love-prompted strain
—'Twixt thee and thine a never-failing bond—
Thrills not the less the bosom of the plain:
Yet mightst thou seem, proud privilege! to sing
All independent of the leafy spring.

Leave to the nightingale her shady wood;
A privacy of glorious light is thine,
Whence thou dost pour upon the world a flood
Of harmony, with instinct more divine;
Type of the wise, who soar, but never roam—
True to the kindred points of Heaven and Home.

W. Wordsworth

18 *Avaro*, man too fond of money: here, perhaps, a fierce dog
19 *iron*, cruel   21 *divest*, take off   1 *singer of the air, and wanderer through the sky*   3 *aspire*, mount
8 *prompted*, caused by   12 without waiting for the leaves, like most birds   14 *privacy*, solitude   17 *type*, figure

* 40 *

THE LAST OF THE FLOCK

IN distant countries have I been,
And yet I have not often seen
A healthy man, a man full grown,
Weep in the public roads alone ;
But such a one, on English ground,
And in the broad highway I met ;
Along the broad highway he came,
  His cheeks with tears were wet ;
Sturdy he seem'd, though he was sad,
And in his arms a lamb he had.

He saw me, and he turn'd aside,
As if he wish'd himself to hide :
And with his coat did then essay
To wipe those briny tears away.
I follow'd him and said, ' My friend,
' What ails you ? wherefore weep you so ?'
—' Shame on me, sir ! this lusty lamb,
  ' He makes my tears to flow.
' To-day I fetch'd him from the rock ;
' He is the last of all my flock.

' When I was young, a single man,
' And after youthful follies ran,
' Though little given to care and thought,
' Yet so it was, an ewe I bought ;
' And other sheep from her I raised,
' As healthy sheep as you might see ;
' And then I married, and was rich
   ' As I could wish to be ;
' Of sheep I number'd a full score,
' And every year increased my store.

' Year after year my stock it grew ;
' And from this one, this single ewe,

'Full fifty comely sheep I raised,
'As fine a flock as ever grazed!
'Upon the Quantock Hills they fed;
'They throve, and we at home did thrive:
—'This lusty lamb of all my store
   'Is all that is alive;
'And now I care not if we die,
'And perish all of poverty.

'Six children, sir, had I to feed;
'Hard labour, in a time of need!
'My pride was tamed, and in our grief,
'I of the parish ask'd relief;
'They said I was a wealthy man,
'My sheep upon the uplands fed,
'And it was fit that thence I took
   'Whereof to buy us bread.
'*Do this; how can we give to you,*
'They cried, *what to the poor is due?*

'I sold a sheep as they had said,
'And bought my little children bread,
'And they were healthy with their food:
'For me – it never did me good.
'A woful time it was for me,
'To see the end of all my gains,
'The pretty flock which I had rear'd
   'With all my care and pains,
'To see it melt like snow away—
'For me it was a woful day!

'Another still! and still another!
'A little lamb, and then its mother!
'It was a vein that never stopp'd—
'Like blood-drops from my heart they dropp'd
'Till thirty were not left alive;
'They dwindled, dwindled, one by one;

'And I may say that many a time
  'I wish'd they all were gone ;
'Reckless of what might come at last,
'Were but the bitter struggle past.

'To wicked deeds I was inclined,
'And wicked fancies cross'd my mind ;
'And every man I chanced to see,
'I thought he knew some ill of me.
'No peace, no comfort could I find,
'No ease within doors or without ;
'And crazily and wearily
  'I went my work about :
'And oft was moved to flee from home
'And hide my head where wild beasts roam.

'Sir, 'twas a precious flock to me,
'As dear as my own children be ;
'For daily with my growing store
'I loved my children more and more.
'Alas! it was an evil time ;
'God cursed me in my sore distress ;
'I pray'd, yet every day I thought
  'I loved my children less ;
'And every week, and every day,
'My flock it seem'd to melt away.

'They dwindled, sir, sad sight to see !
'From ten to five, from five to three,
'A lamb, a wether, and a ewe :
'And then at last from three to two ;
'And, of my fifty, yesterday
  'I had but only one :
'And here it lies upon my arm—
  'Alas, and I have none ;
'To-day I fetch'd it from the rock—
'It is the last of all my flock !'

W. Wordsworth

THE SHEPHERD IN WINTER

When red hath set the beamless sun,
Through heavy vapours dark and dun;
When the tired ploughman, dry and warm,
Hears, half-asleep, the rising storm
Hurling the hail, and sleeted rain,
Against the casement's tinkling pane;
—The sounds that drive wild deer, and fox,
To shelter in the brake and rocks,
Are warnings which the shepherd ask
To dismal and to dangerous task!
Oft he looks forth, and hopes, in vain,
The blast may sink in mellowing rain;
Till, dark above, and white below,
Decided drives the flaky snow,
And forth the hardy swain must go.
Long, with dejected look and whine,
To leave the hearth his dogs repine;
Whistling and cheering them to aid,
Around his back he wreathes the plaid;
His flock he gathers, and he guides
To open downs, and mountain-sides,
Where fiercest though the tempest blow,
Least deeply lies the drift below.
The blast, that whistles o'er the fells,
Stiffens his locks to icicles:
Oft he looks back, while streaming far,
His cottage window seems a star,—
Loses its feeble gleam,—and then
Turns patient to the blast again,
And, facing to the tempest's sweep,
Drives through the gloom his lagging sheep.
If fails his heart, if his limbs fail,
Benumbing death is in the gale:

24 *fells*, moors, high open ground

His paths, his landmarks, all unknown,
Close to the hut, no more his own,
Close to the aid he sought in vain,
The morn may find the stiffen'd swain :
The widow sees, at dawning pale,
His orphans raise their feeble wail ;
And, close beside him, in the snow,
Poor Yarrow, partner of their woe,
Couches upon his master's breast,
And licks his cheek to break his rest.
Sir W. Scott

* 42 *

THE DOG AND THE WATER-LILY

The noon was shady, and soft airs
   Swept Ouse's silent tide,
When, 'scaped from literary cares,
   I wander'd on his side.

My spaniel, prettiest of his race,
   And high in pedigree, —
(Two nymphs adorn'd with every grace
   That spaniel found for me.)

Now wanton'd lost in flags and reeds,
   Now, starting into sight,
Pursued the swallow o'er the meads
   With scarce a slower flight.

It was the time when Ouse display'd
   His lilies newly blown ;
Their beauties I intent survey'd,
   And one I wish'd my own.

With cane extended far I sought
   To steer it close to land ;
But still the prize, though nearly caught,
   Escaped my eager hand.

---

3 *literary cares*, studying and writing   6 of a good breed
7 *nymphs*, girls   15 *intent*, attentively

Beau mark'd my unsuccessful pains
  With fix'd considerate face,
And puzzling set his puppy brains
  To comprehend the case.

But with a cherup clear and strong
  Dispersing all his dream,
I thence withdrew, and follow'd long
  The windings of the stream.

My ramble ended, I return'd ;
  Beau, trotting far before,
The floating wreath again discern'd,
  And plunging left the shore.

I saw him with that lily cropp'd
  Impatient swim to meet
My quick approach, and soon he dropp'd
  The treasure at my feet.

Charm'd with the sight, 'The world,' I cried
  ' Shall hear of this thy deed ;
' My dog shall mortify the pride
  ' Of man's superior breed ;

' But chief myself I will enjoin,
  ' Awake at duty's call,
' To show a love as prompt as thine
  ' To Him who gives me all.'

W. Cowper

* 43 *

TO A FIELD MOUSE

WEE, sleekit, cow'rin', tim'rous beastie,
O what a panic's in thy breastie !
Thou need na start awa sae hasty,
  Wi' bickering brattle !

---

24 *comprehend*, make out   26 *dream*, thinking
39 *mortify*, take down   41 *enjoin*, remind
1 *sleekit*, sleek   2 *panic*, sudden fear
3 *na*, not   4 *bickering brattle*, flittering race

I wad be laith to rin and chase thee
    Wi' murd'ring pattle!

I'm truly sorry man's dominion
Has broken Nature's social union,
And justifies that ill opinion
    Which makes thee startle
At me, thy poor earth-born companion,
    And fellow-mortal!

I doubt na, whyles, but thou may thieve;
What then? poor beastie, thou maun live!
A daimen icker in a thrave
    's a sma' request:
I'll get a blessin' wi' the lave,
    And never miss't!

Thy wee bit housie, too, in ruin!
Its silly wa's the win's are strewin':
And naething, now, to big a new ane,
    O' foggage green!
And bleak December's winds ensuin,'
    Baith snell and keen!

Thou saw the fields laid bare and waste,
And weary winter coming fast;
And cozie here, beneath the blast,
    Thou thought to dwell,
Till, crash! the cruel coulter past
    Out thro' thy cell.

That wee bit heap o' leaves and stibble
Has cost thee mony a weary nibble!

5 *laith*, loath: *rin*, run   6 *pattle*, ploughstaff
7 man's cruelty to animals   13 *whyles*, at times
14 *maun*, must   15 a corn-ear now and then from a double shock
17 *lave*, rest   20 *wa's*, walls   21 *big*, build
22 *foggage*, after-grass   23 *ensuing*, following
24 *snell*, biting   29 *coulter*, plough-iron   30 *cell*, nest

Now thou's turn'd out for a' thy trouble
    But house or hald,
To thole the winter's sleety dribble
    And cranreuch cauld !

But, Mousie, thou art no thy lane
In proving foresight may be vain :
The best laid schemes o' mice and men
    Gang aft a-gley,
And lea'e us nought but grief and pain,
    For promised joy.

Still thou art blest, compared wi' me !
The present only toucheth thee :
But, och ! I backward cast my e'e
    On prospects drear !
And forward, tho' I canna see,
    I guess and fear.
                                    R. Burns

* 44 *

THE WORM

TURN, turn thy hasty foot aside,
    Nor crush that helpless worm !
The frame thy wayward looks deride
    Required a God to form.

The common lord of all that move,
    From whom thy being flow'd,
A portion of His boundless love
    On that poor worm bestow'd.

The sun, the moon, the stars, He made
    For all His creatures free ;
And spread o'er earth the grassy blade,
    For worms as well as thee.

---

34 *but hald*, without dwelling-place   35 *thole*, bear
36 *cranreuch*, hoarfrost   37 *thy lane*, alone
39 *schemes*, plans   40 often go awry   41 *lea'e*, leave

Let them enjoy their little day,
Their humble bliss receive ;
O ! do not lightly take away
The life thou canst not give !

T. Gisborne

* 45 *

THE GIRL DESCRIBES HER FAWN

WITH sweetest milk and sugar first
I it at my own fingers nursed ;
And as it grew, so every day
It wax'd more white and sweet than they—:
It had so sweet a breath ! and oft
I blush'd to see its foot more soft
And white,—shall I say,—than my hand?
Nay, any lady's of the land !
  It is a wondrous thing how fleet
'Twas on those little silver feet :
With what a pretty skipping grace
It oft would challenge me the race :—
And when 't had left me far away
'Twould stay, and run again, and stay :
For it was nimbler much than hinds,
And trod as if on the four winds.

I have a garden of my own,
But so with roses overgrown
And lilies, that you would it guess
To be a little wilderness :
And all the spring-time of the year
It only lovéd to be there.
Among the beds of lilies I
Have sought it oft, where it should lie ;
Yet could not, till itself would rise,
Find it, although before mine eyes :—
For in the flaxen lilies' shade
It like a bank of lilies laid.

24 *should*, might

Upon the roses it would feed,
Until its lips e'en seem'd to bleed:
And then to me 'twould boldly trip,
And print those roses on my lip.
But all its chief delight was still
On roses thus itself to fill,
And its pure virgin limbs to fold
In whitest sheets of lilies cold :—
Had it lived long, it would have been
Lilies without,—roses within.
A. Marvell

· 46 ·

THE CHILD AND THE SNAKE

HENRY was every morning fed
With a full mess of milk and bread.
One day the boy his breakfast took,
And ate it by a purling brook.
His mother lets him have his way.
With free leave Henry every day
Thither repairs, until she heard
Him talking of a fine *gray bird*.
This pretty bird, he said, indeed,
Came every day with him to feed ;
And it loved him and loved his milk,
And it was smooth and soft like silk.
—On the next morn she follows Harry,
And carefully she sees him carry
Through the long grass his heap'd-up mess.
What was her terror and distress
When she saw the infant take
His bread and milk close to a snake !
Upon the grass he spreads his feast,
And sits down by his frightful guest,

Who had waited for the treat ;
And now they both began to eat.
Fond mother ! shriek not, O beware
The least small noise, O have a care—
The least small noise that may be made
The wily snake will be afraid —
If he hear the slightest sound,
He will inflict th' envenom'd wound.
—She speaks not, moves not, scarce does breathe,
As she stands the trees beneath.
No sound she utters ; and she soon
Sees the child lift up his spoon,
And tap the snake upon the head,
Fearless of harm ; and then he said,
As speaking to familiar mate,
' Keep on your own side, do, Gray Pate ; '
The snake then to the other side,
As one rebukéd, seems to glide ;
And now again advancing nigh,
Again she hears the infant cry,
Tapping the snake, ' Keep further, do ;
' Mind, Gray Pate, what I say to you.'
The danger's o'er ! she sees the boy
(O what a change from fear to joy !)
Rise and bid the snake ' Good-bye ' ;
Says he, ' Our breakfast's done, and I
' Will come again to-morrow day ' ;
—Then, lightly tripping, ran away.

M. Lamb

* 47 *

THE TRAVELLER'S RETURN

SWEET to the morning traveller
   The song amid the sky,
Where, twinkling in the dewy light,
   The skylark soars on high.

And cheering to the traveller
　The gales that round him play,
When faint and heavily he drags
　Along his noontide way.

And when beneath the unclouded sun
　Full wearily toils he,
The flowing water makes to him
　A soothing melody.

And when the evening light decays,
　And all is calm around,
There is sweet music to his ear
　In the distant sheep-bell's sound.

But O! of all delightful sounds
　Of evening or of morn,
The sweetest is the voice of love
　That welcomes his return.

　　　　　　　　　　　R. Southey

* 48 *

A FAREWELL

Go fetch to me a pint o' wine,
　And fill it in a silver tassie;
That I may drink before I go
　A service to my bonnie lassie:
The boat rocks at the pier of Leith,
　Fu' loud the wind blaws frae the Ferry,
The ship rides by the Berwick-law,
　And I maun leave my bonnie Mary.

The trumpets sound, the banners fly,
　The glittering spears are rankèd ready;
The shouts o' war are heard afar,
　The battle closes thick and bloody:

2 *tassie*, cup　　4 *a service*, a health　　8 *maun*, must

But it's not the roar o' sea or shore
  Wad make me langer wish to tarry;
Nor shouts o' war that's heard afar—
  It's leaving thee, my bonnie Mary.

R. Burns

* 49 *
ABSENCE

WHEN I think on the happy days
  I spent wi' you, my dearie;
And now what lands between us lie,
  How can I be but eerie!

How slow ye move, ye heavy hours,
  As ye were wae and weary!
It was na sae ye glinted by
  When I was wi' my dearie.

Unknown

* 50 *
TO ALTHEA FROM PRISON

WHEN Love with unconfinéd wings
  Hovers within my gates,
And my divine Althea brings
  To whisper at the grates;
When I lie tangled in her hair,
  And fetter'd to her eye,
The birds that wanton in the air
  Know no such liberty.

When flowing cups run swiftly round
  With no allaying Thames,
Our careless heads with roses crown'd,
  Our hearts with loyal flames:

4 *eerie*, in low spirits   6 *As ye*, as if; *wae*, sad
    7 *na*, not; *glinted*, went brightly
3 *Althea*, his lady-love   10 with no water in the wine
    12 *flames*, feelings

When thirsty grief in wine we steep,
  When healths and draughts go free—
Fishes that tipple in the deep
  Know no such liberty.

When, linnet-like confinéd, I
  With shriller throat shall sing
The sweetness, mercy, majesty
  And glories of my King;
When I shall voice aloud how good
  He is, how great should be,
Enlargéd winds that curl the flood
  Know no such liberty.

Stone walls do not a prison make,
  Nor iron bars a cage;
Minds innocent and quiet take
  That for an hermitage:
If I have freedom in my love,
  And in my soul am free,
Angels alone, that soar above,
  Enjoy such liberty.
                            Colonel Lovelace

* 51 *

THE FORSAKEN

THOU hast left me ever, Jamie,
  Thou hast left me ever;
Thou hast left me ever, Jamie,
  Thou hast left me ever.
Aften hast thou vow'd that death
  Only should us sever;
Now thou'st left thy lass for aye—
  I maun see thee never, Jamie,
    I'll see thee never!

20 *King*, Charles I.   28 a prison for a place of rest
              2 *ever*, for ever

Thou hast me forsaken, Jamie,
   Thou hast me forsaken ;
Thou hast me forsaken, Jamie,
   Thou hast me forsaken.
Thou canst love anither jo,
   While my heart is breaking ;
Soon my weary e'en I'll close—
   Never mair to waken, Jamie,
   Ne'er mair to waken !
                                        R. Burns

* 52 *

THE BRAES OF YARROW

THY braes were bonny, Yarrow stream,
   When first on them I met my lover ;
Thy braes how dreary, Yarrow stream,
   When now thy waves his body cover !
For ever now, O Yarrow stream !
   Thou art to me a stream of sorrow ;
For never on thy banks shall I
   Behold my Love, the flower of Yarrow.

He promised me a milk-white steed
   To bear me to his father's bowers ;
He promised me a little page
   To squire me to his father's towers ;
He promised me a wedding-ring,—
   The wedding-day was fix'd to-morrow ;—
Now he is wedded to his grave,
   Alas, his watery grave, in Yarrow !

Sweet were his words when last we met ;
   My passion I as freely told him ;
Clasp'd in his arms, I little thought
   That I should never more behold him !

14 *jo*, sweetheart   16 *e'en*, eyes
1 *braes*, sloping sides   12 *squire*, go with and guard

Scarce was he gone, I saw his ghost;
It vanish'd with a shriek of sorrow;
Thrice did the water-wraith ascend,
And gave a doleful groan thro' Yarrow.

His mother from the window look'd
With all the longing of a mother;
His little sister weeping walk'd
The green-wood path to meet her brother;
They sought him east, they sought him west,
They sought him all the forest thorough;
They only saw the cloud of night,
They only heard the roar of Yarrow.

No longer from thy window look—
Thou hast no son, thou tender mother!
No longer walk, thou lovely maid;
Alas, thou hast no more a brother!
No longer seek him east or west
And search no more the forest thorough;
For, wandering in the night so dark,
He fell a lifeless corpse in Yarrow.

The tear shall never leave my cheek,
No other youth shall be my marrow—
I'll seek thy body in the stream,
And then with thee I'll sleep in Yarrow.
—The tear did never leave her cheek,
No other youth became her marrow;
She found his body in the stream,
And now with him she sleeps in Yarrow.

J. Logan

23 *wraith*, ghost of person about to die   42 *marrow*, mate

* 53 *
ADAM OF GORDON

It fell about the Martinmas,
   When the wind blew shrill and cold,
Said Adam of Gordon to his men,
   'We maun draw to a hold.

'And whatna hold shall we draw to,
   ' My merry men and me?
'We will go to the house of Rodes,
   ' To see that fair ladye.'

The lady stood on her castle wall ;
   Beheld both dale and down ;
There she was aware of a host of men
   Came riding towards the town.

' O see ye not, my merry men all,
   ' O see ye not what I see?
' Methinks I see a host of men :
   ' I marvel who they be.'

She had no sooner buskit herself,
   And putten on her gown,
Till Adam of Gordon and his men
   Were round about the town.

The lady ran to her tower-head,
   As fast as she could hie,
To see if by her fair speeches
   She could with him agree.

' Give o'er your house, ye lady fair,
   ' Give o'er your house to me !
' Or I shall burn yourself therein,
   ' But and your babies three.'

4 *maun draw to a hold*, must go to a castle   7 *Rodes*, Rothes
   12 *town*, walled dwelling-place.   17 *buskit*, dressed
      28 *but and*, and also

'I winna give o'er, ye false Gordon,
  'To no sic traitor as thee;
'And if ye burn my ain dear babes,
  'My lord shall mak' ye dree.

—'Woe worth, woe worth ye, Jock, my man;
  'I paid ye well your fee;
'Why pull ye out the grund-wa' stone,
  'Lets in the reek to me?

'And e'en woe worth ye, Jock, my man!
  'I paid ye well your hire;
'Why pull ye out the grund-wa' stone,
  'To me lets in the fire?'

—'Ye paid me well my hire, ladye,
  'Ye paid me well my fee;
'But now I'm Adam of Gordon's man,—
  'Must either do or dee.'

O then bespake her little son,
  Sat on the nurse's knee;
Says, 'O mither dear, give o'er this house!
  'For the reek it smothers me.'

—'I winna give up my house, my dear,
  'To no sic traitor as he:
'Come weel, come woe, my jewel fair,
  'Ye maun take share with me.'

O then bespake her daughter dear,—
  She was both jimp and small:
'O row me in a pair of sheets,
  'And tow me o'er the wall!'

29 *winna*, will not   32 *dree*, suffer for it   34 *fee*, wages
35 *grund-wa'*, foundation   36 *reek*, smoke   44 *dee*, die
54 *jimp*, slender   55 *row*, roll

They row'd her in a pair of sheets,
    And tow'd her o'er the wall;
But on the point of Gordon's spear
    She gat a deadly fall.

O bonnie, bonnie was her mouth,
    And cherry were her cheeks,
And clear, clear was her yellow hair,
    Whereon the red blood dreeps!

Then with his spear he turn'd her o'er;
    O gin her face was wan!
He said, 'Ye are the first that e'er
    'I wish'd alive again.

'Busk and boun, my merry men all,
    'For ill dooms I do guess;—
'I cannot look on that bonnie face
    'As it lies on the grass.'

But when the ladye saw the fire
    Come flaming o'er her head,
She wept, and kiss'd her children twain,
    Says, 'Bairns, we be but dead.'

— O this way look'd her own dear lord,
    As he came o'er the lea;
He saw his castle all in a lowe,
    So far as he could see.

'Put on, put on, my mighty men,
    'As fast as ye can dri'e!
'For he that's hindmost of the thrang
    'Shall ne'er get good of me!'

66 *gin*, if   69 *busk and boun*, prepare and get ready
70 I see evil coming   79 *lowe*, red flame   82 *dri'e*, drive

Then some they rade, and some they ran,
    Out-o'er the grass and bent ;
But ere the foremost could win up,
    Both lady and babes were brent.

And after the Gordon he is gane,
    Sae fast as he might dri'e ;
And soon i' the Gordon's foul heart's blood
    He's wroken his fair ladye.
Unknown

54

HUNTING SONG

THE hunt is up, the hunt is up,
    And it is well nigh day ;
And Harry our king is gone hunting
    To bring his deer to bay.

The east is bright with morning light,
    And darkness it is fled ;
And the merry horn wakes up the morn
    To leave his idle bed.

Behold the skies with golden dyes
    Are glowing all around ;
The grass is green, and so are the treen
    All laughing at the sound.

The horses snort to be at sport,
    The dogs are running free,
The woods rejoice at the merry noise
    Of Hey tantara tee ree !

The sun is glad to see us clad
    All in our lusty green,
And smiles in the sky as he riseth high
    To see and to be seen.

87 *win*, come   92 *wroken*, revenged   11 *treen*, trees
    18 *green*, dress

Awake all men, I say again,
  Be merry as you may;
For Harry our king is gone hunting,
  To bring his deer to bay.

Unknown

* 55 *

THE RETIRED CAT

A POET'S cat, sedate and grave
As poet well could wish to have,
Was much addicted to inquire
For nooks to which she might retire,
And where, secure as mouse in chink,
She might repose, or sit and think.
Sometimes ascending, debonair,
An apple-tree, or lofty pear,
Lodged with convenience in the fork,
She watch'd the gardener at his work:
Sometimes her ease and solace sought
In an old empty watering-pot;
There, wanting nothing save a fan
To seem some nymph in her sedan,
Apparell'd in exactest sort,
And ready to be borne to court.

But love of change it seems has place
Not only in our wiser race;
Cats also feel, as well as we,
That passion's force, and so did she.
Her climbing, she began to find,
Exposed her too much to the wind,
And the old utensil of tin
Was cold and comfortless within:

1 *sedate*, sober   3 *addicted*, fond of
7 *debonair*, cheerful   11 *solace*, comfort   14 *nymph*, young lady
15 dressed in the height of fashion   23 *utensil*, the watering-pot

She therefore wish'd, instead of those,
Some place of more serene repose,
Where neither cold might come, nor air
Too rudely wanton with her hair,
And sought it in the likeliest mode,
Within her master's snug abode.
   A drawer, it chanced, at bottom lined
With linen of the softest kind,
With such as merchants introduce
From India, for the ladies' use—
A drawer impending o'er the rest,
Half open, in the topmost chest,
Of depth enough, and none to spare,
Invited her to slumber there.
Puss, with delight beyond expression,
Survey'd the scene and took possession.
Recumbent at her ease, ere long,
And lull'd by her own hum-drum song,
She left the cares of life behind,
And slept as she would sleep her last;
When in came, housewifely inclined,
The chambermaid, and shut it fast;
By no malignity impell'd,
But all unconscious whom it held.
   Awaken'd by the shock, cried Puss,
'Was ever cat attended thus!
'The open drawer was left, I see,
'Merely to prove a nest for me;
'For soon as I was well composed,
'Then came the maid, and it was closed.
'How smooth these kerchiefs, and how sweet!
'Oh! what a delicate retreat.
'I will resign myself to rest,

---

28 *wanton*, ruffle   30 *abode*, home   35 *impending*, hanging out
41 *recumbent*, lying down   45 *housewifely*, to make things neat
48 *unconscious*, not knowing   50 *attended*, waited on

'Till Sol, declining in the west,
'Shall call to supper, when, no doubt,
'Susan will come and let me out.'

The evening came, the sun descended,
And Puss remain'd still unattended.
The night roll'd tardily away,
(With her, indeed, 'twas never day,)
The sprightly morn her course renew'd,
The evening gray again ensued ;
And Puss came into mind no more
Than if entomb'd the day before.
With hunger pinch'd, and pinch'd for room,
She now presaged approaching doom,
Nor slept a single wink or purr'd,
Conscious of jeopardy incurr'd.

That night, by chance, the poet watching,
Heard an inexplicable scratching ;
His noble heart went pit-a-pat,
And to himself he said, 'What's that ?'
He drew the curtain at his side,
And forth he peep'd, but nothing spied ;
Yet, by his ear directed, guess'd
Something imprison'd in the chest,
And, doubtful what, with prudent care
Resolved it should continue there.
At length a voice which well he knew,
A long and melancholy mew,
Saluting his poetic ears,
Consoled him and dispell'd his fears.
He left his bed, he trod the floor,
And 'gan in haste the drawers explore,
The lowest first, and without stop

58 *Sol*, the sun   63 *tardily*, slowly   65 *ensued*, followed
68 *entomb'd*, buried   70 *presaged*, prophesied : *doom*, death
72 *jeopardy*, danger   *incurr'd*, run into   73 *poet*, Cowper
74 *inexplicable*, what he could not make out   86 *dispelled*, drove away   88 *'gan*, began

The rest in order, to the top ;
For 'tis a truth well known to most,
That whatsoever thing is lost,
We seek it, ere it come to light,
In every cranny but the right.
—Forth skipp'd the cat, not now replete,
As erst, with airy self-conceit,
Nor in her own fond apprehension
A theme for all the world's attention :
But modest, sober, cured of all
Her notions hyperbolical,
And wishing for a place of rest
Anything rather than a chest.
Then stepp'd the poet into bed
With this reflection in his head :—

Moral

Beware of too sublime a sense
Of your own worth and consequence !
The man who dreams himself so great,
And his importance of such weight,
That all around, in all that's done,
Must move and act for him alone,
Will learn in school of tribulation,
The folly of his expectation.

W. Cowper

* 56 *

THE HARPER

On the green banks of Shannon when Sheelah was nigh,
No blithe Irish lad was so happy as I ;
No harp like my own could so cheerily play,
And wherever I went was my poor dog Tray.

95 *replete*, filled   96 *erst*, before   97 *apprehension* thought
98 *theme*, matter   100 *hyperbolical*, ridiculously grand
105 *sublime*, grand   111 *tribulation*, suffering

When at last I was forced from my Sheelah to part,
She said, (while the sorrow was big at her heart,)
Oh! remember your Sheelah when far, far away:
And be kind, my dear Pat, to our poor dog Tray.

Poor dog! he was faithful and kind to be sure,
And he constantly loved me although I was poor;
When the sour-looking folk sent me heartless away
I had always a friend in my poor dog Tray.

When the road was so dark, and the night was so cold,
And Pat and his dog were grown weary and old,
How snugly we slept in my old coat of gray,
And he lick'd me for kindness—my poor dog Tray.

Though my wallet was scant, I remember'd his case,
Nor refused my last crust to his pitiful face;
But he died at my feet on a cold winter day,
And I play'd a sad lament for my poor dog Tray.

Where now shall I go, poor, forsaken, and blind?
Can I find one to guide me, so faithful and kind?
To my sweet native village, so far, far away,
I can never more return with my poor dog Tray.
T. Campbell

ELEGY ON THE DEATH OF A MAD DOG

Good people all, of every sort,
   Give ear unto my song;
And if you find it wondrous short,
   It cannot hold you long.

In Islington there was a Man,
   Of whom the world might say,
That still a godly race he ran—
   Whenc'er he went to pray.

A kind and gentle heart he had,
 To comfort friends and foes :
The naked every day he clad,—
 When he put on his clothes.

And in that town a Dog was found,
 As many dogs there be,
Both mongrel, puppy, whelp, and hound,
 And curs of low degree.

This Dog and Man at first were friends ;
 But when a pique began,
The Dog, to gain some private ends,
 Went mad, and bit the Man.

Around from all the neighbouring streets
 The wondering neighbours ran,
And swore the Dog had lost his wits,
 To bite so good a Man !

The wound it seem'd both sore and sad
 To every Christian eye :
And while they swore the Dog was mad,
 They swore the Man would die.

But soon a wonder came to light,
 That show'd the rogues they lied :—
The Man recover'd of the bite,
 The Dog it was that died !

O. Goldsmith

* 58 *

THE PARROT

A True Story

THE deep affections of the breast
 That Heaven to living things imparts,
Are not exclusively possess'd
 By human hearts.

18 *pique*, quarrel   19 *ends*, objects   3 *exclusively*, only

A Parrot, from the Spanish main,
  Full young and early caged came o'er,
With bright wings, to the bleak domain
  Of Mulla's shore.

To spicy groves where he had won
  His plumage of resplendent hue,
His native fruits, and skies, and sun,
  He bade adieu.

For these he changed the smoke of turf,
  A heathery land and misty sky,
And turn'd on rocks and raging surf
  His golden eye.

But petted in our climate cold,
  He lived and chatter'd many a day:
Until with age, from green and gold
  His wings grew gray.

At last when blind, and seeming dumb,
  He scolded, laugh'd, and spoke no more,
A Spanish stranger chanced to come
  To Mulla's shore;

He hail'd the bird in Spanish speech,
  The bird in Spanish speech replied;
Flapp'd round the cage with joyous screech,
  Dropt down, and died.

T. Campbell

* 59 *

ROBIN REDBREAST

GOOD-BYE, good-bye to Summer!
  For Summer's nearly done;
The garden smiling faintly,
  Cool breezes in the sun;

---

5 *Spanish main*, mainland of South America near West Indies, belonging to Spain 8 *Mulla*, island of Mull
10 *plumage*, feathers: *resplendent*, brilliant 12 *adieu*, farewell
13 *changed*, took instead: *turf*, the fuel of the Hebrides

Our thrushes now are silent,
　Our swallows flown away,—
But Robin's here with coat of brown,
　And ruddy breast-knot gay.
　　Robin, Robin Redbreast,
　　　O Robin dear!
　　Robin sings so sweetly
　　　In the falling of the year.

Bright yellow, red, and orange,
　The leaves come down in hosts;
The trees are Indian princes,
　But soon they'll turn to ghosts;
The scanty pears and apples
　Hang russet on the bough;
Its Autumn, Autumn, Autumn late,
　T'will soon be Winter now.
　　Robin, Robin Redbreast,
　　　O Robin dear!
　　And what will this poor Robin do?
　　　For pinching days are near.

The fire-side for the cricket,
　The wheatstack for the mouse,
When trembling night-winds whistle
　And moan all round the house.
The frosty ways like iron,
　The branches plumed with snow,—
Alas! in winter dead and dark,
　Where can poor Robin go?
　　Robin, Robin Redbreast,
　　　O Robin dear!
　　And a crumb of bread for Robin,
　　　His little heart to cheer!
　　　　　　　　W. Allingham

15 covered with gold　　　30 *plumed*, feathery

* 60 *

ODE TO AUTUMN

SEASON of mists and mellow fruitfulness!
Close bosom-friend of the maturing sun;
Conspiring with him how to load and bless
With fruit the vines that round the thatch-eaves run:
To bend with apples the moss'd cottage-trees,
And fill all fruit with ripeness to the core;
To swell the gourd, and plump the hazel shells
With a sweet kernel; to set budding more
And still more, later flowers for the bees,
Until they think warm days will never cease;
For Summer has o'erbrimm'd their clammy cells.

Who hath not seen Thee oft amid thy store?
Sometimes whoever seeks abroad may find
Thee sitting careless on a granary floor,
Thy hair soft-lifted by the winnowing wind;
Or on a half-reap'd furrow sound asleep,
Drowsed with the fume of poppies, while thy hook
Spares the next swath and all its twinéd flowers;
And sometime like a gleaner thou dost keep
Steady thy laden head across a brook;
Or by a cider-press, with patient look,
Thou watchest the last oozings, hours by hours.

Where are the songs of Spring? Ay, where are they?
Think not of them,—thou hast thy music too,
While barréd clouds bloom the soft-dying day
And touch the stubble-plains with rosy hue;
Then in a wailful choir the small gnats mourn
Among the river-sallows, borne aloft
Or sinking as the light wind lives or dies;

---

2 *maturing*, ripening   3 *conspiring*, planning
12 *Thee*, Autumn   17 *drowsed*, made drowsy : *fume*, sleepy smell
25 *bloom*, cast a soft light upon   27 *wailful*, wailing

And full-grown lambs loud bleat from hilly bourn ;
Hedge-crickets sing, and now with treble soft
The redbreast whistles from a garden-croft,
And gathering swallows twitter in the skies.

J. Keats

* 61 *

THE DEATH OF THE FLOWERS

THE melancholy days are come, the saddest of the year,
Of wailing winds, and naked woods, and meadows brown and sear.
Heap'd in the hollows of the grove, the autumn leaves lie dead ;
They rustle to the eddying gust, and to the rabbit's tread.
The robin and the wren are flown, and from the shrubs the jay,
And from the wood-top calls the crow through all the gloomy day.

The wind-flower and the violet, they perish'd long ago,
And the brier-rose and the orchis died amid the summer glow ;
But on the hill the golden-rod, and the aster in the wood,
And the yellow sun-flower by the brook in autumn beauty stood,
Till fell the frost from the clear cold heaven, as falls the plague on men,
And the brightness of their smile was gone, from upland, glade, and glen.

30 *bourn*, hill bounding the view   31 *treble*, piping
7 *wind-flower*, Anemone nemorosa

And now, when comes the calm mild day, as still
  such days will come,
To call the squirrel and the bee from out their
  winter home ;
When the sound of dropping nuts is heard, though
  all the trees are still,
And twinkle in the smoky light the waters of the rill,
The south wind searches for the flowers whose
  fragrance late he bore,
And sighs to find them in the wood and by the
  stream no more.
                              W. C. Bryant

* 62 *

TO DAFFODILS

FAIR Daffodils, we weep to see
    You haste away so soon :
As yet the early-rising Sun
    Has not attain'd his noon.
        Stay, stay,
    Until the hasting day
        Has run
    But to the even-song ;
And, having pray'd together, we
    Will go with you along.

We have short time to stay, as you,
    We have as short a Spring ;
As quick a growth to meet decay
    As you, or any thing.
        We die,
    As your hours do, and dry
        Away
    Like to the Summer's rain ;
Or as the pearls of morning's dew
    Ne'er to be found again.
                              R. Herrick

16 *smoky*, misty   17 *fragrance*, sweet smell
 4 *attained*, reached   13 we grow as fast towards death

* 63 *

CHRISTMAS IN OLD TIME

HEAP on more wood!—the wind is chill;
But let it whistle as it will,
We'll keep our Christmas merry still.

Each age has deem'd the new-born year
The fittest time for festal cheer:
And well our Christian sires of old
Loved when the year its course had roll'd,
And brought blithe Christmas back again,
With all his hospitable train.
Domestic and religious rite
Gave honour to the holy night;
On Christmas Eve the bells were rung;
On Christmas Eve the mass was sung:
That only night in all the year,
Saw the stoled priest the chalice rear.
The damsel donn'd her kirtle sheen;
The hall was dress'd with holly green;
Forth to the wood did merry-men go,
To gather in the mistletoe.
Then open'd wide the baron's hall
To vassal, tenant, serf, and all;
Power laid his rod of rule aside,
And Ceremony doff'd his pride.
The heir, with roses in his shoes,
That night might village partner choose;
The lord, underogating, share
The vulgar game of 'post and pair.'
All hail'd, with uncontroll'd delight
And general voice, the happy night,

  4 *deemed*, thought   10 *rite*, observance
  13 *mass*, divine service   15 *stoled*, robed
16 *kirtle sheen*, gay gown   21 *vassal, serf*, countrymen under
  landlord   26 *underogating*, without losing his place
     27 a game at cards

That to the cottage, as the crown,
Brought tidings of Salvation down.

The fire, with well-dried logs supplied,
Went roaring up the chimney wide ;
The huge hall-table's oaken face,
Scrubb'd till it shone, the day to grace,
Bore then upon its massive board
No mark to part the squire and lord.
Then was brought in the lusty brawn,
By old blue-coated serving-man ;
Then the grim boar's head frown'd on high,
Crested with bays and rosemary.
Well can the green-garb'd ranger tell,
How, when, and where, the monster fell ;
What dogs before his death he tore,
And all the baiting of the boar.
The wassel round, in good brown bowls,
Garnish'd with ribbons, blithely trowls.
There the huge sirloin reek'd ; hard by
Plum-porridge stood, and Christmas pie ;
Nor fail'd old Scotland to produce,
At such high tide, her savoury goose.
Then came the merry maskers in,
And carols roar'd with blithesome din ;
If unmelodious was the song,
It was a hearty note, and strong.
Who lists may in their mumming see
Traces of ancient mystery ;
White shirts supplied the masquerade,
And smutted cheeks the visors made ;—
But, O ! what maskers, richly dight,
Can boast of bosoms half so light !
England was merry England, when
Old Christmas brought his sports again.

42 *green-garbed*, foresters were dressed in green
46 *wassel*, comfortable drink : probably old ale   56 *lists*, likes
57 *mystery*, rough stage-play   59 *visors*, masks   60 *dight*, dressed

'Twas Christmas broach'd the mightiest ale ;
'Twas Christmas told the merriest tale ;
A Christmas gambol oft could cheer
The poor man's heart through half the year.
                                            Sir W. Scott

* 64 *

RULE BRITANNIA

WHEN Britain first, at Heaven's command,
   Arose from out the azure main,
This was the charter of her land,
   And guardian angels sung the strain :
Rule Britannia ! Britannia rules the waves !
   Britons never shall be slaves.

The nations not so blest as thee
   Must in their turn to tyrants fall :
Whilst thou shalt flourish, great and free,
   The dread and envy of them all.

Still more majestic shalt thou rise,
   More dreadful from each foreign stroke ;
As the loud blast that tears the skies
   Serves but to root thy native oak.

Thee haughty tyrants ne'er shall tame ;
   All their attempts to bend thee down
Will but arouse thy generous flame,
   And work their woe and thy renown.

To thee belongs the rural reign ;
   Thy cities shall with commerce shine ;
All thine shall be the subject main,
   And every shore it circles thine !

The Muses, still with Freedom found,
   Shall to thy happy coast repair ;

---

64 *broached*, opened the cask
2 *azure main*, blue sea   3 *charter*, law   12 *foreign stroke*, attack
  17 *flame*, spirit   19 *rural reign*, excellence in farming
  21 *main*, sea   23 *the Muses*, arts and learning   24 *repair*, come

Blest Isle, with matchless beauty crown'd,
And manly hearts to guard the fair :—
Rule Britannia ! Britannia rules the waves !
Britons never shall be slaves !
J. Thomson

* 65 *

BATTLE OF THE BALTIC

OF Nelson and the North
Sing the glorious day's renown,
When to battle fierce came forth
All the might of Denmark's crown,
And her arms along the deep proudly shone ;
By each gun the lighted brand
In a bold determined hand,
And the Prince of all the land
Led them on.

Like leviathans afloat
Lay their bulwarks on the brine ;
While the sign of battle flew
On the lofty British line :
It was ten of April morn by the chime :
As they drifted on their path
There was silence deep as death ;
And the boldest held his breath
For a time.

But the might of England flush'd
To anticipate the scene ;
And her van the fleeter rush'd
O'er the deadly space between.
' Hearts of oak ! ' our captains cried, when each gun
From its adamantine lips
Spread a death-shade round the ships,
Like the hurricane eclipse
Of the sun.

4 all the power of the Danes 6 *brand*, torch 11 *bulwarks*, Danish ships 19, 20 our sailors rejoiced at what was coming 21 *van*, foremost ships 24 *adamantine*, very hard 26 like the sun hidden by a southern storm

Again! again! again!
And the havoc did not slack,
Till a feeble cheer the Dane
To our cheering sent us back;—
Their shots along the deep slowly boom :—
Then ceased—and all is wail,
As they strike the shatter'd sail;
Or in conflagration pale
Light the gloom.

Out spoke the victor then
As he hail'd them o'er the wave,
' Ye are brothers! ye are men!
' And we conquer but to save :—
' So peace instead of death let us bring:
' But yield, proud foe, thy fleet
' With the crews, at England's feet,
' And make submission meet
' To our King.'

Then Denmark blest our chief
That he gave her wounds repose;
And the sounds of joy and grief
From her people wildly rose,
As death withdrew his shades from the day:
While the sun look'd smiling bright
O'er a wide and woeful sight,
Where the fires of funeral light
Died away.

Now joy, old England, raise!
For the tidings of thy might,
By the festal cities' blaze,
Whilst the wine-cup shines in light;
And yet amidst that joy and uproar,
Let us think of them that sleep

29 *havoc*, destruction   33 *wail*, sorrow   37 *victor*, conqueror
50 as the battle-smoke cleared off   57 *festal*, rejoicing

Full many a fathom deep
By thy wild and stormy steep,
Elsinore !

Brave hearts ! to Britain's pride
Once so faithful and so true.
On the deck of fame that died
With the gallant good Riou :
Soft sigh the winds of heaven o'er their grave !
While the billow mournful rolls,
And the mermaid's song condoles,
Singing, Glory to the souls
Of the brave !
T. Campbell

* 66 *

TOM BOWLING

HERE, a sheer hulk, lies poor Tom Bowling,
 The darling of our crew ;
No more he'll hear the tempest howling,
 For death has broach'd him to.
His form was of the manliest beauty,
 His heart was kind and soft ;
Faithful, below, he did his duty ;
 But now he's gone aloft.

Tom never from his word departed,
 His virtues were so rare,
His friends were many and true-hearted,
 His Poll was kind and fair :
And then he'd sing, so blithe and jolly,
 Ah, many's the time and oft !
But mirth is turn'd to melancholy,
 For Tom is gone aloft.

7 *condoles*, joins in lamenting
1 *sheer hulk*, ship without masts   4 *broach to*, brought him suddenly up so as to go over   8 *aloft*, up to heaven   12 his wife

Yet shall poor Tom find pleasant weather,
   When He, who all commands,
Shall give, to call life's crew together,
   The word to pipe 'all hands.'
Thus Death, who kings and tars despatches,
   In vain Tom's life has doff'd :
For though his body's under hatches,
   His soul has gone aloft.
                              C. Dibdin

* 67 *

THE LAWLANDS OF HOLLAND

THE Love that I have chosen
   I'll therewith be content ;
The salt sea shall be frozen
   Before that I repent.
Repent it shall I never
   Until the day I dee !
But the Lawlands of Holland
   Have twinn'd my Love and me.

My Love he built a bonny ship,
   And set her to the main ;
With twenty-four brave mariners
   To sail her out and hame.
But the weary wind began to rise,
   The sea began to rout,
And my Love and his bonny ship
   Turn'd withershins about.

There shall no mantle cross my back,
   No comb go in my hair,
Neither shall coal nor candle-light
   Shine in my bower mair ;

20 *pipe*, whistle 22 *doffed*, ended
23 *under hatches*, below the deck, buried
7 *the Lawlands*, probably here the flat sands of the coast
8 *twinn'd*, parted 16 *withershins*, the wrong way ; probably
   here, right over 20 *bower*, girl's room

Nor shall I choose another Love
  Until the day I dee,
Since the Lawlands of Holland
  Have twinn'd my Love and me.

' Now haud your tongue, my daughter dear,
' Be still, and bide content !
' There's other lads in Galloway ;
· Ye needna sair lament.'
—O there is none in Galloway,
  There's none at all for me :—
I never loved a lad but one,
  And he's drown'd in the sea.

Unknown

* 68 *

THE ANCHORSMITHS

LIKE Aetna's dread volcano, see the ample forge
Large heaps upon large heaps of jetty fuel gorge,
While, salamander-like, the ponderous anchor lies
Glutted with vivid fire, through all its pores that
    flies :—
The dingy anchorsmiths, to renovate their strength,
Stretch'd out in death-like sleep, are snoring at
    their length,
Waiting the master's signal when the tackle's force
Shall, like split rocks, the anchor from the fire
    divorce ;
While, as old Vulcan's Cyclops did the anvil bang,
In deafening concert shall their ponderous hammers
    clang,
And into symmetry the mass incongruous beat,
To save from adverse winds and waves the gallant
    British fleet.

2 *gorge*, swallow greedily 3 *salamander*, reptile fabled to live in fire
4 *glutted*, filled through and through   5 *renovate*, refresh
8 *divorce*, withdraw   9 see end   11 *symmetry*, accurate form:
  incongruous, shapeless   12 *adverse*, opposing

Now, as more vivid and intense each splinter flies,
The temper of the fire the skilful master tries;
And, as the dingy hue assumes a brilliant red,
The heated anchor feeds that fire on which it fed:
The huge sledge-hammers round in order they arrange,
And waking anchorsmiths await the look'd-for change,
Longing with all their force the ardent mass to smite,
When issuing from the fire array'd in dazzling white;
And, as old Vulcan's Cyclops did the anvil bang,
To make in concert rude their ponderous hammers clang,
So the misshapen lump to symmetry they beat,
To save from adverse winds and waves the gallant British fleet.

The preparations thicken; with forks the fire they goad;
And now twelve anchorsmiths the heaving bellows load;
While arm'd from every danger, and in grim array,
Anxious as howling demons waiting for their prey:—
The forge the anchor yields from out its fiery maw,
Which, on the anvil prone, the cavern shouts hurraw!
And now the scorch'd beholders want the power to gaze,
Faint with its heat, and dazzled with its powerful rays;
While, as old Vulcan's Cyclops did the anvil bang,
To forge Jove's thunderbolts, their ponderous hammers clang;—

  15 as the dark iron grows red 19 *ardent*, white-hot
  30 *prone*, lying flat: *cavern*, the smiths in their smithy

And, till its fire's extinct, the monstrous mass they beat
To save from adverse winds and waves the gallant British fleet.
C. Dibdin

* 69 *

THE VISION OF BELSHAZZAR

THE King was on his throne,
　The Satraps throng'd the hall;
A thousand bright lamps shone
　O'er that high festival.
A thousand cups of gold,
　In Judah deem'd divine—
Jehovah's vessels hold
　The godless Heathen's wine.

In that same hour and hall
　The fingers of a Hand
Came forth against the wall,
　And wrote as if on sand:
The fingers of a man;—
　A solitary hand
Along the letters ran,
　And traced them like a wand.

The monarch saw, and shook,
　And bade no more rejoice;
All bloodless wax'd his look,
　And tremulous his voice:—
'Let the men of lore appear,
　'The wisest of the earth,
'And expound the words of fear,
　'Which mar our royal mirth.'

35 *extinct*, gone out
2 *Satraps*, chief governors　　19 *wax'd*, grew
20 *tremulous*, trembling　21 *lore*, wisdom　23 *expound*, explain
24 *mar*, spoil

Chaldea's seers are good,
  But here they have no skill;
And the unknown letters stood
  Untold and awful still.
And Babel's men of age
  Are wise and deep in lore;
But now they were not sage,
  They saw—but knew no more.

A Captive in the land,
  A stranger and a youth,
He heard the king's command,
  He saw that writing's truth;
The lamps around were bright,
  The prophecy in view;
He read it on that night,—
  The morrow proved it true!

' Belshazzar's grave is made,
  ' His kingdom pass'd away,
' He, in the balance weigh'd,
  ' Is light and worthless clay;
' The shroud, his robe of state;
  ' His canopy, the stone;
' The Mede is at his gate!
  ' The Persian on his throne!'
              Lord Byron

· 70 ·

EDWIN AND PAULINUS:

The Conversion of Northumbria

THE black-hair'd gaunt Paulinus
  By ruddy Edwin stood :—
' Bow down, O king of Deira,
  ' Before the blesséd Rood!

---

25 *seers*, prophets   46 *canopy*, covering of throne *stone*, tombstone
4 *Rood*, crucifix

'Cast out thy heathen idols,
  "And worship Christ our Lord.'
—But Edwin look'd and ponder'd,
  And answer'd not a word.

Again the gaunt Paulinus
  To ruddy Edwin spake :
' God offers life immortal
  ' For his dear Son's own sake !
' Wilt thou not hear his message,
  ' Who bears the keys and sword ? '
—But Edwin look'd and ponder'd,
  And answer'd not a word.

Rose then a sage old warrior ;
  Was five-score winters old ;
Whose beard from chin to girdle
  Like one long snow-wreath roll'd :—
' At Yule-time in our chamber
  ' We sit in warmth and light,
' While cold and howling round us
  ' Lies the black land of Night.

' Athwart the room a sparrow
  ' Darts from the open door :
' Within the happy hearth-light
  ' One red flash,—and no more !
' We see it come from darkness,
  ' And into darkness go :—
' So is our life, King Edwin !
  ' Alas, that it is so !

' But if this pale Paulinus
  ' Have somewhat more to tell :
' Some news of Whence and Whither,
  ' And where the soul will dwell ;—

13 *his*, the Bishop of Rome, who sent the mission to England

'If on that outer darkness
  'The sun of Hope may shine ;—
'He makes life worth the living !
  'I take his God for mine !'

So spake the wise old warrior ;
  And all about him cried
'Paulinus' God hath conquer'd !
  'And he shall be our guide :—
'For he makes life worth living
  'Who brings this message plain,
'When our brief days are over,
  'That we shall live again.'
Unknown

* 71 *
TO A FLY
Busy, curious, thirsty Fly,
Drink with me, and drink as I !
Freely welcome to my cup,
Could'st thou sip and sip it up :
Make the most of life you may !
Life is short and wears away.

Both alike are mine and thine,
Hast'ning quick to their decline :—
Thine's a summer : mine's no more,
Though repeated to three-score :—
Three-score summers, when they're gone,
Will appear as short as one.
W. Oldys

* 72 *
THE LIGHT OF OTHER DAYS
Oft in the stilly night
  Ere slumber's chain has bound me,
Fond Memory brings the light
  Of other days around me :

<small>2 before Sleep has made me his prisoner</small>

The smiles, the tears
   Of boyhood's years,
The words of love then spoken ;
   The eyes that shone,
   Now dimm'd and gone,
The cheerful hearts now broken !
Thus in the stilly night
   Ere slumber's chain has bound me,
Sad Memory brings the light
   Of other days around me.

When I remember all
   The friends so link'd together
I've seen around me fall
   Like leaves in wintry weather,
   I feel like one
   Who treads alone
Some banquet-hall deserted,
   Whose lights are fled,
   Whose garlands dead,
And all but he departed !
Thus in the stilly night
   Ere slumber's chain has bound me,
Sad Memory brings the light
   Of other days around me.
                                T. Moore

* 73 *

THE POPLAR FIELD

THE poplars are fell'd, farewell to the shade
And the whispering sound of the cool colonnade ;
The winds play no longer and sing in the leaves,
Nor Ouse on his bosom their image receives.

16 *link'd*, joined   21 *banquet*, feast
2 *colonnade*, row

Twelve years have elapsed since I last took a view
Of my favourite field, and the bank where they grew:
And now in the grass behold they are laid,
And the tree is my seat that once lent me a shade.

The blackbird has fled to another retreat
Where the hazels afford him a screen from the heat ;
And the scene where his melody charm'd me before
Resounds with his sweet-flowing ditty no more.

My fugitive years are all hasting away,
And I must ere long lie as lowly as they,
With a turf on my breast and a stone at my head,
Ere another such grove shall arise in its stead.

'Tis a sight to engage me, if anything can,
To muse on the perishing pleasures of man ;
Short-lived as we are, our enjoyments, I see.
Have a still shorter date, and die sooner than we.

         W. Cowper

* 74 *

FRIENDS DEPARTED

THEY are all gone into the world of light !
 And I alone sit lingering here !
Their very memory is fair and bright,
 And my sad thoughts doth clear.

It glows and glitters in my cloudy breast
 Like stars upon some gloomy grove,
Or those faint beams in which this hill is drest
 After the Sun's remove.

5 *elapsed*, passed   11 *melody*, music   13 *fugitive*, flying
   17 *engage*, lead   18 *muse*, reflect
   5 *It*, memory   8 *remove*, setting

I see them walking in an air of glory,
   Whose light doth trample on my days ;
My days, which are at best but dull and hoary,
   Mere glimmerings and decays.

O holy hope ! and high humility !
   High as the Heavens above !
These are your walks, and you have show'd them me,
   To kindle my cold love.

Dear, beauteous Death ; the jewel of the just !
   Shining nowhere but in the dark ;
What mysteries do lie beyond thy dust,
   Could man outlook that mark !

He that hath found some fledged birdes nest may know
   At first sight if the bird be flown ;
But what fair dell or grove he sings in now,
   That is to him unknown.

And yet, as Angels in some brighter dreams
   Call to the soul when man doth sleep,
So some strange thoughts transcend our wonted themes,
   And into glory peep.

                              H. Vaughan

* 75 *

THE LAND OF DREAMS

'AWAKE, awake, my little boy !
'Thou wast thy mother's only joy ;
'Why dost thou weep in thy gentle sleep ?
'O wake ! thy father does thee keep.'

10 *trampl on*, surpass greatly   17 *just*, good   19 *mysteries*, wonders   27 *transcend*, go above ou usual thoughts

—' O what land is the Land of Dreams?
' What are its mountains, and what are its streams?
' O father! I saw my mother there,
' Among the lilies by waters fair.

'Among the lambs, clothèd in white,
' She walk'd with her Thomas in sweet delight:
' I wept for joy; like a dove I mourn :—
' O when shall I again return!'

—' Dear child! I also by pleasant streams
' Have wander'd all night in the Land of Dreams :—
' But, though calm and warm the waters wide,
' I could not get to the other side.'

—' Father, O father! what do we here,
' In this land of unbelief and fear?—
' The Land of Dreams is better far,
' Above the light of the morning star.'

W. Blake

* 76 *

DEATH IN LIFE

How soon doth man decay!
When clothes are taken from a chest of sweets
   To swaddle infants, whose young breath
      Scarce knows the way,
Those clouts are little winding-sheets,
Which do consign and send them unto death.

When boys go first to bed,
They step into their voluntary graves;
   Sleep binds them fast; only their breath
      Makes them not dead.
Successive nights, like rolling waves,
Convey them quickly, who are bound for death.

6 *consign*, mark them for :- the thought of the poem is, that every-
    thing in Life foreshows and longs for Death
      11 *successive*, one after the other

When youth is frank and free,
And calls for music, while his veins do swell,
  All day exchanging mirth and breath,
    In company;
  That music summons to the knell,
Which shall befriend him at the house of death.

When man grows staid and wise,
Getting a house and home, where he may move
  Within the circle of his breath,
    Schooling his eyes;
  That dumb inclosure maketh love
Unto the coffin, that attends his death.

When age grows low and weak,
Marking his grave, and thawing every year,
  Till all do melt, and drown his breath
    When he would speak;
  A chair or litter shows the bier
Which shall convey him to the house of death.

Man, ere he is aware,
Hath put together a solemnity,
  And drest his hearse, while he has breath
    As yet to spare:—
  Yet, Lord! instruct us so to die,
That all these dyings may be life in death.
                                    G. Herbert

* 77 *

TO-MORROW

IN the downhill of life, when I find I'm declining,
  May my lot no less fortunate be
Than a snug elbow-chair can afford for reclining,
  And a cot that o'erlooks the wide sea;

---

15 *breath*, song   22 *schooling*, training
23 the walls of his house form themselves beforehand into a coffin
24 *attends*, is waiting for   29 *shows*, figures beforehand

With an ambling pad-pony to pace o'er the lawn,
    While I carol away idle sorrow,
And blithe as the lark that each day hails the dawn,
    Look forward with hope for to-morrow.

With a porch at my door, both for shelter and shade too,
    As the sun-shine or rain may prevail ;
And a small spot of ground for the use of the spade too,
    With a barn for the use of the flail :
A cow for my dairy, a dog for my game,
    And a purse when a friend wants to borrow ;
I'll envy no nabob his riches or fame,
    Nor what honours await him to-morrow.

From the bleak northern blast may my cot be completely
    Secured by a neighbouring hill ;
And at night may repose steal upon me more sweetly
    By the sound of a murmuring rill :
And while peace and plenty I find at my board,
    With a heart free from sickness and sorrow,
With my friends may I share what to-day may afford,
    And let them spread the table to-morrow.

And when I at last must throw off this frail covering
    Which I've worn for three-score years and ten,
On the brink of the grave I'll not seek to keep hovering,
    Nor my thread wish to spin o'er again :
But my face in the glass I'll serenely survey,
    And with smiles count each wrinkle and furrow;
As this old worn-out stuff, which is thread-bare to-day,
    May become everlasting to-morrow.

J. Collins

15 *nabob*, newly rich man   28 *thread to spin*, live my life
    29 *serenely*, calmly   31 *stuff*, his body

* 78 *

HUMAN LIFE

This Life, which seems so fair,
Is like a bubble blown up in the air
By sporting children's breath,
Who chase it everywhere,
And strive who can most motion it bequeath
And though it sometimes seem of its own might
Like to an eye of gold to be fix'd there,
And firm to hover in that empty height,
That only is because it is so light.
— But in that pomp it doth not long appear;
For when 'tis most admired, in a thought,
Because it erst was nought, it turns to nought.

W. Drummond

* 79 *

ADORATION

Sweet is the dew that falls betimes,
And drops upon the leafy limes;
   Sweet Hermon's fragrant air:
Sweet is the lily's silver bell,
And sweet the wakeful tapers smell
   That watch for early prayer.

Sweet the young nurse, with love intense,
Which smiles o'er sleeping innocence;
   Sweet when the lost arrive:
Sweet the musician's ardour beats,
While his vague mind's in quest of sweets,
   The choicest flowers to hive.

---

5 *bequeath*, give   10 *pomp*, glory   12 *erst*, at first
10 *ardour*, passion for his work   11 *vague*, wandering: *quest*, search
                12 *flowers*, of music

Strong is the horse upon his speed;
Strong in pursuit the rapid glede,
  Which makes at once his game:
Strong the tall ostrich on the ground;
Strong through the turbulent profound
  Shoots xiphias to his aim.

Strong is the lion—like a coal
His eyeball—like a bastion's mole
  His chest against the foes:
Strong the gier-eagle on his sail;
Strong against tide the enormous whale
  Emerges as he goes.

But stronger still, in earth and air,
And in the sea, the man of prayer,
  And far beneath the tide:
And in the seat to Faith assign'd,
Where ask is, have; where seek is, find;
  Where knock is, open wide.
C. Smart

✱ 80 ✱

ELEGY WRITTEN IN A COUNTRY CHURCH-YARD

THE curfew tolls the knell of parting day,
The lowing herd winds slowly o'er the lea,
The ploughman homeward plods his weary way,
And leaves the world to darkness and to me.

Now fades the glimmering landscape on the sight,
And all the air a solemn stillness holds,
Save where the beetle wheels his droning flight,
And drowsy tinklings lull the distant folds:

---

14 *glede*, kite   17 *turbulent profound*, stormy sea
18 *xiphias* sword-fish   20 *bastion's mole*, projecting piece of fortification   22 *gier-eagle*, large
2 *emerges*, rises above surface   1 *curfew*, evening bell
7 *droning*, long low humming

Save that from yonder ivy-mantled tower
The moping owl does to the moon complain
Of such as, wandering near her secret bower,
Molest her ancient solitary reign.

Beneath those rugged elms, that yew-tree's shade
Where heaves the turf in many a mouldering heap,
Each in his narrow cell for ever laid,
The rude Forefathers of the hamlet sleep.

The breezy call of incense-breathing morn,
The swallow twittering from the straw-built shed,
The cock's shrill clarion, or the echoing horn,
No more shall rouse them from their lowly bed.

For them no more the blazing hearth shall burn,
Or busy housewife ply her evening care:
No children run to lisp their sire's return,
Or climb his knees the envied kiss to share.

Oft did the harvest to their sickle yield,
Their furrow oft the stubborn glebe has broke;
How jocund did they drive their team afield!
How bow'd the woods beneath their sturdy stroke!

Let not Ambition mock their useful toil,
Their homely joys, and destiny obscure;
Nor Grandeur hear with a disdainful smile
The short and simple annals of the Poor.

The boast of heraldry, the pomp of power,
And all that beauty, all that wealth e'er gave,
Await alike th' inevitable hour :—
The paths of glory lead but to the grave.

12 *molest*, trouble her solitude   15 *cell*, chamber, the grave
17 *incense-breathing*, smelling sweetly   19 *clarion*, trumpet
22 *ply her care*, do her work   26 *glebe*, plough land
27 *jocund*, cheerful   30 *destiny*, mode of life :
obscure, little known of   32 *annals*, history of years
35 *inevitable*, that which cannot be escaped

Nor you, ye Proud, impute to these the fault
If Memory o'er their tomb no trophies raise,
Where through the long-drawn aisle and fretted vault
The pealing anthem swells the note of praise.

Can storied urn or animated bust
Back to its mansion call the fleeting breath?
Can Honour's voice provoke the silent dust,
Or Flattery soothe the dull cold ear of Death?

Perhaps in this neglected spot is laid
Some heart once pregnant with celestial fire;
Hands, that the rod of empire might have sway'd,
Or waked to ecstasy the living lyre:

But Knowledge to their eyes her ample page,
Rich with the spoils of time, did ne'er unroll;
Chill Penury repress'd their noble rage,
And froze the genial current of the soul.

Full many a gem of purest ray serene
The dark unfathom'd caves of ocean bear:
Full many a flower is born to blush unseen,
And waste its sweetness on the desert air.

Some village-Hampden, that with dauntless breast
The little tyrant of his fields withstood,
Some mute inglorious Milton here may rest,
Some Cromwell, guiltless of his country's blood.

Th' applause of list'ning senates to command,
The threats of pain and ruin to despise,
To scatter plenty o'er a smiling land,
And read their history in a nation's eyes

---

37 *impute fault*, blame   38 *trophies*, great monuments
39 *fretted*, carved   41 *storied urn*, monument with inscription
43 *provoke*, call out again to life   46 *pregnant with*, full of
48 *lyre*, harp   51 *Penury*, poverty: *rage*, genius   53 *ray*, radiance
59 *mute*, silent   61 *applause*, shouts of praise: *senates*, parliaments

Their lot forbade : nor circumscribed alone
Their growing virtues, but their crimes confined ;
Forbade to wade through slaughter to a throne,
And shut the gates of mercy on mankind ;

The struggling pangs of conscious truth to hide,
To quench the blushes of ingenuous shame,
Or heap the shrine of Luxury and Pride
With incense kindled at the Muse's flame.

Far from the madding crowd's ignoble strife,
Their sober wishes never learn'd to stray ;
Along the cool sequester'd vale of life
They kept the noiseless tenour of their way.

Yet e'en these bones from insult to protect
Some frail memorial still erected nigh,
With uncouth rhymes and shapeless sculpture deck'd,
Implores the passing tribute of a sigh.

Their name, their years, spelt by th' unletter'd Muse,
The place of fame and elegy supply :
And many a holy text around she strews
That teach the rustic moralist to die.

For who, to dumb forgetfulness a prey,
This pleasing anxious being e'er resign'd,
Left the warm precincts of the cheerful day,
Nor cast one longing, lingering look behind ?

On some fond breast the parting soul relies,
Some pious drops the closing eye requires ;
E'en from the tomb the voice of Nature cries,
E'en in our ashes live their wonted fires.

65 *circumscribed*, bounded   71, 72 flatter with poetry the rich
75 *sequester'd*, quiet   76 *tenour*, character   80 *tribute*, offering
81 *unletter'd Muse*, untaught village poet   82 *elegy*, poem upon
       a person dead   84 *moralist*, thoughtful person
86 *this being*, this life   87 *precincts*, abodes   89 *parting*, departing
         90 *pious drops*, tears of affection
      91, 92 the dead have affections and desires

For thee, who, mindful of th' unhonour'd dead,
Dost in these lines their artless tale relate ;
If chance, by lonely Contemplation led,
Some kindred spirit shall inquire thy fate,--

Haply some hoary-headed swain may say,
' Oft have we seen him at the peep of dawn
' Brushing with hasty steps the dews away,
' To meet the sun upon the upland lawn ;

' There at the foot of yonder nodding beech
' That wreathes its old fantastic roots so high,
' His listless length at noon-tide would he stretch,
' And pore upon the brook that babbles by.

' Hard by yon wood, now smiling as in scorn,
' Muttering his wayward fancies he would rove ;
' Now drooping, woeful-wan, like one forlorn,
' Or crazed with care, or cross'd in hopeless love.

' One morn I miss'd him on the custom'd hill,
' Along the heath, and near his favourite tree ;
' Another came ; nor yet beside the rill,
' Nor up the lawn, nor at the wood was he ;

' The next with dirges due in sad array
' Slow through the church-way path we saw him
    ' borne,—
' Approach and read (for thou canst read) the lay
' Graved on the stone beneath yon agéd thorn.'

The Epitaph

Here rests his head upon the lap of Earth
A Youth, to Fortune and to Fame unknown ;
Fair Science frown'd not on his humble birth,
And Melancholy mark'd him for her own.

93 *thee*, the Poet   94 *artless*, simple   96 *kindred spirit*, thoughtful man   97 *swain*, countryman   102 *fantastic*, twisted   104 *pore*, look steadily   105 *Hard by*, close to   113 *dirges*, funeral service   115 *lay*, epitaph   119 though poor, he was well educated

Large was his bounty, and his soul sincere;
Heaven did a recompense as largely send:
He gave to Misery all he had, a tear,
He gain'd from Heaven, 'twas all he wish'd, a friend.

No farther seek his merits to disclose,
Or draw his frailties from their dread abode,
(There they alike in trembling hope repose,)
The bosom of his Father and his God.
T. Gray

* 81 *
TO A SKYLARK

HAIL to thee, blithe Spirit!
  Bird thou never wert,
That from heaven, or near it,
  Pourest thy full heart
In profuse strains of unpremeditated art.

  Higher still and higher
    From the earth thou springest,
  Like a cloud of fire,
    The blue deep thou wingest,
And singing still dost soar, and soaring ever singest.

  In the golden lightning
    Of the sunken sun
  O'er which clouds are bright'ning,
    Thou dost float and run,
Like an unbodied Joy whose race is just begun.

  The pale purple even
    Melts around thy flight;
  Like a star of heaven
    In the broad daylight
Thou art unseen, but yet I hear thy shrill delight:

---

122 *recompense*, reward   125 *disclose*, make known
5 *profuse*, abundant; *unpremeditated*, not thought of before

    Keen as are the arrows
      Of that silver sphere,
    Whose intense lamp narrows
      In the white dawn clear
Until we hardly see, we feel that it is here.

    All the earth and air
      With thy voice is loud,
    As, when night is bare,
      From one lonely cloud
The moon rains out her beams, and heaven is over-
    flow'd.

    What thou art we know not;
      What is most like thee?
    From rainbow clouds there flow not
      Drops so bright to see
As from thy presence showers a rain of melody.

    Like a poet hidden
      In the light of thought,
    Singing hymns unbidden,
      Till the world is wrought
To sympathy with hopes and fears it heeded not:

    Like a high-born maiden
      In a palace tower,
    Soothing her love-laden
      Soul in secret hour
With music sweet as love, which overflows her
    bower:

    Like a glow-worm golden
      In a dell of dew,
    Scattering unbeholden
      Its aerial hue
Among the flowers and grass, which screen it from
    the view:

    21 *arrows*, rays   22 *sphere*, star
23 *intense lamp*, brilliant light   40 *to sympathy*, to feel
49 *aerial hue*, the faint light of the glow-worm

Like a rose embower'd
  In its own green leaves,
By warm winds deflower'd,
  Till the scent it gives
Makes faint with too much sweet these heavy-wingéd thieves.

Sound of vernal showers
  On the twinkling grass,
Rain-awaken'd flowers,
  All that ever was
Joyous, and clear, and fresh, thy music doth surpass.

Teach us, sprite or bird,
  What sweet thoughts are thine :
I have never heard
  Praise of love or wine
That panted forth a flood of rapture so divine.

Chorus hymeneal
  Or triumphal chaunt
Match'd with thine, would be all
  But an empty vaunt—
A thing wherein we feel there is some hidden want.

What objects are the fountains
  Of thy happy strain?
What fields, or waves, or mountains?
  What shapes of sky or plain?
What love of thine own kind? what ignorance of pain?

---

55 *thieves*, the winds that steal the scent of the rose
56 *vernal*, in spring   65 *rapture*, delight   66, 67 marriage-song or song of victory   69 *vaunt*, boast

T

With thy clear keen joyance
    Languor cannot be :
Shadow of annoyance
    Never came near thee :
Thou lovest ; but ne'er knew love's sad satiety.

Waking or asleep
    Thou of death must deem
Things more true and deep
    Than we mortals dream,
Or how could thy notes flow in such a crystal stream ?

We look before and after,
    And pine for what is not :
Our sincerest laughter
    With some pain is fraught ;
Our sweetest songs are those that tell of saddest thought.

Yet if we could scorn
    Hate, and pride, and fear ;
If we were things born
    Not to shed a tear,
I know not how thy joy we ever should come near.

Better than all measures
    Of delightful sound,
Better than all treasures
    That in books are found,
Thy skill to poet were, thou scorner of the ground !

Teach me half the gladness
    That thy brain must know,
Such harmonious madness
    From my lips would flow
The world should listen then, as I am listening now !

P. B. Shelley

82 *deem*, think   89 *fraught*, laden   95 *measures*, music

* 82 *

A CRADLE SONG

Hush ! my dear, lie still and slumber ;
    Holy angels guard thy bed !
Heavenly blessings without number
    Gently falling on thy head.

Sleep, my babe ; thy food and raiment,
    House and home, thy friends provide ;
All without thy care or payment
    All thy wants are well supplied.

How much better thou'rt attended
    Than the Son of God could be,
When from Heaven he descended,
    And became a child like thee !

Soft and easy is thy cradle :
    Coarse and hard thy Saviour lay :
When his birth-place was a stable,
    And his softest bed was hay.

See the kindly shepherds round him,
    Telling wonders from the sky !
Where they sought him, there they found him,
    With his Virgin-Mother by.

See the lovely babe a-dressing :
    Lovely infant, how he smiled !
When he wept, the mother's blessing
    Soothed and hush'd the holy child.

Lo, he slumbers in his manger,
    Where the hornéd oxen fed ;
— Peace, my darling ! here's no danger !
    Here's no ox a-near thy bed !

9 *attended*, waited on

May'st thou live to know and fear him,
  Trust and love him all thy days :
Then go dwell for ever near him ;
  See his face, and sing his praise.

I could give thee thousand kisses,
  Hoping what I most desire :
Not a mother's fondest wishes
  Can to greater joys aspire.

I. Watts

* 83 *

ON THE MORNING OF CHRIST'S NATIVITY

THIS is the month, and this the happy morn
Wherein the Son of Heaven's Eternal King
Of wedded maid and virgin mother born,
Our great redemption from above did bring ;
For so the holy sages once did sing
That he our deadly forfeit should release,
And with his Father work us a perpetual peace.

That glorious Form, that Light unsufferable,
And that far-beaming blaze of Majesty
Wherewith he wont at Heaven's high council-table
To sit the midst of Trinal Unity,
He laid aside ; and, here with us to be,
Forsook the courts of everlasting day,
And chose with us a darksome house of mortal clay.

Say, heavenly Muse, shall not thy sacred vein
Afford a present to the Infant God ?
Hast thou no verse, no hymn, or solemn strain
To welcome him to this his new abode,
Now while the heaven, by the sun's team untrod,

---

36 *aspire*, hope   6 *forfeit*, punishment due for sin
    15, 16 shall not this sacred subject be sung
  19 *team*, chariot and horses, supposed to carry the sun

Hath took no print of the approaching light,
And all the spangled host keep watch in squadrons bright?
See how from far, upon the eastern road,
The star-led wizards haste with odours sweet :
O run, prevent them with thy humble ode
And lay it lowly at his blessèd feet :
Have thou the honour first thy Lord to greet,
And join thy voice unto the angel quire
From out his secret altar touch'd with hallow'd fire.

The Hymn

It was the winter wild
While the heaven-born Child
All meanly wrapt in the rude manger lies ;
Nature in awe to him
Had doff'd her gaudy trim,
With her great Master so to sympathize :
It was no season then for her
To wanton with the sun, her lusty paramour.

Only with speeches fair
She woos the gentle air
To hide her guilty front with innocent snow ;
And on her naked shame,
Pollute with sinful blame,
The saintly veil of maiden white to throw ;
Confounded, that her Maker's eyes
Should look so near upon her foul deformities.

But he, her fears to cease,
Sent down the meek-eyed Peace ;
She, crown'd with olive green, came softly sliding
Down through the turning sphere,

21 *host*, stars : *squadrons*, bands   23 *wizards*, the three kings
24 *prevent*, go before : *ode*, solemn song   33 *doff'd*, put off
34 *sympathize*, show similar feeling   36 *paramour*, lover
39 *front*, forehead   48 *turning sphere*, see end

His ready harbinger,
With turtle wing the amorous clouds dividing ;
And waving wide her myrtle wand,
She strikes a universal peace through sea and land.

No war, or battle's sound
Was heard the world around :
The idle spear and shield were high up hung ;
The hookéd chariot stood
Unstain'd with hostile blood ;
The trumpet spake not to the arméd throng :
And kings sat still with awful eye,
As if they surely knew their sovran Lord was by.

But peaceful was the night
Wherein the Prince of Light
His reign of peace upon the earth began :
The winds, with wonder whist,
Smoothly the waters kist,
Whispering new joys to the mild oceán—
Who now hath quite forgot to rave,
While birds of calm sit brooding on the charméd wave.

The stars, with deep amaze,
Stand fix'd in steadfast gaze,
Bending one way their precious influence ;
And will not take their flight
For all the morning light,
Or Lucifer that often warn'd them thence ;
But in their glimmering orbs did glow
Until their Lord himself bespake, and bid them go.

And though the shady gloom
Had given day her room.
The sun himself withheld his wonted speed,
And hid his head for shame,

49 *harbinger* herald 50 *turtle*, dove 56 *hookéd*, with hooks at axletree 59 *awful*, full of fear 64 *whist*, hushed
71 *influence*, supposed power 74 *Lucifer*, the morning-star

As his inferior flame
The new-enlighten'd world no more should need :
He saw a greater Sun appear
Than his bright throne, or burning axletree, could bear.

The shepherds on the lawn
Or ere the point of dawn
Sate simply chatting in a rustic row ;
Full little thought they than
That the mighty Pan
Was kindly come to live with them below ;
Perhaps their loves, or else their sheep
Was all that did their silly thoughts so busy keep.

When such music sweet
Their hearts and ears did greet
As never was by mortal finger strook—
Divinely-warbled voice
Answering the stringéd noise,
As all their souls in blissful rapture took :
The air, such pleasure loth to lose,
With thousand echoes still prolongs each heavenly close.

Nature, that heard such sound
Beneath the hollow round
Of Cynthia's seat the aery region thrilling,
Now was almost won
To think her part was done,
And that her reign had here its last fulfilling ;
She knew such harmony alone
Could hold all heaven and earth in happier union

81 *As*, as if   86 *Or ere*, before   88 *than*, then
92 *silly*, simple   95 *strook*, struck   98 delighted their souls
100 *close*, cadence   102 within the Moon's (*Cynthia's*) orbit
103 *aery region*, the atmosphere

At last surrounds their sight
A globe of circular light
That with long beams the shamefaced night array'd ;
The helmèd Cherubim
And sworded Seraphim
Are seen in glittering ranks with wings display'd,
Harping in loud and solemn quire
With unexpressive notes, to Heaven's new-born Heir.

Such music (as 'tis said)
Before was never made
But when of old the Sons of Morning sung,
While the Creator great
His constellations set
And the well balanced world on hinges hung ;
And cast the dark foundations deep,
And bid the weltering waves their oozy channel keep.

Ring out, ye crystal spheres !
Once bless our human ears,
If ye have power to touch our senses so ;
And let your silver chime
Move in melodious time ;
And let the bass of Heaven's deep organ blow ;
And with your ninefold harmony
Make up full consort to the angelic symphony.

For if such holy song
Enwrap our fancy long,
Time will run back, and fetch the age of gold ;
And speckled vanity
Will sicken soon and die,
And leprous sin will melt from earthly mould ;
And Hell itself will pass away,
And leave her dolorous mansions to the peering day.

116 *unexpressive*, such as no one could express
124 *weltering*, rolling   125 see end   132 *consort*, agreement :
   symphony, choral song   134 be audible to man
   136 *speckled*, perhaps, plague-spotted   140 *dolorous*, sad

Yea, Truth and Justice then
Will down return to men,
Orb'd in a rainbow ; and, like glories wearing.
Mercy will sit between
Throned in celestial sheen,
With radiant feet the tissued clouds down steering ;
And Heaven, as at some festival,
Will open wide the gates of her high palace hall.

But wisest Fate says No ;
This must not yet be so ;
The Babe yet lies in smiling infancy
That on the bitter cross
Must redeem our loss ;
So both himself and us to glorify :
Yet first, to those y-chain'd in sleep,
The wakeful trump of doom must thunder through
    the deep ;

With such a horrid clang
As on mount Sinai rang
While the red fire and smouldering clouds outbrake :
The aged Earth aghast
With terrour of that blast
Shall from the surface to the centre shake,
When, at the world's last sessión,
The dreadful Judge in middle air shall spread his
    throne.

And then at last our bliss
Full and perfect is,
But now begins ; for from this happy day
The old Dragon, under ground
In straiter limits bound,
Not half so far casts his usurpéd sway ;

143 *Orb'd in*, encircled by   145 *sheen*, brightness
146 *tissued*, variegated   155 *y-chained*. *y* is a participial prefix
163 *session*, assembly for trial   168 *Dragon*, Satan

And wroth to see his kingdom fail,
Swindges the scaly horrour of his folded tail.

The oracles are dumb ;
No voice or hideous hum
Runs thro' the archéd roof in words deceiving:
Apollo from his shrine
Can no more divine,
With hollow shriek the steep of Delphos leaving :
No nightly trance or breathéd spell
Inspires the pale-eyed priest from the prophetic cell.

The lonely mountains o'er,
And the resounding shore,
A voice of weeping heard, and loud lament ;
From haunted spring and dale
Edged with poplar pale
The parting Genius is with sighing sent ;
With flower-inwoven tresses torn
The nymphs in twilight shade of tangled thickets mourn.

In consecrated earth
And on the holy hearth
The Lars and Lemures moan with midnight plaint ;
In urns, and altars round
A drear and dying sound
Affrights the Flamens at their service quaint;
And the chill marble seems to sweat,
While each peculiar Power forgoes his wonted seat.

Peor and Baalim
Forsake their temples dim,
With that twice batter'd god of Palestine ;
And moonéd Ashtaroth

172 *swindges*, lash es 177 *divine*, utter oracles ; see end
186 *Genius*, Spirit of the place 191 *Lars and Lemures*, household gods and spirits of the dead 194 *Flamens*, Roman priests : *quaint*, here, usual 196 *forgoes*, quits 199 Dagon

Heaven's queen and mother both,
Now sits not girt with tapers' holy shine;
The Lybic Hammon shrinks his horn;
In vain the Tyrian maids their wounded Thammuz
    mourn.

And sullen Moloch, fled,
Hath left in shadows dread
His burning idol all of blackest hue:
In vain with cymbals' ring
They call the grisly king,
In dismal dance about the furnace blue;
The brutish gods of Nile as fast
Isis, and Orus, and the dog Anubis, haste.

Nor is Osiris seen
In Memphian grove, or green,
Trampling the unshower'd grass with lowings
    loud:
Nor can he be at rest
Within his sacred chest;
Nought but profoundest hell can be his shroud;
In vain with timbrell'd anthems dark
The sable-stoléd sorcerers bear his worshipt
    ark.

He feels from Juda's land
The dreaded infant's hand;
The rays of Bethlehem blind his dusky eyn;
Not all the gods beside
Longer dare abide,
Not Typhon huge ending in snaky twine:
Our Babe, to show his Godhead true,
Can in his swaddling bands control the damnéd
    crew.

  215 *unshower'd*, watered by the Nile only
 219 *timbrell'd anthems*, sacred songs, accompanied by timbrels
 220 *stoléd*, mantled 223 *eyn*, eyes 226 *twine*, twists

So, when the sun in bed
Curtain'd with cloudy red
Pillows his chin upon an orient wave,
The flocking shadows pale
Troop to the infernal jail,
Each fetter'd ghost slips to his several grave ;
And the yellow-skirted fays
Fly after the night-steeds, leaving their moon-loved
   maze.

But see, the Virgin blest
Hath laid her Babe to rest ;
Time is, our tedious song should here have ending :
Heaven's youngest-teeméd star
Hath fix'd her polish'd car,
Her sleeping Lord with hand-maid lamp attending :
And all about the courtly stable
Bright-harness'd angels sit in order serviceable.

J. Milton

* 84 *

THE BURNING BABE

As I in hoary winter's night stood shivering in the
   snow,
Surprised I was with sudden heat, which made my
   heart to glow :
And lifting up a fearful eye to view what fire was
   near,
A pretty babe, all burning bright, did in the air
   appear ;
Who, scorchéd with excessive heat, such floods of
   tears did shed,
As though his floods should quench his flames
   which with his tears were fed :—

---

231 *orient*, in the east   232 *see* end   235 *fays*, fairies
236 *steeds*, mares : *maze*, dancing-ground   239 *tedious*, long
240 *teem'd*, born   241 the star is resting   244 *harness'd*, armoured

Alas!' quoth He, 'but newly born, in fiery heats I fry,
'Yet none approach to warm their hearts or feel my fire but I!
'My faultless breast the furnace is, the fuel wounding thorns;
'Love is the fire, and sighs the smoke, the ashes shame and scorns;
'The fuel Justice layeth on, and Mercy blows the coals,
'The metal in this furnace wrought are men's defiléd souls,
'For which, as now on fire I am, to work them to their good.
'So will I melt into a bath to wash them in my blood.'—
With this He vanish'd out of sight, and swiftly shrunk away;
And straight I calléd unto mind that it was Christmas-day.

R. Southwell

7 *fry*, old use of the word for *burn*   12 *defiled*, sinful

End of Second Part

NOTES:

MAINLY HISTORICAL AND CRITICAL

PART I.

PAGE	NO.	
6	4	Most copies of Cowper's poems contain an account of these hares, written in the exquisite prose of which he was master.
13	9	The poetry which Blake, an artist of very high and rare powers, wrote during his youth, shows the same qualities as his art ; simple yet often majestic imagination, spiritual insight, profound feeling for grace and colour. Like his art also, his verse is narrow in its range, and at times eccentric to the neighbourhood of madness. But, whatever he writes, his eye is always straight upon his subject.
26	12	So many beautiful pieces in prose and verse have been written in the Scots or North Country language that a great source of pleasure is lost by readers who will not take the small pains required to master the peculiarities of spelling and vocabulary: it is hoped that the very numerous notes added here will tempt children to give themselves this pleasure. The original ballads by unknown poets appear generally to have taken their present form within the two hundred years before 1700.
33	16	Casabianca was son to a French Admiral commanding the flag-ship *L'Orient* at the battle of the Nile, 1798.
34	17	The *Birkenhead*, steam troop-ship, struck near Simon's Bay, Cape of Good Hope, 25th of February, 1852. Four hundred and thirty-eight officers, soldiers, and seamen, were lost : including the military commander, Colonel Seton of the 74th. For some alterations which make this fine poem more intelligible to children, readers are indebted to the author's kindness.
37	19	These gallant lines are almost worthy of Campbell.
38	20	The *Royal George*, of 108 guns, commanded by Admiral Kempenfelt, whilst undergoing a partial careening in Portsmouth Harbour, was overset about 10 A.M. Aug. 29, 1782. The total loss was believed to be near 1,000 souls. These lines were written (Sept. 1782) to the music of the March in Handel's *Scipio*. For tenderness and grandeur under the form of severe simplicity they have few rivals. They are Greek after the manner in which a modern English poet should be Greek:—Readers who admire them are on the right way to high and lasting pleasure.
39	21	Burns justly named this 'one of the most beautiful songs in the Scots or any other language.'
41	23	'I never saw anything like this funeral dirge,' says Charles Lamb, 'except the ditty which reminds Ferdinand of his drowned father in the *Tempest*. As that is of the water, watery ; so this is of the earth, earthy. Both have that intenseness of feeling, which seems to resolve itself into the element which it contemplates.'
42	24	Alexander Selkirk's life of four years in the desolate

Notes 287

PAGE	NO.	
		island, *Juan Fernandez*, may have been in De Foe's mind when he wrote 'Robinson Crusoe.'
48	28	Line 66, *Cockrood*, unexplained, so far as the Editor can learn. It would seem to mean either a *road* or *run*, as we say, for woodcocks; or a wooden stage for them, by a vague use of *rood*.
49	29	A justly famous specimen of the allegorical style prevalent in Elizabeth's time: the Shepherd's life being poetically glorified and described as a type of life in general. This piece should be compared with the charming truthfulness of Herrick's country scenes in the preceding piece, or Wordsworth's following:—Marlowe's has much beauty; but how much more beautiful is Truth, in the hands of a genuine poet!
63	41	The tale of Lord Leicester's private marriage with Amy Robsart, her imprisonment and fearful death at Cumnor Hall, near Oxford, partially confirmed by history, has been made more real to us than most historical realities by Sir Walter Scott's *Kenilworth*: the most splendid of the three tragic romances left by that great writer.
78	47	This spirited poem, which blazes throughout with the highhearted patriotism of its distinguished author, should be read accompanied by some history of the period, and the map of England.
		Line 10, *Pinta*; the Editor can find no Spanish vessel recorded under this name; nor does the word, in Spanish, bear any sense applicable to a ship. Medina Sidonia, who commanded the Armada, sailed in the *Saint Martin*.
		Line 23, At Cressy, .. Picardy, the king of Bohemia, and a body of Genoese soldiers, fought in the army of Philip. *Cæsar's eagle shield* appears to be an allusion to some German troops who also served. The eagle is the ancient bearing of the empire.
		Line 42, Mines of lead and zinc exist in the Mendip Hills.
		Line 43, *Longleat, Cranbourne*; houses in Wilts and Dorset belonging to Lords Bath and Salisbury.
		Line 71, *Belvoir*, house of the Duke of Rutland near Grantham.
		Line 73, *Gaunt's embattled pile*, Lancaster Castle, built by John of Gaunt about 1363.
82	48	This battle was fought December 2, 1800, between the Austrians under Archduke John and the French under Moreau, in a forest near Munich. *Hohen Linden* means *High Limetrees*.
86	51	Belisarius, a Thracian peasant, became general of the Roman Empire under Justinian. He fought against the Vandals, Moors, Goths, Bulgarians, and other enemies; but was finally dismissed ungratefully by the Emperor, and died A.D. 565.
		The writer of this rough, but truly noble and original poem, died soon after 1800. The version here given from Plumtre's 'Songs,' 1806) differs from that published by Collins in his very rare little book, 'Scripscrapologia,' 1804.
80	53	Lines 22, 24, These places are in the S.W. promontory of

PAGE	NO.	
		Donegal, Ireland. *Slieveleague* is a mountain; *Columbkill* a glen between Slieveleague and the *Rosses* islands.
96	56	The poet professed that these fine, wildly musical lines came to him in his sleep, and that all he did on waking was to write them down. Coleridge, in his magic world, is the most imaginative and romantic of all our poets, Shakespeare (always exceptional) excepted. Seeing how little he wrote in this class, we must regret that he did not dream oftener.
100	59	In this one poem the Editor has ventured to make some changes, in order to simplify the language, which (in the original does not appear to him to do full justice to the admirable simplicity and pathos of the picture presented.
102	60	During the last three centuries, the poetry written in the North Country or Scots form of English has been so much more important than that written in other forms, as to obscure the peculiar merits which each of them possesses. But the series of poems from which this piece and the next are taken proves the pathos and picturesqueness which the Dorset dialect has when handled by a gifted countryman.
105	62	The death of a young man wandering on Helvellyn in the Lake country, in 1805, supplied Scott with his subject. In this poem the thoughts are much simpler than the language: a rare fault with Scott, or, indeed, with any really great poet.
112	70	An admirable specimen of the Allegorical style which, under the first two Stuart kings, took the place of the pastoral Elizabethan allegory represented by No. 29. Few poets, in C. Lamb's language, are more 'matterful' than Herbert, or express their thoughts with fewer words, introduced only for ornament or metre's sake.
118	72	Remarkable for its close and scientific enumeration of natural phenomena.
119	73	An extract from the long poem said to have been written by poor Smart when confined as a madman. It is full of glorious wildness and intense imagination. Many of its strange phrases (as line 10 here) might probably be traced to, if not explained by, the writings of the 'mystical' theologians.
120	74	It is remarkable how much Addison here anticipates the exquisite suavity and elegance of Cowper's style in similar pieces.
121	75	Wordsworth has left no more consummate specimen of the singular art by which he presents us with a thought which strikes the mind as, at once, perfectly original, and yet, perfectly familiar. The *Cuckoo* (No. 78), on the other hand, paints a fervour of imaginative delight which would be felt only by a highly poetical nature.
128	81	*Arethusa*, with the two poems which follow it, will probably be found difficult at first reading, and may give older children a glimpse into that world of poetry in general to which this book is meant as an introduction. Shelley has here put into verse, so brilliant that we easily forgive its occasional commonplace and carelessness of phrase, a Greek mythical legend.

> Divine Alpheus, who by secret sluice
> Stole under seas to meet his Arethuse,

—a river rising near Mount Erymanthus in Arcadia,

PAGE	NO	
		the ancient central province of Southern Greece, is feigned to pursue the stream Arethusa ; they pass through a rent in Mount Erymanthus, cross under the sea to Sicily (opposite to the coast of Greece), and now form one stream in the harbour of Syracuse (Ortygia). *Aceroceraunia*, a mountain tract in Northern Greece, must have been named by Shelley inadvertently, or on account of the re-onance of the name. This poem is a fine example of Shelley's singular power in *personification*: he paints the rivers as vividly as if they had been real human creatures
131	82	*L'Allegro* and *Il Penseroso*. It is a striking proof of Milton's astonishing power, that these, the earliest pure descriptive lyrics in our language, should still remain the best in a style which so many great poets have since attempted. The bright and the thoughtful aspects of nature are their subjects ; but each is preceded by a mythological introduction in a mixed Classical and Italian manner. The meaning of the first is that gaiety is the child of nature and of spring ; of the second, that pensiveness is the daughter of solitude and wisdom.
132	—	Line 36, Milton calls Liberty a *mountain-nymph* in allusion to ancient Greece, Switzerland, and other similar countries in which national freedom has been defended by the hardy inhabitants. Wordsworth has a fine sonnet on this subject
135	—	Line 132, The *sock* was the low shoe worn by actors in the ancient comedies ; the *buskin* (line 102 of the *Penseroso*, No. 83) the high shoe worn in tragedies, to give the figure a more commanding air. Line 133. *Fancy*: probably used for what we speak of as Imagination. Milton is here alluding to Shakespeare through the mouth of the 'Cheerful Man ;' he hence refers to Shakespeare's lighter qualities. Line 145, Orpheus in Greek story was a divine musician who redeemed his wife Eurydice from death (Pluto) by song ; but lost her when on the boundary line of life by turning back to look on her before she had passed it. See also *Penseroso*, No. 83, line 105.
137	83	Line 46, *Spare Fast*: Milton elsewhere has expressed his belief that the mind is made clear and fit for high and divine thoughts by fasting.
138	—	Line 87, The *Great Bear*, in English latitudes being always above the horizon, is here used for Night. Line 98, *Sceptred pall*: Ancient tragedies turned generally on the fortunes of heroic persons, kings, and gods ; hence the actors appeared robed and with sceptres. *Thebes*, &c. are names referring to the great Athenian tragedies.
139	—	Line 110. *Cambuscan*, &c., these names occur in Chaucer's unfinished 'Squire's Tale.' Line 116, *Great bards* ; referring to such poets as the Italian Ariosto and Tasso, and to our own Spenser.
141	84	This fine poem, recently printed from manuscript, has been ascribed to Robert Devereux, Earl of Essex. It does not appear whether the first of that name (beheaded 1600) or his son (with whom the peerage ended in 1646) be intended. The lines, at any rate, belong to the 'Elizabethan' period or a few years later.

U

NOTES:

PART II.

MAINLY HISTORICAL AND CRITICAL

PAGE	NO.	
143	1	This rough but spirited poem, with a very few more, give Drayton a claim to remembrance, which his long and laborious chronicles in rhyme have failed to secure. Agincourt was fought October 25, 1415. A history of England, and Shakespeare's *Henry the Fifth* should be read with this poem.
145	—	Line 48, The *lilies* are the Fleur-de-Lys, long the arms of France, as the Lions are of England.
147	2	Southey, like Drayton, has left little work vividly penetrated with the spirit of poetry, in comparison with his many pages of skilful and industrious manufacture. This piece has something of the merit shown in Wordsworth's tales; but it wants Wordsworth's exquisiteness
149	3	Simple as *Lucy Gray* seems, a mere narrative of what 'has been and may be again,' yet every detail in it is marked by the deepest and purest 'ideal' character. Hence it is not strictly a pathetic poem, pathetic as the situation is. So far as this element has a place, Wordsworth asks that we should feel for the parents, rather than for the child: she is painted as a creature, 'made one with Nature' in her death, not less than in her life.
152	5	This little poem, again, within, its sphere, in ideal perfection rivals the most perfect work of the world's greatest lyrical poets.—Readers who smile, are invited to try to 'do likewise.'
163	12	Within its range, the *Ancient Mariner* is 'alone in its glory':—but the crown must have been given to *Christabel*, had Coleridge completed that poem, and completed it in the style of the two parts which we have. The *Memoirs* of Wordsworth give an interesting narrative of the mode in which the *Ancient Mariner* was written: The dream of a friend, according to Coleridge, was the foundation; but by far the greatest part of the story is due to the poet's mind. The introduction of the Albatross, and the working of the ship by the dead sailors, were motives suggested by Wordsworth, who also supplied a very few lines, as the friends walked together over the lovely Quantock Hills in the autumn of 1797.—Such were the external circumstances under which this masterpiece was created: it is pleasant to know them; but all that made it such is the poet's secret.
185	14	Line 5, It is not clear whether by *fairy-flax* the poet means *graceful* and *fairylike*, or whether it be a local name for some species of the plant.

PAGE	NO	
190	16	Glencoe, the 'Valley of Weeping,' is a savage glen on the north-western coast of Argyllshire. The murder of the Macdonalds who were settled in it, by the Earls of Breadalbane and Argyll, and (most prominently) Sir John Dalrymple of Stair, has been told by Macaulay with equal historical force and judicial fairness.
191	17	Line 12, Marvell belonged to the 'Puritan' party ; and the Emigrants here intended are persons of that party flying from ecclesiastical pressure during the first half of the seventeenth century. Lines 35, 36 present a curious example of ' anti-climax ' ; but the poem, as a whole, is very sweet and original.
193	18, 19	Noble, if rough, pieces of work. In Bunyan's, there may be an echo of Shakespeare's *Under the greenwood tree*, No. 31.
197	23	Very full explanatory notes have been subjoined to this and to other poems written in local dialect, in hope that children may thus be tempted to conquer (to their own great advantage the sense of difficulty and repulsion which the first sight of a vocabulary, differing slightly from the common literary form, never fails to rouse.
198	24	After the capture of Madrid by Napoleon, Sir J. Moore retreated before Soult and Ney, the French commanders, to Corunna, in North-west Spain, and was killed whilst covering the embarkation of his troops. His tomb, built by Ney, bears this inscription— 'John Moore, leader of the English armies, slain in battle, 1809.'
199	25	Founded on a real story of the English campaign in China, 1860.
205	29	Eminently characteristic of Scott in its music. It has an airy freedom and freshness, a certain magical quality ; one might fancy that the actual voice of the wildwood was audible in it.
208	34	The *Thanksgiving*, and No 36, are delightful pictures of English country life two centuries ago.
222	44	There is something of the sublime in the severe and pathetic simplicity of this little piece.
223	45	Perhaps no poem in this collection is more delicately fancied, more exquisitely finished. By placing the description of the Fawn in a young girl's mouth, Marvell has legitimated that abundance of ' imaginative hyperbole ' to which he is always partial ; he makes us feel it quite natural that the maiden's favourite should be whiter than milk, sweeter than sugar, ' lilies without, roses within.' The poet's imagination is, as it were, justified in its seeming extravagance by the intensity and unity with which it invests the poem — and the reader's pleasure is proportionately intensified.

The verdict of Time is not always just and conclusive, even after many years. Undeserved contemporary fame is sometimes traditionally prolonged ; sometimes, though less often, the crown, fairly won, is withheld for centuries. Of this latter injustice, Marvell is an example. We cannot place him among our ' greater gods ' of song ; yet, within his own sphere, no one has more decided originality, more vivid imagination, more attractive and enduring charm. |

U 2

PAGE	NO	
224	46	This poem (inserted on the ground of its *naïveté* and originality) is one of a series described as by Charles and Mary Lamb. The style seems to warrant its ascription to the latter.
226	48	An old fragment, completed with exquisite skill by Burns. His version of No. 49 is not equally successful. It would, indeed, hardly be possible to improve such a little masterpiece of music, tenderness, and simplicity.
227	50	A justly-famous piece of 'Cavalier' poetry: Lovelace was brought twice to prison by his devotion to Charles I. *Thames* (line 10), by a classical form of metaphor, is used for *water*.
228	51	Compare the note on Nos. 48, 49 :—These poems may (perhaps) a little exceed the boundary line laid down in the Preface; but the Editor did not know how to omit them.
235	55	Our collection has much loftier pieces of poetry than Cowper's *Cat*, but none in which poetical skill is more consummate.
249	65	Sir Hyde Parker commanded in this battle, fought in April 1801 in order to detach Denmark from the Northern coalition which hindered the singlehanded attempt of England to curb Napoleon Bonaparte. Nelson's spirit of heroic gallantry never blazed higher than here. Riou was killed in command of a squadron.
253	63	The insertion of these grandly-simple, almost Homeric stanzas is due to the suggestion of Mr W. E. Gladstone :— of No. 79, equally fine in its wild intensity of imagination, to Mr R. Browning. The Cyclops were the assistants of Vulcan, the god of the forge, in old mythology: Jove was the king of all
256	70	The vivid incident (A.D 627), characteristic in every way of the English mind, upon which the poem is founded, is told by the old English historian Bede.
260	74	The subjects chosen by Vaughan and Herbert have mostly placed their poems beyond the limits of this selection; but they will be found 'treasures for ever' by readers who find more attraction in the matter than in the manner of poetry. Line 17 refers either to the imagined carbuncle, or to the brief luminosity which the diamond retains after exposure to sunshine.
266	80	For wealth of condensed thought and imagery, fused into one equable stream of golden song by intense fire of genius, the Editor knows no poem superior to this *Elegy*,— none quite equal. Nor has the difficulty of speaking well on common topics, without exaggeration yet with unfailing freshness and originality, been ever met with greater success. Line after line has the perfection of a flawless jewel: it is hard to find a word that could have been spared, or changed for the better. This condensation, however, has injured the clearness of the poem: the specific gravity of the gem, if we may pursue the image, has diminished its translucent qualities. Many notes have hence been added ;—the useful but prosaic task of paraphrase is best left to the reader, who may make one for his benefit, and then burn it for his pleasure.
275	82	Shelley's masterpiece, in the shorter form of lyric (as, if such a judgment be permissible, all things considered, the Editor would hold the *Skylark*,) follows Gray's:

and in No. 63 we have one of the most stately and musical odes in our or any language. With these, Watts' verses come like the child they describe into a company of kings and conquerors. Indeed, the admirable author of the *Cradle Song* almost apologized for publishing it ;—yet within its little sphere, this also is a masterpiece.—Reynolds himself does not paint childhood with a more absolute tenderness.

Here, as in other instances within our selection, it will be useful if the reader pauses and considers how many ways true art offers for reaching excellence. The 'House of Poetry,' if we may so call it, truly has 'many mansions': size and splendour are not the only elements of success: here, as elsewhere, the poet's words are true—

> In small proportions we just beauties see ;
> And in short measures life may perfect be.

276   83   Milton imagined this magnificent ode at dawn of Christmas-day 1629, having then lately passed his twenty-first birthday, and completed his Cambridge course. The poem, if compared with *L'Allegro* or *Comus*, moves somewhat heavily at times, and as if embarrassed by its weight of historical allusion: Milton has proved his armour, but does not yet wear it with perfect ease. Yet this stateliness of movement, as in sacred music, befits the subject.

277   83   Line 37, Nature is here treated by Milton as 'guilty,' as impersonating a 'fallen world.' The heathen religions, in the latter part of the Ode, are similarly regarded rather as demon-worship than as the imperfect and corrupted efforts of man to reach the truth.

—   —   Line 47, The *olive* and the *myrtle* (line 51) have for many centuries been regarded as emblems of Peace and her blessings.

—   —   Line 48, *turning sphere;* the whole Universe is here thought of as a whirling orb, hung from heaven.

278   —   Line 68, The 'halcyon days,' when the king-fishers were breeding, and the sea supposed to be supernaturally calm, were placed by the ancients in midwinter.

279   —   Line 89, *Pan*, God of shepherds, here used for the Lord of All.

280   —   Line 110, *globe;* here seemingly bears the military sense of body of troops.

—   —   Line 125, The Universe was by the Greeks supposed to consist of crystal spheres concentrically arranged, the sound of which as they moved formed a heavenly music, too fine for human hearing.

—   —   Line 135, By the 'age of gold' the old poets meant the earliest and best time of the world.

282   —   Lines 173—236, Milton here works out at length the tradition that the power of the heathen gods ended with the birth of Our Saviour. *Oracles* were answers given to enquirers at certain holy places, as Delphos (line 178): *Nymphs* (line 183) goddesses of wood and field.

283   —   Line 204, *Thammuz* or Adonis was feigned to die and revive yearly in Lebanon. *Osiris* (line 213) was the god of the Nile, torn to pieces by Typhon, and embalmed in a

PAGE	NO.	
		sacred chest. The Bull-form belongs, however, to Apis, another Egyptian deity.
284	83	Line 232, The old belief was, that spirits fled away at dawning to their prisons underground.
—	—	Line 243, *courtly*, the stable of Bethlehem being figured as a palace.
284	84	Ben Jonson, a man who rated himself highly, said If he had written that piece, the *Burning Babe*, he would have been content to destroy many of his own poems :—and Jonson's enthusiasm is well justified by the passionate intensity and picturesqueness of this lovely mystical lyric.

INDEX OF WRITERS.

PART I.

FIRST PERIOD

FLETCHER, John (1576—1625) 27

HERBERT, George (1593—1632) 70
HERRICK, Robert (1591—1674?) 28

JONSON, Ben (1574—1637) 67

KING, Henry (1591—1669) 64

MARLOWE, Christopher (1562—1593) 29
MILTON, John (1608—1674) 82, 83

NASH, Thomas (1567—1600?) 26

SHAKESPEARE, William (1564—1616) 22, 36, 52

WEBSTER, John (— —1638?) 23

UNKNOWN : 12, 13, 33, 40, 44, 54, 69, 84

SECOND PERIOD

ADDISON, Joseph (1672—1719) 74

BLAKE, William (1757—1827) 1, 3, 9, 57, 58
BURNS, Robert (1759—1796) 5, 34, 65

CIBBER, Colley (1671—1757) 7
COLLINS, John (18th century) 51
COWPER, William (1731—1800) 4, 6, 10, 20, 24

GOLDSMITH, Oliver (1728—1774) 39

LINDSAY, Anne (1750—1825) 43
LOGAN, John (1748—1788) 77

MALLET, David (1700?—1765) 11
MICKLE, William Julius (1734—1788) 21, 41

SKELTON, Philip (1707—1787) 72
SMART, Christopher (1722—1770) 73

THIRD PERIOD

ALLINGHAM, William (———) 53

BARNES, William (———) 60, 61
BRYANT, William Cullen (———) 79
BYRON, George Gordon Noel (1788—1824) 46

CAMPBELL, Thomas (1777—1844) 14, 45, 48, 50, 76
COLERIDGE, Samuel Taylor (1772—1834) 56
CUNNINGHAM, Allan (1784-1842) 25

DIBDIN, Charles (1745-1814) 15
DOYLE, Francis Hastings Charles (———) 17

HEMANS, Felicia Dorothea (1794—1835) 16

MACAULAY, Thomas Babington (1800—1859) 47

NEWMAN, John Henry (———) 68

SCOTT, Walter (1771—1832) 37, 38, 42, 49, 55, 62, 63, 80
SHELLEY, Percy Bysshe (1792—1822) 32, 81

WORDSWORTH, William (1770—1850) 2, 8, 30, 31, 35, 66, 71, 75, 78

UNKNOWN: 18, 19, 59

INDEX OF WRITERS.

PART II.

FIRST PERIOD

BUNYAN, John (1628—1688) 18

CAREW, Elizabeth (16th and 17th centuries) 19

DRAYTON, Michael (1563—1631) 1
DRUMMOND, William (1585—1649) 78

HERBERT, George (1593—1632) 76
HERRICK, Robert (1591—1674?) 32, 34, 36, 62
HEYWOOD, Thomas (—— 1649?) 1, 30

LOVELACE, Richard (1618—1658) 50

MARVELL, Andrew (1621—1678) 17, 45
MILTON, John (1608—1674) 83

SHAKESPEARE, William (1564—1616) 9, 31
SHIRLEY, James (1596—1666) 22
SOUTHWELL, Robert 1560—1595) 84

VAUGHAN, Henry (1621—1695) 74

WOTTON, Henry (1568—1639) 20

UNKNOWN: 10, 11, 13, 28, 53, 54, 67

SECOND PERIOD

BLAKE, William (1757—1827) 4, 5, 7, 21, 75
BURNS, Robert (1759—1796) 43, 48,

COLLINS, John (18th century) 77
COWPER, William (1731—1800) 42, 55, 73

GISBORNE, Thomas (1758—1846) 44
GOLDSMITH, Oliver (1728—1774) 57
GRAY, Thomas (1716—1771) 80

LANGHORNE, John (1735—1779) 38
LOGAN, John (1748—1788) 52

OLDYS, W—— (18th century) 71

SMART, Christopher (1722—1770) 79
SMITH, Charlotte (1749—1806) 37

THOMSON, James (1700—1748) 64

WARTON, Thomas (1728—1790) 35
WATTS, Isaac (1674—1748) 82

UNKNOWN : 49

THIRD PERIOD

ALLINGHAM, William (———— ————) 59

BARNES, William (———— ————) 23
BRYANT, William Cullen (———— ————) 61
BYRON, George Gordon Noel (1788—1824) 69

CAMPBELL, Thomas (1777—1844) 56, 58, 65
COLERIDGE, Samuel Taylor (1772—1834) 12

DIBDIN, Charles (1745—1814) 66, 68
DOYLE, Francis Hastings Charles (———— ————) 25

KEATS, John (1795—1821) 60

LAMB, Mary (1765 ?—1847) 46
LATTO, T—— C—— (19th century) 6
LONGFELLOW, Henry Wadsworth (———— ————) 14

MOORE, Thomas (1780—1852) 72

SCOTT, Walter (1771—1832) 15, 16, 26, 27, 29, 41, 63
SHELLEY, Percy Bysshe (1792—1822) 81
SOUTHEY, Robert (1774—1843) 2, 47

WOLFE, Charles (1791—1823) 24
WORDSWORTH, William (1770—1850) 3, 8, 33, 39, 40

UNKNOWN : 70

INDEX OF FIRST LINES.

	PAGE
A Chieftain to the Highlands bound	75
A fair maid sat at her bower-door	26
A poet's cat, sedate and grave	235
A weary lot is thine, fair maid	205
A wet sheet and a flowing sea	43
Agincourt, Agincourt! know ye not Agincourt	143
And are ye sure the news is true	39
Annan Water's wading deep	204
*Arethusa arose	128
As I in hoary winter's night stood shivering in the snow	284
As I wer readèn ov a stwone	197
*A spaniel, Beau, that fares like you	8
Attend all ye who list to hear our noble England's praise	78
Awake, awake, my little boy	261
A whirl-blast from behind the hill	54
Behold her, single in the field	50
Busy, curious, thirsty fly	258
Call for the robin-redbreast and the wren	41
*Come live with me and be my Love	49
Come unto these yellow sands	88
Come, sons of summer, by whose toil	211
Down in yon garden sweet and gay	73
Ethereal minstrel! pilgrim of the sky	214
Ever after summer shower	210
Fair Daffodils, we weep to see	245
Fair pledges of a fruitful tree	207
From Oberon, in fairy land	158
Full fathom five thy father lies	41
*Glad sight, wherever new with old	51
Go fetch to me a pint o' wine	226
Good bye, good-bye to Summer	241
Good people all, of every sort	239
Hail, beauteous stranger of the grove	124
Hail to thee, blithe Spirit!	271
Happy were he could finish forth his fate	141
Heap on more wood!—the wind is chill	246
*Heaven's gifts are unequal in this world awarded	86
*Hence loathèd Melancholy	131
*Hence, vain deluding Joys	135
Henry was every morning fed	224
Here, a sheer hulk, lies poor Tom Bowling	251
Here lies, whom hound did ne'er pursue	6
He sang of God, the mighty source	119

	PAGE
How are thy servants blest, O Lord	120
How happy is he born and taught	194
How soon doth man decay	262
Hush! my dear, lie still and slumber	275
I am monarch of all I survey	44
*I climb'd the dark brow of the mighty Helvellyn	105
I have no name	152
I heard a thousand blended notes	121
I reach'd the village on the plain	100
I wander'd lonely as a cloud	208
In distant countries have I been	215
In the southern clime	13
*In Xanadu did Kubla Khan	96
In the downhill of life, when I find I'm declining	263
In the sweet shire of Cardigan	154
Inhuman man! curse on thy barbarous art	7
It fell about the Martinmas	231
It is an Ancient Mariner	121
It is not growing like a tree	110
It was a summer evening	147
It was intill a pleasant time	160
It was the schooner *Hesperus*	185
John Anderson my jo, John	109
John Gilpin was a citizen	16
Last night among his fellow roughs	199
Like Aetna's dread volcano, see the ample forge	253
Like to the falling of a star	108
Little bird, with bosom red	213
Little Lamb, who made thee	5
Lord, thou hast given me a cell	208
Merry it is in the good greenwood	92
My mind to me a kingdom is	111
No soul did hear her lips complain	104
Not a drum was heard, not a funeral note	198
O, aye! they had woone chile bezide	102
*O blithe new comer! I have heard	125
O Brignall banks are wild and fair	56
O hark to the strain that sae sweetly is ringin'	152
O listen, listen, ladies gay	188
O lovers' eyes are sharp to see	203
O say what is that thing call'd light	10
O tell me, Harper, wherefore flow	190
O well is me, my gay goshawk	28
O who will shoe my bonny foot	64
O where have ye been, my long-lost lover	183
O, young Lochinvar is come out of the West	201
Of Nelson and the North	249
Oft I heard of Lucy Gray	149
Oft in the stilly night	258
*On came the whirlwind—like the last	83
On Linden, when the sun was low	82
On the green banks of Shannon when Sheelah was nigh	238
Our bugles sang truce, for the night-cloud had lowered	85
Pack, clouds, away, and welcome day	206
*Prune thou thy words; the thoughts control	111
*Right on our flank the crimson sun went down	34
Season of mists and mellow fruitfulness	243
See the day begins to break	45
Sleep, sleep, beauty bright	99

Index of First Lines.

	PAGE
Spring, the sweet Spring is the year's pleasant king	44
Sweet country life, to such unknown	46
Sweet is the dew that falls betimes	265
Sweet peace, where dost thou dwell? I humbly crave	112
Sweet to the morning traveller	225
*That way look my Infant, lo	114
The Assyrian came down like the wolf on the fold	77
The black-hair'd gaunt Paulinus	256
The boy stood on the burning deck	33
The curfew tolls the knell of parting day	266
The deep affections of the breast	240
The dew was falling fast, the stars began to blink	1
*The dews of summer night did fall	68
The fairest action of our human life	193
The glories of our blood and state	196
The gorse is yellow on the heath	213
The hunt is up, the hunt is up	234
The King was on his throne	255
The Love that I have chosen	252
The melancholy days are come, the saddest of the year	244
The noon was shady, and soft airs	219
The 'Northern Star'	36
The poplars are fell'd, farewell to the shade	259
The signal to engage shall be	32
The sun descending in the West	153
The sun does arise	98
The sun upon the lake is low	127
The post-boy drove with fierce career	11
The warm sun is failing, the bleak wind is wailing	51
*There is a flower, the Lesser Celandine	109
There is in the lone, lone sea	37
There lived a wife at Usher's Well	91
They are all gone into the world of light	260
This is the month, and this the happy morn	276
This Life, which seems so fair	265
Thou hast left me ever, Jamie	228
Thy braes were bonny, Yarrow stream	229
'To God, ye choir above, begin	158
Toll for the Brave	38
Triumphal arch, that fill'st the sky	122
'Turn, gentle Hermit of the dale	53
Turn, turn thy hasty foot aside	222
'Twas at the silent, solemn hour	24
Under the greenwood tree	206
Up the airy mountain	89
Wee, modest, crimson tipped flower	53
Wee, sleekit, cow'rin', tim'rous beastie	230
What pleasures have great princes	52
When Britain first, at Heaven's command	248
When icicles hang by the wall	55
When I think on the happy days	227
When Love with unconfined wings	227
When my mother died I was very young	105
'When, musing on companions gone	107
When red hath set the beamless sun	218
When the green woods laugh with the voice of joy	1
When the sheep are in the fauld, and the kye at hame	72
When the voices of children are heard on the green	151
Where the bee sucks, there suck I	88

	PAGE
Where the remote Bermuda's ride	191
*Where shall the lover rest	70
Whither, 'midst falling dew	126
Who wou'd true valour see?	193
Why weep ye by the tide, ladie	55
With sweetest milk and sugar first	223
*Ye Mariners of England	31
You spotted snakes with double tongue	157

www.ingramcontent.com/pod-product-compliance
Lightning Source LLC
Chambersburg PA
CBHW022055230426
43672CB00008B/1176